Politics in the Lifeboat

Politics in the Lifeboat

Immigrants and the American Democratic Order

John C. Harles

Westview Press

BOULDER • SAN FRANCISCO • OXFORD

Copyright © 1993 by Westview Press, Inc.

Published in 1993 in the United States of America by Westview Press, Inc., 5500 Central Avenue, Boulder, Colorado 80301-2877, and in the United Kingdom by Westview Press, 36 Lonsdale Road, Summertown, Oxford OX2 7EW

Library of Congress Cataloging-in-Publication Data
Harles, John C.
  Politics in the lifeboat : immigrants and the American democratic
order / John C. Harles.
    p. cm.
  Includes bibliographical references and index.
  ISBN 0-8133-8368-4
  1. Immigrants—United States—Political activity. 2. Political
participation—United States. 3. United States—Politics and
government. I. Title
JV6477.H37 1993
323.3′293′0973—dc20   92-23617
CIP

Printed and bound in the United States of America

⊗ The paper used in this publication meets the requirements of the
American National Standard for Permanence of Paper for Printed
Library Materials Z39.48-1984.

10 9 8 7 6 5 4 3 2

It is a drama that goes on, without a pause, day-by-day and year by year, this visible act of ingurgitation on the part of our body politic and social, and constituting really an appeal to amazement beyond that of any sword-swallowing or fire-swallowing of the circus.

—Henry James, *The American Scene*

Contents

Preface

In a bibliographic essay appended to his book, *The Nature of American Politics,* Professor H.G. Nicholas observes, "Surprisingly, no comprehensive assessment of immigration's impact on American politics exists." The present study, although by no means claiming to be comprehensive, aspires to make at least a small contribution to that end.

Clearly, there is no shortage of scholarship exploring the relationship between immigration and American politics. Numerous students of the subject have traced the effect of immigrant-stock voters on partisan alignment and the politics of the urban machine. Still others have examined the political dimensions of nativism—those episodes in American history during which anti-immigrant sentiment has been at its height. Further research has considered whether immigrants have advanced or impeded the development of American working-class politics, socialism in particular. So too has immigration been surveyed from the prospect of assimilation, a process, in light of the extraordinary cultural diversity of American society as enhanced and replenished by successive flows of immigration, that is widely regarded as the crucial unifying, and arguably moderating, force of the American polity. Certainly, all such themes would need to be addressed in any truly thorough political assessment of immigration; if the current volume does not do so systematically, it is not for reason of unimportance but concision.

What follows is meant to complement, not supplant, these well-established historical and sociological approaches to immigration and American politics. Thus the essay's claim to distinctiveness is not so much the ground it covers but its effort to view what may be familiar about immigrants and immigration in a new way—through the lens of empirical democratic theory. That this perspective is rarely confronted explicitly in standard accounts of the politics of immigration is the major reason recommending it here. But more boldly, in its macro-level or "top-down" consideration of the topic, democratic theory also promises an integrative framework for analysis, potentially one making for a more inclusive appraisal of immigration's political consequences.

To anticipate the direction of the text, its point of departure is the theoretical case against ethnic heterogeneity and, by implication, the immigration producing it. As Chapter 2 maintains, students of democracy have tended to be wary of cultural diversity and immigration; first, because it threatens to undermine the sense of political community necessary to political stability; second, because it suggests a *dissensus* on political values unsettling to democracy's cultural equilibrium; and third, because once cultural diversity becomes an entrenched feature of the social environment, governments have difficulty fighting its alleged ill effects. Chapter 3 introduces the specifically American version of this scholarly wisdom, realized both in the theory and practice of American government and centering on the role of ideological consensus as a guarantor of the democratic order, hence a standard to which immigrants must be made to conform. In response, Chapter 4 contends that although immigrants to the United States may not always possess the precise combination of political values believed to be the key to American stability, circumstances inherent in the process of immigration tend to make the foreign-born highly allegiant and undemanding residents of the republic. Chapter 5 supplements that hypothesis with a qualitative study of Laotian immigrants and concludes that if the Laotian experience is in any sense representative, from the viewpoint of political stability immigrants have not been simply a mixed blessing for the United States but a positive good. The essay is bracketed by brief introductory and concluding chapters, the former foreshadowing the central lines of argument and clarifying several of the concepts employed, the latter speculating as to the work's theoretical and practical implications.

One further prefatory note seems warranted. Given that immigration historically has been a topic of no small partisan debate, it would be natural if the author's political convictions were the subject of speculation. In particular, a reliance on the consensus paradigm of American politics, as well as the assertion that in the view of many immigrants the United States appears to be a "lifeboat" promising relief from the anxieties of the homeland, may indicate to some readers that a relatively uncritical view of American political history is being offered. At the risk of revealing more than is necessary, that is neither this study's intention nor its author's inclination. There is no desire to underplay the very real hardships of American life for the foreign-born or to suggest that all has been well in the immigrant ghetto. If anything, the fact that immigrant life has frequently been so difficult makes it all the more remarkable that immigrants typically are such committed and supportive citizens. The only political perspective the volume consciously intends to express may be found in its concluding paragraph: "Not only have immigrants built America and defined the texture of American life, but they have been instrumental in the preservation of the democratic order." Should any loyalties be communicated in that, they are to the immigrants themselves.

John C. Harles

Acknowledgments

This book's early stages of development were advantaged by the nurture of Jim Sharpe of Nuffield College, Oxford. Jim never failed to respond promptly and extensively to innumerable drafts of the manuscript and was consistently able to strike the judicious balance between criticism (invariably constructive) and encouragement. One could not have wished for a better mentor; I continue to benefit from his advice and friendship. Byron Shafer, also of Nuffield College, offered insights and efforts that have been a major catalyst in the transformation of the draft manuscript into a book, and I am deeply appreciative of his substantive and moral support. I might mention, as well, the help extended by Seymour Martin Lipset of Stanford and George Mason Universities; his confidence in the manuscript has been gratifying.

My work with Laotian immigrants was expedited by the able assistance of Helen Sawyer and Sisouphanh Ratthahao. Through their linguistic and cultural facility, they provided me with a conduit to the Laotian community. To the degree that my fieldwork has been at all successful, they are in large part responsible.

At Messiah College I have had the great privilege of working with three very bright and amiable research assistants: Laurie Bernotsky, Dennis Hoover, and Naomi Johnson. They participated in the preparation of this book in myriad ways: typing the manuscript, compiling bibliographies, tracking down citations, and serving as a general sounding board for my musings about immigration; I hope they did not find it all too tedious. Many thanks, too, to Pamela Snyder, who provided invaluable technical assistance in the final stages of the manuscript's production. A sizable debt of gratitude is also due to my good friend and colleague, Bill Trollinger. Drawing on his field of specialization in American social history, Bill not only saved me from several factual errors but also introduced me to a literature on immigration and ethnicity that I might otherwise have missed. He was generous with his time as well, reading a version of the manuscript in its entirety and offering congenial and honest critical comment.

In ways great and small, all of these people made this book far better than if left to me alone. Should the work be found wanting, they, of course, must be absolved; it is my errors in judgment that are responsible.

This book is lovingly dedicated to Ellen, about whom there was no error in judgment.

J.C.H.

1

Introduction

As an ethnically heterogeneous but stable democracy, the United States is a puzzle for students of politics. According to the received wisdom of democratic theory, ethnic diversity is not conducive to stable government. Indeed, the infrequency of ethnically heterogeneous but stable democracies suggests there is much to be said in favor of this proposition.[1] The United States, however, is a conspicuous exception to the general rule. Whereas ethnically based conflict is not foreign to the American political experience, the United States has been able to avoid the system-threatening consequences of heterogeneity known in other democracies. Moreover, of the handful of countries that are both heterogeneous and stable, America appears distinctive in the extent of its political integration, possessing an extraordinary ability to create the sentiments of political solidarity necessary to counteract the centrifugal forces of an ethnically diverse society. It is for the source of the United States' power of political transformation, this capacity to change an ethnically heterogeneous mass into a politically consolidated and stable whole, that the present study seeks.

This essay will contend that a secret to America's success lies in the immigrant origins of its population. It is, of course, a truism that the United States is a nation of immigrants—over 54 million arrived between 1820, when the government began to keep statistics on immigration, and 1988—yet it is a truism of critical political consequence.[2] In many, perhaps most, democracies, ethnically diverse populations are largely the legacy of state-building processes that coercively solder together culturally different geographical elements. By contrast, in the United States, with a few important qualifications—namely, the conquest of Native American and Spanish territory and the traffic in slaves—ethnic heterogeneity is primarily the result of the voluntary migration of ethnically distinct peoples. With respect to political stability, the outcomes of these two processes, forcible incorporation on the one hand and self-determined affiliation on the other, promise to be fundamentally different. In the former instance, political rule may be exercised over resentful and recalcitrant ethnic contingents, groups with little positive commitment to the state of which they, or their forbearers, have been forced to become a part. But when immigration is the major source of heterogeneity, as it is in America, the bonds of political community would seem more firmly established, the act of immigration itself suggesting an intent to identify politically with the host country. On this view, because the United States is a nation of immigrants, it has been able to escape the ill-effects of heterogeneity that theorists of democracy predict.

In arguing that immigrants promote political stability, the present essay departs from conventional scholarly assessments of immigration. In the literature of American democratic theory, the foreign-born have often been considered a potentially destabilizing political force. Not that theorists holding such views are necessarily anti-immigrant; rather they anticipate the disruptive ideological divisions immigrants promise to introduce into a consensual American polity. Examinations of the republic's political culture typically maintain that Americans are to a remarkable degree united on the tenets of a central political value system, a national creed whose origins and precise content are subject to scholarly debate, yet which is most often defined in terms of a variety of liberalism. Given that American society is extremely heterogeneous with respect to ethnicity, this liberal ethos is judged to be the social adhesive of the polity, providing the ideological unity required to integrate a culturally diverse society. That said, it is by no means certain that upon arrival in the United States immigrants will be good liberals. Having come from other places and having been socialized to alien political norms, it is unlikely that the majority will possess the necessary ideological credentials. Consequently, the stability of the United States is believed to turn on its capacity to assimilate the foreign-born. Left to their own devices, it is reasoned, immigrants would in fact destroy America's political equilibrium; it is only by virtue of the United States' ability to educate immigrants in the unifying political creed that such a fate has been averted.

Although not denying the political significance of assimilation, the present study asserts that this traditional reading of the immigrant experience is in some sense incomplete. Far from being an inherently unsettling influence on the American democratic order, immigrants have been a positive factor making for stability, the influence of assimilation aside. The political character of immigrants is shaped profoundly by what this essay calls the "politics of the lifeboat," a metaphor suggesting the perspective from which many immigrants view the American political system. At the limit, no doubt, the image risks exaggeration—that immigrants are necessarily the "wretched refuse" of humanity, as the poem affixed to the base of the Statue of Liberty would have it, has always been something of a caricature. Nevertheless, for countless immigrants America has promised deliverance from a homeland environment judged unacceptable. And to the extent that the foreign-born believe their country of adoption rescues them from various conditions of political, economic, and cultural distress—and the circumstances of immigration incline them to see things this way—they are keen to offer it their steadfast political allegiance. Other than displaying an enthusiastic patriotism, however, immigrants are improbable participants in American public life, both because they are reticent to engage in any activities that might antagonize their American hosts, and because they normally do not have the resources that would facilitate their participation. Thus, the conventional manner in which political theorists have understood the immigrant experience is wanting on two accounts: (1) immigrant loyalties do not need to be manufactured, as they are ready-made, and (2) immigrants are unlikely to disrupt the political process, as they have little inclination to participate in it at all.

In the context of American political practice, this revised interpretation of immigrant politics suggests a certain irony. Over the course of American history, public officials and private citizens alike have often viewed immigrants as politically suspect, the bearers of values inconsistent with American norms. Senator Alan Simpson, a major legislative force behind the immigration reform effort of the last decade, has observed:

> Although the subject of the immediate economic impact of immigration receives great attention, assimilation to fundamental American public values and institutions may be of far more importance to the future of the United States. If immigration is continued at a high level and yet a substantial portion of newcomers and their descendants do not assimilate, they may create in America some of the same social, political, and economic problems which existed in the country they have chosen to depart.[3]

Such cautionary appraisals do not negate the fact, of course, that the United States has administered a comparatively magnanimous immigration policy or that it takes official pride in its immigrant roots, frequently publicizing the economic and cultural contributions the foreign-born have made to the tenor of American life. Yet as concerns their political qualities, immigrants have been regarded with considerably less enthusiasm. So it is that numerous laws have been passed excluding immigrants from America for fear of their political characteristics, and concerted public efforts have been made to reformulate immigrant attitudes in a manner consonant with American political beliefs. Immigrants must be made politically acceptable, it is imagined, because upon coming to America they are likely to be politically unacceptable.

The present study will contend that such conclusions are inappropriate. In an elementary sense, immigrants are already faithful Americans when they first set foot on American soil. The process of assimilation, widely regarded as the primary means of affecting the immigrant's political metamorphosis, does not so much evangelize the pagan as it preaches to the converted. In fact, purely from the standpoint of American public officials, it would seem that immigrants might make the best political subjects—they ask little from government yet are fervently loyal to it. To turn a phrase reminiscent of Oscar Handlin in his Pulitzer Prize–winning account of immigration, *The Uprooted,* America need not fear the immigrant's politics; the immigrant's politics *is* the politics of America.[4]

Before these arguments can receive a more thorough exposition, it is necessary to define several of the terms that are basic to the ensuing discussion. In truth, only an attempt to define them can be made as their referents are, perhaps inevitably, imprecise and subject to scholarly debate. "Democracy" is certainly in this category of contested concepts. For the duration of the present study, democracy will indicate what is sometimes called "liberal democracy," as distinct from "socialist democracy" or "people's democracy"—other claimants to the democratic title.[5] At its core, liberal democracy consists of three political principles: (1) maximization of individual freedom and, relatedly, the restriction of government power; (2) equality of influence of all competent citizens over the political decision-making process; (3) toleration of political dissent and opposition. Undoubtedly, these ideals are only imperfectly implemented in the practice of liberal democratic governments. But for present purposes, it is not necessary to debate whether liberal democracies are reliably democratic, only to take note of the essential norms of liberal-democratic rule and to recognize the United States as a member of the democratic club sharing these tenets.

"Ethnicity" is a concept similarly difficult to specify; the *Harvard Encyclopedia of American Ethnic Groups* uses fourteen separate measures to determine whether a given social group is eligible for inclusion in the volume.[6] Originally, ethnicity indicated the idea of race, but this biological connotation now tends to be deemphasized in favor of a definition centering on cultural criteria. To that end, a common language, religion, history, and territory of residence are all used to delimit ethnic boundaries, each thought to give rise to the shared beliefs essential to group identity. Nevertheless, at its heart ethnicity indicates a psychological sense of belonging to a social group having some of these cultural features, and it is in this manner that the concept will be employed.[7] Clearly, American society is highly heterogeneous with regard to ethnicity: 106 separate ethnic group entries are included in the *Harvard Encyclopedia*, while the *World Handbook of Political and Social Indicators* places the United States in fifty-fourth place among 135 countries on the basis of ethnic fractionalization (first place indicating the most fractionalized political system) and among liberal democracies cites only Belgium and Canada as more fractionalized.[8]

"Political stability" is a further term possessing a multi-dimensional quality. Although political scientists are by no means united in their use of the concept, at least four notions of stability seem representative.[9] First, a stable political system is one not plagued by domestic political violence, one in which political life proceeds in an orderly and institutionalized fashion. Second, political stability is indicated by a low rate of turnover in the chief executive offices, the durability of governments lending continuity to the political process. Third, a stable state is characterized by the existence of a widely supported constitutional order, which establishes the norms of political interaction and legitimizes the outputs of the political process. Fourth, a stable polity is one in which the basic structures of government, the fundamental relationships among political institutions, remain relatively constant over time.

By at least three of these standards, and probably the most telling, the United States possesses the hallmarks of a politically stable state. Undeniably, the United States has often been a very violent country, in terms of both overall level of violent crime and specifically political violence.[10] Yet such violence has not seemed to diminish America's ability to achieve political order on other accounts. In comparative perspective, the longevity of American governments is impressive. Strictly speaking, of course, in the United States all administrations complete their tenure, but even so, only five of fifty presidential terms (1789—1989) have been cut short due to irregular political causes, while transfers of executive power have always been on the basis of well-established legal procedures.[11] Furthermore, the legal order of the United States is widely regarded as legitimate; at just one point in American history has that order been severely challenged (the Civil War), and although political protest is not an infrequent feature of American life, such protest rarely questions the appropriateness of the fundamental rules of the political system. Even more impressively, as embodied in the Constitution, the oldest document of its kind in the world, the basic structures of American politics, if modified, have remained much the same over two centuries of existence. To be sure, that the United States is politically stable seems so self-evidently true as hardly to warrant examination were it not for its usefulness as a comparative object lesson. In other countries, ethnic conflict has caused governments to fall, constitutions to be reformulated, and separatist movements to challenge the integrity of the state. As an ethnically heterogeneous but stable polity, America is unusual among democracies.

In pursuing a particular path of analysis, the present work necessarily leaves several avenues of investigation unexplored. First, immigration to colonial America will not be directly addressed in the pages that follow. This omission does not signify that the matter of colonial immigration has no bearing on the thesis. America has been an immigrant society since its inception, and it is to be expected that immigration's political effect on colonial America should show continuity with its impact on an independent United States. But it is also to be expected that the politics of immigration to an imperial possession will be far different from the politics of immigration to a sovereign state, and it is the latter with which this discussion is concerned.

Second, a consideration of the majority of the black American population, comprising those individuals who trace their origins to Africa via the slave trade, will not be undertaken in the present study. As the official traffic in slaves ended soon after American independence, the historical constraints just mentioned put much of the Afro-American ethnic group beyond the scope of the discussion. But more than this, those Africans who came to America through the slave trade were immigrants by reason of coercion. The present investigation, however, wishes to explore the politics of individuals who have voluntarily determined to come to the United States. Again, this is not to suggest that the Afro-American experience is irrelevant to the thesis under consideration. Indeed, it may be hypothesized that the black American population has posed a vigorous challenge to the political order precisely because its progenitors were unwillingly incorporated into America. Testing that hypothesis, however, is a task reserved for future research.

Finally, the subject of illegal immigration, so prominent in contemporary American public debate, will not receive direct attention in this study. Once more, this is not to imply that the experience of illegal immigrants is of no theoretical significance. It may be that illegal immigrants will have an even greater inclination to political quiescence than will legal immigrants or naturalized citizens; for illegal immigrants, to participate in politics is to risk attracting the attention of government authorities and suffering subsequent deportation. But the focus of the present study is on immigrants who have arrived in America with the full knowledge and authority of the United States government. It is among legal immigrants that the political dynamics of the "lifeboat" are most clearly observed; for illegal immigrants that lifeboat can never be completely secure.

Notes

1. See, for example, Robert A. Dahl, *Polyarchy: Participation and Opposition* (New Haven: Yale University Press, 1971), pp. 108–10; Arend Lijphart, *Democracies: Patterns of Majoritarian and Consensus Government in Twenty-One Countries* (New Haven: Yale University Press, 1984), p. 43; G. Bingham Powell, *Contemporary Democracies: Participation, Stability, Violence* (Cambridge: Harvard University Press, 1982), pp. 42–45, 73–96.

2. United States Bureau of the Census, *Statistical Abstract of the United States: 1990* (Washington, D.C.: G.P.O., 1990), p. 9.

3. The Select Commission on Immigration Policy, *U.S. Immigration Policy and the National Interest* (Washington, D.C.: G.P.O., 1981), pp. 412–13. Simpson cites with approval Almond and Verba's *The Civic Culture* and D. C. McClelland's *The Achieving Society* as scholarship drawing the connection between cultural attributes and stable democracy.

4. Handlin writes, "Once I thought to write a history of the immigrants in America. Then I discovered that immigrants *were* American history." Oscar Handlin, *The Uprooted* (Boston: Little, Brown, 1951), p. 3.

5. See, for example, C. B. MacPherson, *The Real World of Democracy* (Toronto: Canadian Broadcasting Company, 1965).

6. *Harvard Encyclopedia of American Ethnic Groups* (1980), p. vi.

7. William Petersen, "Concepts of Ethnicity," *Harvard Encyclopedia* (1980), pp. 234–42.

8. Charles Lewis Taylor and Michael C. Hudson, *World Handbook of Political and Social Indicators* (New Haven: Yale University Press, 1972), p. 272.

9. See Uriel Rosenthal, *Political Order* (Aalphen an den Rijn: Sijthoff and Noordhoff, 1978); Leon Hurwitz, "Contemporary Approaches to Political Stability," *Comparative Politics,* 5 (1973), 449–63.

10. See Taylor and Hudson, *World Handbook,* pp. 94–110; Dane Archer and Rosemary Gartner, *Violence and Crime in Cross-National Perspective* (New Haven: Yale University Press, 1984); Franklin L. Ford, *Political Murder: From Tyrannicide to Terrorism* (Cambridge: Harvard University Press, 1985), chapter 15.

11. See Taylor and Hudson, *World Handbook,* pp. 128–50. The five interrupted presidential tenures have been: Lincoln, Garfield, McKinley, and Kennedy by reason of assassination (though at least four other presidents—Jackson, Truman, Ford, and Reagan—and one president-elect—Franklin Roosevelt—have been the targets of attempted assassination) and Nixon by reason of resignation.

2

Ethnic Heterogeneity and Stable Democracy

With few exceptions, immigration entails the emergence of an ethnically heterogeneous population. Such sociocultural diversity is, of course, an enduring legacy of immigration to the settler societies of the New World, where at a minimum Europeans confronted aboriginal/Indian populations, but it is not only a New World phenomenon. The same ethnic pluralism has become characteristic of the more established European states, where, by virtue of imperial obligations or demand for unskilled labor, sizable numbers of foreign nationals have acquired residence. In the latter half of the twentieth century, not many democracies have been left untouched by the cultural diversity brought on by immigration.

When political theorists have considered the political consequences of immigration, they have usually done so in the context of its relationship with ethnic heterogeneity. As much of the contemporary public debate centers on immigration's economic impact, this issue of heterogeneity is often obscured. But in fact, the emphasis placed on the economic aspect of immigration is a relatively recent development. When labor was scarce, natural resources were plentiful, and governments took little responsibility for the material welfare of their citizens, arguments regarding the detrimental economic impact of immigration were seldom heard or at least lacked the intensity and moral certitude of those made at present. It is the matter of heterogeneity that has been the more enduring concern among students of politics.

The following discussion examines the relationship between ethnic heterogeneity and stable democracy as illuminated by the insights of political theory. It will be discovered that the bulk of scholarly opinion weighs in on the side of ethnic homogeneity as a social condition of political stability. The charge against heterogeneity is threefold: (1) heterogeneity undermines the sense of political community necessary to stable democracy; (2) heterogeneity suggests the valuational *dissensus* unsettling to the democratic order; (3) once heterogeneity is a feature of the social environment, governments have only a restricted latitude to fight its political ill-effects. To the degree that immigration is a source of ethnic diversity, it is subject to the same indictment that political theory makes against diversity as a condition for democracy. If largely by implication, theories concerning the social prerequisites of a democratic state take a dim view of immigration.

Ethnic Heterogeneity and the Question of Community

A sense of common political identity is essential to the stability of the state. The reason is clear: periodically the state requires individual citizens to make sacrifices for the good of the entire political community. Should the feeling of a collective destiny with other citizens be absent, individuals will find it difficult to subordinate private interests to public welfare. The call to military service is the most dramatic, and the most elementary, example of this general point. The decision to risk death in defense of the interests of the community turns, in part, on whether an individual believes the community sufficiently expresses his or her own identity and thus is worthy of protection. But the issue of sacrifice also applies to the more mundane matter of taxation. Not even the most doctrinaire capitalists will readily argue that the free market can provide all desired public goods and services; the state must undertake some of the required functions that the market cannot or will not do. At the very least, the state must make provision for domestic security, though in the modern era its catalog of services is likely to be far more extensive. And all of these services must be funded, in large measure, by tax revenues collected from individuals whose remittances may be quite disproportional to the public benefits they bring. In fact, citizens are taxed to support public goods for which they may not receive full advantage. Yet if a state is to fulfill its agenda, it must have the compliance of those who do not directly profit from its services. A belief in a common identity among members of the body politic is one reason to forego current satisfactions for diffuse benefits. It is this sense of a shared political fate that, from the perspective of the state, may be termed national integration, and from the perspective of the citizenry, political community.[1]

That ethnic diversity undermines the communal spirit necessary to political stability is the most basic and enduring indictment against a culturally heterogeneous state. The assumption that political order requires cultural unity is a well-developed theme of political theory, a prejudice with a considerable history. Aristotle sets the tone when in *The Politics* he describes the life of the ideal polis. Excluded from political participation are all those of foreign birth, including slaves obtained through conquest of foreign states and metics who carry on commercial enterprises to the benefit of native Athenians. As Aristotle's model of political excellence is the self-contained polis, it stands to reason he is wary of ethnic diversity; the intimacy of the city-state would seem especially vulnerable to the disruptive effects of heterogeneity. But although the fate of the Greek polis has been sealed for two millennia, in the corpus of political thought the notion that heterogeneity threatens stability has not diminished. Certainly elements of this perspective can be found in the work of Machiavelli, Montesquieu, and Rousseau, as well as that of other more contemporary political theorists.

This traditional interpretation of ethnic heterogeneity as threatening to stability is understandable. Without question, heterogeneity complicates the search for political community. By its very nature, ethnicity suggests particularity, a focus for personal identity with the ability to dissolve common political commitments. Indeed, the essence of ethnicity is the sense of being set apart on the basis of cultural distinctives. In conditions of cultural homogeneity, when the state serves the interest of only a single ethnic group, this disruptive potential is neutralized. As the boundaries of ethnic and political community are one and the same, ethnic and political loyalties coincide. But when a single state encompasses two or more culturally distinct social groups, the political consequences can be far more serious. No longer does the state unambiguously promote the interests of a single ethnic group; now there are competitors in the field. As discrete ethnic contingents vie for political recognition, a coherent sense of political community may be replaced by a public arena rife with mutual suspicion. Citizens are unlikely to make sacrifices in the name of the state when it is no longer clear in whose interest the state operates—their own or that of a contending ethnic group.

Ethnicity is often the primary source of an individual's self-identification; for that reason alone it is of political consequence. This is perhaps most evident with respect to linguistic and religious affiliation, two aspects of ethnic identity. Each is a major determinant of an individual's sense of selfhood and thus an important variable in calculations of political interest. Small wonder, then, that in heterogeneous states ethnic issues are prominent and the political debate surrounding them intense; the stakes of conflict are high because they penetrate to the core of personal identity. Predictably, a crusading spirit infuses the public realm when matters of ethnicity are raised. Thus, when presenting the watershed Bill 101 to Quebec's National

Assembly, the Parti Québécois minister of cultural development declared with conviction that "the charter of the French language in Quebec is the supreme affirmation of the French fact in America, the victory of the Québécois nation over the Anglophone occupiers, the annulment of the defeat upon the Plains of Abraham, and the cultural Magna Charta of the Québécois."[2] And if the matter of linguistic rights can evoke such a response, religiously inspired activism, which may have chiliastic import in the eyes of the faithful, may be entered into with an even greater level of commitment—Lebanon provides a tragic example.

Of course, ethnically based conflict may extend beyond issues of language and religion. In a heterogeneous society, any social good can become a focal point for interethnic conflict. Harold Laswell's famous list enumerates eight such collective goods—power, wealth, respect, knowledge, well-being, skill, affection and rectitude—any one of which can provide the impetus for ethnic groups to mobilize politically. Whatever is deemed necessary to secure the welfare of a given ethnic group, or to promote group interests, can quickly become an ethnic issue. In fact, religion or language may simply come to symbolize an interethnic debate conducted on other grounds. Thus, in Belgium ethnic conflict is often understood in terms of linguistic divisions when the distribution of economic power between the Walloons and the Flemish is truly at issue, and in Northern Ireland conflict is frequently expressed in terms of confessional groups when the underlying problems concern more strictly economic and political circumstances. But no matter its source, ethnic heterogeneity makes the process of governing more difficult by bringing culturally specific issues to the top of the political agenda, issues that are zealously advanced.

For this reason ethnic conflict may be especially resistant to resolution. If compromise is a key to orderly political rule, it is a goal difficult to attain should ethnic conflict be salient. In the first instance, commitment to the ethnic cause betrays attempts at compromise; when politics is passionate, compromise is the refuge of the impotent. But more than this, certain ethnic demands do not permit compromise. Ethnic conflicts suggest zero-sum games: either French is accepted as a language co-equal with English, or it is not; either Catholics are to be given political power on a par with Protestants, or they are not. Furthermore, the incommensurability of much ethnic politics increases the perception of distance between contending factions, making mutual understanding between the aggrieved parties even more remote. Fear and distrust of the opposition are a likely result, as is an escalation in the intensity of debate. Prospects for cultivating the communal spirit necessary to political stability are to that degree diminished.

Should ethnicity coincide with other social cleavages, political conflict may be all the more volatile and the destruction of the political community all the more likely. In the worst-case scenario, a particular ethnic community is on average of low socioeconomic status—at least compared to rival ethnic groups in the same state—and is geographically concentrated in a relatively well-defined territorial unit. Under such an arrangement, the ethnic group in question may take its disadvantaged socioeconomic position to be prima facie evidence of political prejudice. As the group is geographically self-contained, demands for greater political autonomy are natural; better to rule oneself in one's own interests than to allow the present injustices to continue. At the extreme, demands are made for complete independence from the parent state, but even calls for devolution are symptomatic. Over the last three decades, this model of ethnic dissensus approximates the experience of the Québécois in Canada, the Scots in Great Britain, the Basques in Spain, and the Wallonians in Belgium, among others. In all of these instances, the sense of common allegiance on which the central (i.e., Canadian, British, Spanish, and Belgian) political order rests, if indeed such allegiance obtains any longer at all, is severely attenuated.

Specifically democratic political theory likewise affirms the importance of common identity to stability but is not content to let the matter rest there. Not just any type of common bond will do—what must be achieved on the democratic logic is a community of equals. Democracy aspires to a parity of influence in the process of collective decisionmaking, its character defined by an effort to achieve the political equality of all competent citizens. Moreover, to the degree that political equality is a function of social and economic equality, the democratic state must consider the broader mandate of its central principle. In his *Reflections on Government*, Ernest Barker makes the case that equality must inform the common vision holding together the democratic polity:

> There must be some accepted language of social intercourse, and some common stock of historical tradition, before there can be discussion which is conducted in common terms. . . . If a country made up of different nationalities has no common medium of discussion, the same is true of two different nations of rich and poor, unable to comprehend one another, or to speak to one another across a gulf of difference. The ideal discussion is that between equals; and a community in which discussion moves easily must also be a community animated by a spirit of social equality.[3]

As Barker suggests, it is for reason of equality that ethnic heterogeneity is most often viewed as an impediment to democratic governance. To be sure, the consequences of heterogeneity on a distinctly democratic political order may be especially severe, given the nature of the democratic project. To begin with, ethnic heterogeneity complicates the search for the democratic ideal simply by multiplying the number of constituent social groups to whom political power must be equally distributed. But more than this, should constituent ethnic groups believe that the cardinal principle of equality is not observed in the decisionmaking process, they may well seek to undermine the democratic order itself. This is particularly relevant with respect to the vote-counting device of majority rule, a procedure that is required in the democratic process of decisionmaking, but that can operate in a highly prejudicial fashion. Rather than be subject to the dictates of majority rule, a minority ethnic group may prefer to see the restriction of democracy or may even more dramatically redirect its political allegiance; the alternative is to run the risk of being consistently outvoted on issues about which it most deeply cares.[4]

In the annals of democratic theory, John Stuart Mill provides the prototypical discussion of the relationship between ethnicity and democracy. In *Considerations on Representative Government*, Mill argues that the preservation of freedom and democracy dictates the coincidence of state and ethnic boundaries. Describing the difficulties of a multi-national state, he writes:

An altogether different set of leaders have the confidence of one part of the country and another. The same books, newspapers, pamphlets, speeches do not reach them. One section does not know what opinions, or what instigations are circulating in another. The same incidents, the same acts, the same system of government, affect them in different ways; and each fears more injury to itself from the other nationalities than from the common arbiter, the state. Their mutual antipathies are generally much stronger than jealousy of the government. That any one of them feels aggrieved by the policy of the common ruler is sufficient to determine another to support that policy. Even if all are aggrieved, none feel that they can rely on others for fidelity in a joint resistance; the strength of none is sufficient to resist alone, and each may reasonably think that it consults its own advantage most by bidding for the favor of the government against the rest.[5]

In this passage Mill advances the most common criticism of ethnic pluralism in a democratic state: that it impedes the sentiment of political community necessary to the effective operation of government and, by implication, destroys the spirit of equality that must animate a specifically democratic polity. Contending nationalities, keen to have their interests equally met, view one another with suspicion, seek evidence of prejudicial treatment by the public authorities or, alternatively, petition for public favors to secure their position. In the event, democracy itself is imperiled. Gone is the vigilance necessary to limit the power of government and preserve personal freedom. It is in this manner that a multiethnic population lends itself to authoritarianism—this scenario suggests a strategy of divide and rule, in which antagonistic groups are played off against one another and the power of the central authorities is thereby enhanced. On Mill's view, the tension between democracy and heterogeneity is intrinsic. The only solution is assimilation to a single cultural identity or, failing that, separation.[6]

But not only is ethnic homogeneity an important safeguard of the democratic polity, according to Mill it is also a consequence of democratic practice. Mill writes, "Where the sentiment of nationality exists in any force, there is a *prima facie* case for uniting all the members of the nationality under the same government, and a government to themselves apart. This is merely saying that the question of government ought to be decided by the governed."[7] The democratic ethos unleashes the demand among ethnic communities for self-rule to which, on the democratic view, they are entitled. If allowed to choose, Mill believes ethnic communities will join cultural homogeneity and political sovereignty. In a democracy, political autonomy will and should follow the contours of ethnicity.

Twentieth-century political developments reveal the appositeness of Mill's interpretation. In the early years of this century, Woodrow Wilson gave official credence to the notion that democracy and stability require ethnic homogeneity. Believing the Great War to be a consequence of unsatisfied demands for self-governance, Wilson maintained that the peace settlement should re-draw the boundaries of southern Europe along the lines of ethnicity. Similarly, calls for national sovereignty underscore the mid-century colonial independence movements in Asia and Africa—somewhat ironically, perhaps, given that a majority of the colonies at issue were themselves multi-ethnic and after independence were on the receiving end of the same demands for self-determination. So do the recent petitions for devolution and separation lodged in Europe and Canada. In retrospect, Mill's view of the homogenizing consequences of democratic politics seems prescient. Democratic politics has in fact served the interests of ethnic self-determination. As Michael Walzer comments:

Democracy and equality have proven to be the great solvents. In the old empires, the elites of conquered nations tended to assimilate to the dominant culture. They sent their children to be educated by their conquerors; they learned an alien language; they came to see their own culture as parochial and inferior. But ordinary men and woman did not assimilate; and when they were mobilized, first for economic and then for political activity, they turned out to have deep national and ethnic loyalties.... For centuries, perhaps, different nations had lived in peace, side by side, under imperial rule. Now that they had to rule themselves, they found that they could do so (peacefully) only among themselves, adjusting political lines to cultural boundaries.[8]

Lest there be any doubt concerning the accuracy of such judgments, contemporary democratic theorists have taken pains to verify empirically the connection between ethnic homogeneity and stable democracy. Thus, based on a study of 114 countries, Robert Dahl concludes that liberal democracy (in Dahl's terms, polyarchy) is most prevalent in ethnically homogeneous states and least frequent in states with high levels of ethnic heterogeneity.[9] Similarly, Arend Lijphart observes that only one-third of the twenty-one democracies he considers stable (by virtue of their longevity) are ethnically heterogeneous.[10] And affirming Dahl's and Lijphart's general conclusions, but using a more sophisticated statistical analysis, G. Bingham Powell notes that voter turnout is higher, and rates of deadly violence and rioting lower, in homogeneous societies. Powell believes that the volatile character of ethnic conflict makes it difficult to channel into regular modes of political behavior such as voting. Furthermore, he finds that homogeneity is positively associated with executive durability; ethnic pluralism is held to be related to multipartyism and extremism, the latter being the consequence if an ethnically based minority is excluded from power for too long. Again, the case is made for homogeneity as a condition of democratic stability.[11]

To summarize, students of politics tend to argue that ethnic heterogeneity undermines the sentiments of solidarity necessary to the political order. Ethnicity, it is claimed, disrupts the spirit of community necessary to political stability and, even more so, the preservation of a community of equals, as empirical evidence suggests. But in the literature of democratic theory, the concern for heterogeneity does not stop there. Political theorists not only cite the inequalities and separate loyalties that ethnic diversity may introduce into the political system, but also note the potential of ideological dissensus as a concomitant of that diversity. Stable democracy, it is reasoned, rests on a narrow valuational consensus vulnerable to the unsettling effect of ethnic pluralism. Far better, on this account, for democratic rule to be exercised by an ethnically homogeneous citizenry, one with a uniform set of democratic political beliefs.

Ethnic Heterogeneity and the Question of Consensus

Consensus is an imprecise and slippery concept. It concerns the extent of agreement among the citizenry regarding the principles that should govern the political process and that should be reflected in the policies of government. For any particular principle, one hundred percent agreement on its appropriateness indicates a situation of perfect consensus. Apart from unanimity, however, there can always be a dispute as to whether the term is correctly applied. Perhaps the best that can be said is that attributions of consensus become increasingly less satisfactory as agreement on fundamental standards of political judgment descends to the fifty percent mark. Yet the difficulties involved in its deployment aside, consensus remains an important part of the vocabulary of politics and is especially relevant to considerations of the relationship between ethnic diversity and democratic stability.

In *The Democratic Civilization*, Leslie Lipson writes:

> Politics consist in a series of struggles over the beliefs and values which constitute a civilization. In politics men are engaging in controversy about alternative ideas and rival principles. They seek to evoke the emotional allegiance of other men's hearts, the intellectual allegiance of their minds. Anything basic, therefore, that unites human beings makes agreement easier and fosters subjectively that awareness of belonging together which students of politics call a consensus.[12]

For Lipson, as for many political theorists, valuational consensus—"the intellectual allegiance of [men's] minds"—is important to the health of the polity. Without general agreement on the operative values of the political system, the common vision necessary to effective governance is absent. As Lipson indicates, shared standards of political judgment can form the basis for the sense of common political identity that is sometimes called the sentiment of community (as will be noted subsequently, this is precisely the case in the United States). But the two concepts—consensus and community—are analytically distinct: community indicates a diffuse sense of belonging, an emotional attachment that may be established on any one of a number of grounds, whereas consensus pertains to specifically valuational concerns. The difference in approach is subtle but important and provides democratic theorists with further reason for pause relative to ethnic heterogeneity.

When democratic government is at issue, political theorists tend to specify a particularly imposing list of attitudes, delicately configured, as necessary to stability. Gabriel Almond and G. Bingham Powell provide a useful means of cataloging the variety of values and dispositions most frequently mentioned. In a recent formulation, Almond and Powell subdivide the investigation of political culture into three constituent parts—system, process, and policy. System orientations refer to an individual's perspectives on the political system in general, especially the values promoted in the operation of the system; process orientations comprise beliefs, affections, and evaluations concerning the manner of making political decisions, including an individual's ideas about his or her own political participation; and policy orientations indicate the evaluative criteria by which political outcomes are judged.[13] As citizens will tend to judge the dominant values of the political system by the same criteria used to assess public policy, there is a certain amount of overlap between the first and last categories. Hence, the following analysis centers on process and system.

With respect to process orientations, a participatory disposition would appear to be a natural concomitant of democracy. As modern democracy indicates a system of government attempting to maximize the equality of citizens' decisionmaking influence, to deny that the participatory urge is important is tantamount to denying democracy itself. Clearly, the vitality of democracy requires that individuals accept participatory responsibilities and that they be willing to act to preserve institutions affirming the importance of citizen input.

Yet paradoxically, democratic theorists often point out that apathy has its place. Several arguments are advanced in support of this claim. First, apathy may indicate that people are free to interest themselves in political life as they see fit. As such, the apathetic portion of the citizenry is a reminder of the liberal principles of democracy—that governments are restricted in their ability to compel action, even political action.[14] Second, at face value the meaning of apathy is unclear. Apathy may reflect cynicism, inefficacy, and hopelessness, none of which augur well for the continuance of stable government. But apathy may also be generated by a sense of satisfaction with the political and socioeconomic status quo—at least there are no a priori reasons to rule out this possibility.[15] Third, the significance of political participation is equally ambiguous. In a given political system, high levels of participation may indicate widespread commitment to the ideals of democracy; they may also indicate the politicization of conflict between constituent social groups or severe dissatisfaction with current policies or leadership and a realization that compromise or conciliation is beyond the pale.[16] Finally, political theorists have maintained that if a democratic government is to govern, political decisions must not be constantly challenged. This is not to suggest that redress of grievance should be ignored. Nevertheless, political quiescence of a certain fashion—whether called deference, indicating conscious acceptance of government decisions, or apathy, denoting much less than this—seems a necessary counterpart to authoritative decisionmaking. Doubtless such arguments risk overstating the case in favor of apathy, but they do contain an essential truth: apathy is a valid democratic choice.

Given the apparent utility of both participatory and nonparticipatory orientations to the democratic process, how can the circle be squared? For many theorists, pursuit of Aristotle's golden mean provides the answer; the democratic political culture is required to be a hybrid of participatory and nonparticipatory dispositions. Thus Almond and Sidney Verba argue that the ideal political culture—the civic culture—is a participatory/nonparticipatory amalgam. While it is important that the citizenry be favorably oriented to the political system in general, its input structures, and its outputs, and that there be a belief in the importance of participation in decisionmaking, at the same time nonparticipatory orientations, moderating the intensity of the citizen's political activity, provide a healthy check on the participatory urge.[17] For that reason, the archetypal citizen of the civic culture is the potential activist. In a stable democracy, the potential exists to be politically active, involved, and influential, but normally the majority of citizens will defer to the decisionmaking authority of others.[18] On Almond and Verba's view, the civic culture is best suited to stable democracy because stable democracy itself consists of opposed mandates. Specifically, democratic government must have the power and strength of leadership to make decisions yet must remain responsible to the citizenry. The civic culture strikes this balance between elite power and elite responsiveness by furnishing the attitudinal matrix that allows government to govern, though subject to a popular check.

But what of the system orientations of the democratic political culture? In brief, the literature of political theory regards at least three values as essential to democratic government and a democratic citizenry. Individualism is the first of these, indicating both freedom from governmental restraint and the primacy of the person over and above the state. In this manner a democratic polity rests on the consent of the governed; the government's legitimacy, in principle, turns on individual assent to political authority. Second, democracy is animated by the principle of equality, which requires, at a minimum, the negation of special privilege; equal treatment under the law; a recognition of the equal worth of all, politically and otherwise; and, for many theorists, a further commitment to social and economic justice.[19] Third, democracy necessitates the toleration of political dissent. From a democratic perspective, the truths of social life, specifically those concerning the standards of political judgment considered normative, can be known only through the discussion of divergent opinions, not through presumptions. Democratic rule proceeds tentatively and humbly, searching for the best policy by means of a procedure based on freedom of expression and inquiry.

Yet these three values—individualism, equality, toleration of dissent—do not exhaust the attitudinal requirements of stable democracy. The literature of democratic theory cites several other orientations as necessary to political stability, attitudes that are not exclusively related to democratic government but that operate to enhance the prospects of stable democracy. A belief in governmental effectiveness is often mentioned in this regard.[20] As all governments are constrained by time and resources, periodically they fail to produce desired policy outcomes; a popular conviction in the overall effectiveness of government serves to buoy public opinion over these disappointments. Conversely, should perceptions of the government's weakness be prevalent, any policy failure magnifies popular frustration and undermines the government's authority. Likewise, respect for the law is an attitude held propitious for democracy.[21] In a democratic context such respect does not signify slavish devotion to authority. Rather, it indicates that constitutionally defined procedures are the essence of a stable democratic process and that the outcomes of this process must be regarded as binding if a free society is to be made secure. Finally, political theorists often point out the importance of trust to the maintenance of the democratic order.[22] To begin with, because modern democracy is representative democracy, citizens must trust those who claim to be acting on their behalf. But furthermore, as democracy affirms the principle of opposition, it is crucial to trust in the good intentions of political adversaries who seek to hold the reins of power. To be sure, too much trust can mean the loss of vigilance necessary to keep public officials accountable, yet if the entire democratic process were predicated on suspicion, it could not operate at all.

Individualism, egalitarianism, tolerance of opposition, belief in governmental efficiency, respect for the law, and trust—the literature of democratic theory mentions all of these as cultural correlates of stable democracy. For this reason, the impression garnered from much political theory is that the democratic order is precariously situated, requiring the citizenry to embrace an eclectic assortment of attitudes—

at least six as noted here. But it is not enough to find the appropriate set of values scattered throughout the population in question. Instead, they must be embraced by individual members of the citizenry, an even more difficult circumstance to effect. Yet this is what political theorists seem to have in mind when they speak of the necessity of consensus to the democratic order.

The importance of consensus to democracy is a favored, if somewhat controversial, theme of political theory. In volume two of *Democracy in America*, Tocqueville claims:

> [In] order that society should exist and, a fortiori, that a society should prosper it is necessary that the minds of all the citizens should be rallied and held together by certain predominant ideas; and this cannot be the case unless each of them sometimes draws his opinions from the common source and consents to accept certain matters of belief already formed.[23]

There is no lack of twentieth-century theorists who share this perspective. In *The First New Nation*, Seymour M. Lipset maintains that social institutions are under constant pressure to adjust themselves to a central value system and that the failure to do so results in political instability. According to Lipset, legitimacy, and thus stability, is conferred by shared beliefs concerning the proper exercise of political power.[24] Similarly, in a joint article, Ernest Griffiths, John Plamenatz, and J. Roland Pennock, while differing on the precise composition of the required attitudinal orientations, argue for the importance of consensus on these values. The exact measure of consensus is left moot, but the authors exude a common conviction that the values in question be "widespread." Pennock reflects the view of his colleagues when he claims that "democracy, like other forms of government but to a greater extent, must rest upon a measure of consensus, upon a certain community of values."[25] Although the necessary extent of the consensus on any particular issue is difficult to pinpoint, "no commitment to constitutionalism is likely to withstand a persistent deep and wide cleavage on policy. Nor are people so divided likely to be willing to compromise."[26] Echoing this sentiment, William Ebenstein writes that "a condition indispensable to democracy is common agreement on fundamentals. . . . [Where] agreement on fundamentals is lacking, political democracy suffers from stresses and strains that may well become fatal."[27] Giving his blessing to a version of the consensus thesis as well, Joseph Schumpeter writes that agreement on the virtues of democratic control must be diffuse and that "democratic government will work to full advantage only if all the interests that matter are practically unanimous not only in their allegiance to the country but also to the structural principles of the existing society."[28]

Still, among students of politics there is no unanimous and unqualified acceptance of the importance of consensus to democracy. For some, political elites are the guardians of the democratic order and the only group that needs to evince thorough commitment to the democratic belief system. Herbert McClosky, for instance, is convinced that democracy can survive despite popular misunderstanding and disagreement on the application of democratic principles to political life. This survival is possible because the minority of individuals who are most likely to participate in politics, and who have the greatest influence on political decisionmaking, displays the strongest commitment to a democratic value system.[29] Relatedly, Dahl claims that stable democracy depends primarily on the agreement of elites on the essential components of the democratic creed. All that is required of the electorate is that it accepts the general value orientation of democracy, and this it may do simply on pragmatic grounds rather than from moral conviction.[30]

Others minimize the importance of consensus because of their belief in the utility of conflict. Pursuing this theme, Ralf Dahrendorf argues that conflict can contribute to the integration of social systems, serving as a means of resolving tensions between antagonistic parties by releasing submerged grievances that can prevent political unity. Furthermore, as stability requires a political system to respond to changes in its environment, conflict prevents stagnation by supplying the impetus for change. Indeed, political and social systems in which conflict is not regarded as deviant are better able to cope with major conflicts should they arise. If the political system allows for the free expression and consideration of different interests, citizens are more inclined to support the procedures of political decisionmaking as well as the outcomes of those procedures. Dahrendorf notes that it is totalitarian governments that have little tolerance for conflict, not democratic ones.[31]

Alternatively, a number of theorists believe consensus falls short as an explanation for stable democracy because it underplays the role that simple force of habit plays in political life. On this view, the initial submission of political disputes to a democratic procedure of decisionmaking, successful conflict resolution via this procedure, and the habits engendered by repeated participation in this political method can account for political stability apart from any explicitly ideological commitment to democracy. Bernard Crick writes:

Consensus is not a systematic, external and intangible spiritual adhesive, not some metaphysical cement or something mysteriously prior to or above politics; it is the activity of politics itself. In a political system the "public interest," the "common good," and the "general will" are simply pretentious or partisan ways of describing the common interest in preserving the means of making public decisions politically.[32]

Thus, if a consensus on values in fact exists, this may well be a product of the democratic method rather than a requirement for it.

Such reservations notwithstanding, the idea of consensus cannot be easily dismissed. Its validity can perhaps best be realized if the question is put in a negative form: does the absence of consensus have an effect on stable democracy? Asked in this manner, the importance of consensus is more difficult to deny. Even those who challenge the positive effect of consensus on stable democracy are reluctant to disregard the negative effect of the lack of consensus. McClosky, for example, writes, "I do not mean to suggest, of course, that a nation runs no risks when a large number of its citizens fail to grasp the essential principles on which its constitution is founded."[33] "To conclude ... that ideological awareness and consensus are overvalued as determinants of democratic viability," he continues, "is not to imply that they are of no importance."[34] Dahl's comments on the subject of consensus contain a similar disclaimer. Although political elites demonstrate a greater acceptance of the specifics of the democratic ethos, if it were not for considerable popular agreement on that ethos, elites might well be able to depart from the norms of democracy:

> Even if a universal belief in a democratic creed does not guarantee the stability of a democratic system, a substantial decline in the popular consensus would greatly increase the chance of serious instability. How the professionals act, what they advocate, what they are likely to believe, are all constrained by the wide adherence to the creed that exists throughout the community.[35]

Even Dahrendorf, while wishing to distance himself from social theorists who stress the importance of consensus (and the dysfunctionality of conflict), appears to admit the importance of value agreement. When writing of the means to effective conflict regulation, he comments that

> both parties to a conflict have to recognize the necessity and reality of the conflict situation and, in this sense, the fundamental justice of the cause of the opponent. In a way, this is a value premise. .... Wherever

the attempt is made to dispute the case of the opponent by calling it "unrealistic," or denying the opponent the right to make a case at all, effective regulation is not possible.... Without doubt, there are "common interests" in any conflict situation; without community, no conflict, and vice versa.[36]

Granted, this is a far cry from those who understand consensus as a requisite of political stability and conflict as a threat to that stability. But in these passages Dahrendorf seems to acknowledge the importance of shared norms to the maintenance of stability, especially that of toleration for opposition.

Why is it, then, that these individuals hedge on the issue of consensus? The explanation seems to lie in the problematic nature of the alternative to consensus. Common sense indicates that disagreement over the fundamental values informing the political process cannot be in the interest of system maintenance. Such dissent indicates alienation from the political system, a circumstance in which the legitimacy of the system, its right to rule and command obedience, is challenged. Polities that experience deep and persistent divisions regarding the norms of political activity cannot long survive or at least cannot govern effectively. Nor is this simply theoretical speculation. The historical record displays examples of democracies in which the absence of consensus led to instability: the experience of France during the Third and Fourth Republics, Weimar Germany, and postwar Italy is instructive.[37] Conversely, one may point to the consensual nature of political attitudes in countries generally regarded as stable—Sweden, Britain, and the United States, for instance.[38] As Max Weber has argued, the most secure form of political power is that grounded in legitimacy, and legitimacy turns on the extent of popular agreement concerning the norms of the political system.[39]

In light of these considerations, political theorists frequently seek a middle ground. Once more, the principle of balance is offered as a solution, a recognition that consensus and division must accommodate each other in a vital and stable democracy. So, for example, according to Almond and Verba, the civic culture is this hybrid of consensus and conflict. On their view, democratic politics cannot shy away from political conflict as this very conflict produces the policy choices that give democracy its pluralistic quality. Yet if the divisions within a democratic citizenry are too deep, or dissensus is too widespread, political fragmentation and stagnation will follow. Hence, conflict and consensus must effect a certain tension for stable democracy to obtain.[40] In similar fashion, Harry Eckstein argues that democracy presupposes competition between political interests. As the democratic method does not permit the creation of consensus through coercion, in order to resolve such contending interests into workable policy decisions, cohesive social forces must sustain a general public consensus over and above specific instances of conflict.41

Doubtless, there is danger in seeking the "golden mean." To say that both consensus and dissensus are required for stable democracy is to invite the charge that nothing concrete is being said at all. This is particularly the case if empirical measurements of the amount of consensus necessary are not forthcoming, i.e., specification of the key variables to be analyzed and the amount of dissensus permissible. Nevertheless, something eminently sensible *is* being said: social consensus on the norms of democratic government is a more auspicious condition for stable democracy than the alternative. Consensus on the specific application of political principle to the policy and procedures of democratic governments is not required—this is the area where conflict has a crucial role to play in assuring the vitality and responsiveness of democracy. What cannot be recommended, however, is persistent disagreement over the fundamental values by which to judge the policies and procedures of democratic government; at the very least there must not be active antipathy to those values. Even if the concept of consensus proves methodologically inconvenient, its intuitive appeal is difficult to deny.

To review: on the insights of democratic theory, stable democracy relies on a delicate attitudinal equilibrium, which is sufficient reason for its comparative rarity among nations. In the first instance, the list of psychological orientations believed necessary to stable democracy is quite extensive; that alone might suggest the difficulty of achieving the democratic order. But more than this, the relevant values and dispositions should not only be present within a democratic citizenry but should also be in proper alignment. Participatory and non-participatory orientations must coexist. Citizens should be able and willing to participate in politics, but not to the degree that the process of decisionmaking itself is paralyzed—even democratic governments must be allowed to govern. Furthermore, a balance must be achieved between consensus and conflict. Public contestation over issues of public policy is a mark of democratic vitality, yet conflict must not encompass the central principles of political practice, the foundational values on which the structures of government are established and toward which the activities of government are directed. On the strength of such observations, then, as forwarded in the literature of political theory, the dominant image of democratic government is that of fragility.

Consequently, it is not surprising that in the canons of democratic theory, ethnic heterogeneity is often feared for its potential to disturb the valuational equilibrium of a stable political system. Once more, Mill is among the first theorists to make the concern explicit (though traces of the argument may be detected before this—in Montesquieu's discussion of the fall of Rome, for instance). In the *Considerations,* in a passage immediately preceding one already cited, Mill writes:

> Free Institutions are next to impossible in a country made up of different nationalities. Among people without fellow feeling, especially if they read and speak different languages, *the united public opinion, necessary to the working of representative government, cannot exist.* The influences which form opinions and decide the political acts are different in the different sections of the country (emphasis added).[42]

According to Mill, not only does heterogeneity threaten the emotional bonds of political community, but it also suggests an attitudinal dissensus—the lack of "united public opinion"—equally destructive of the polity. Ethnic groups (or in Mill's terms, "nationalities") are culturally distinct, that is to say, they possess group-specific systems of belief. Should such idiosyncracies of belief extend to matters of political principle, ethnic diversity promises political discord and instability.

In the case of a specifically democratic political order, the implications of ethnically induced dissensus would seem all the more severe, if only because the attitudinal requisites of democratic stability are so exacting. It is not to be expected that all ethnic groups will possess the impressive array of psychological attributes believed necessary to sustain a democratic polity. It is difficult enough for an ethnically homogeneous population to possess such an imposing set of political orientations, let alone a population that is culturally, and thus attitudinally, pluralistic. In fact it might be imagined that the greater the number of ethnic groups a single state encompasses, the less likely that state will be to achieve the consensus essential to its preservation. Indeed, the problem of democratic consensus is doubly vexing: stable democracy requires such a carefully balanced set of political orientations, it would seem especially vulnerable to the disruptions of ethnic heterogeneity. Thus, if the standard analyses of democratic political culture are correct, it may be inferred that the prospects for an ethnically diverse but stable democracy are inauspicious. The very fragility of democracy would appear to make it more susceptible than other forms of government to heterogeneity's unsettling consequences.

The Limits of Public Policy

Democratic theory is wary of ethnic heterogeneity for a further reason: once heterogeneity becomes part of a state's social fabric, governments have only a limited ability to moderate its putative ill-effects. Community and consensus are based on a depth of personal conviction, an emotional commitment to other citizens in the first instance and to a particular set of political beliefs in the second. It is this strength of conviction, whether emotional or intellectual, that cannot be readily manufactured through the manipulation of public policy. In this manner, ethnic heterogeneity poses political difficulties especially resistant to resolution. So, while a canvas of the literature of political theory produces several recommendations aimed at diminishing the disruptive political effects of heterogeneity, each is in some sense an unsatisfactory means of addressing the questions that heterogeneity raises.

Consociationalism is a favored remedy among democratic theorists wishing to reconcile political stability and ethnically diverse societies. Consociational political systems possess four major features: (1) a government comprising a grand coalition of the political leaders of all significant segments of the plural society; (2) proportionality as the major standard of all political representation, including civil service appointments; (3) the privilege of mutual veto among the political elites of the various social segments (concurrent majority rule); and (4) a high degree of political autonomy for constituent social groups. With respect to the problem of ethnic heterogeneity, the benefits of such an arrangement appear to be threefold. First, consociationalism is a means of limiting the antagonism between disparate ethnic groups by isolating their membership. In place of popular participation in political decisionmaking at the national level, consociationalism devolves considerable power to ethnic groups in matters that directly relate to their interests. Second, the number of political demands channeled to the central government are thereby reduced, as are the chances of immobilism. Third, decisions reached within a small elite group, with a common set of political assumptions and understandings, are easier to reach and execute. In short, consociationalism is a means of dealing with heterogeneity by institutionalizing it.[43]

Yet consociationalism would seem an extremely difficult solution to put into practice. Even Lijphart, perhaps the greatest advocate of the perspective, confesses that the consociational solution is not universally applicable.[44] Consociationalism itself requires a special mixture of institutional and attitudinal characteristics that Lijphart calls the "favorable conditions" for consociationalism: (1) cross-cutting cleavages to reduce the intensity of a single group loyalty or the potential of unified group policy objectives; (2) a multiple balance of power among the social segments, including a multiparty system of optimally four members; (3) group elites that can command the loyalty and commitment of the constituents for whom they speak; (4) the small size of the state in question, facilitating elite trust and interaction, reducing the import of foreign policy decisions, and limiting the number of demands that the government must manage.[45] From the vantage point of a government considering a consociational solution to heterogeneity, it must appear that one set of impressive requirements—the attitudinal criteria for stable democracy—has been replaced by another, namely those pertinent to consociationalism. Nor does consociationalism do much to address the issues of community and consensus. In fact, it would seem that consociationalism acknowledges the futility of establishing either consensus or community in an ethnically divided polity. At most, consociationalism aspires to reduce the mutual antagonisms of ethnically divided social segments rather than meld them into an emotional or ideological whole.

Beyond consociationalism, democratic theorists may recommend a more equitable distribution of resources as a means of delimiting ethnic conflict. As already noted, a democratic sense of community flourishes only in conditions of equality. Conflict destructive of the sentiment of community often stems from the belief that desired goods and services are inequitably distributed. It is diminished to the degree that ethnic groups do not perceive themselves as disadvantaged. Governments may respond by trying to foster public belief in the equal balance of rewards among constituent social groups. Among the policy measures taken to promote this perception are legal prohibitions on ethnic discrimination, ethnic quotas for public office, school desegregation, affirmative action in employment, official recognition of minority languages, or, more aggressively, an ethnically specific distribution of welfare benefits.[46]

Even though advice to promote equality is appealing, its execution is problematic. In the first place, the particular dimension of equality at issue must be defined. Although social, economic, and political equality are related, they remain distinct concerns and could each be the point of the government's efforts. Second, as complete equality in resource distribution is virtually impossible to achieve in practice (nor would it in all cases be desirable), the measure of equality by which successful public policy is to be judged must be specified. In other words, how much equality is enough? The answer would seem to be related to popular perceptions of equality, but these perceptions may exist quite apart from the objective distribution of goods. Nor are all citizens likely to interpret equality in the same way. Finally, even if these problems could be overcome, there would remain people with an interest in maintaining inequality. As such individuals are likely to be beneficiaries of the unequal distribution of resources, including political power, alienating them may well threaten the very political stability that the equal distribution of resources seeks to accomplish. Again, a possible remedy for the ills of heterogeneity is burdened by the question of implementation.

Assimilation to dominant cultural norms is a further method of coping with heterogeneity, although the literature of democratic theory does not so much advise assimilation as it observes its happy effect—America being the archetypical example. The conventional manner of employing the term *assimilation* is to indicate conformity to the preexisting norms of a particular social segment. Accordingly, assimilation nears its endpoint when other groups come to identify most closely with the cultural imperatives of one social group and when this dominant group is willing to accept individuals who were not originally members as equal participants in group life.[47] Ideally, the values and behavior subsumed in a stable democracy would be transmitted in this assimilation process, as would be a single political identity.

But democratic governments face numerous difficulties in following the path of assimilation. One of them is that government-sponsored assimilation programs suggest autocracy. Imposing uniformity on a fragmented society is opposed, some might claim, to the democratic value of freedom, including freedom of association. Hence attempts at Russification have been pointed to as instances of tsarist, and subsequently Soviet, illiberalism. But even more fundamentally, efforts to assimilate foreign-born populations may fail because of the native population's general unwillingness to engage in them. Although eugenics has become otiose, the principal of cultural exclusivity remains strong. It is especially vital in the states of Europe that have been the source of so much of the human wave of immigration to the Western Hemisphere. Indeed the idea of becoming English, French, or German without having been born a national and possessing the correct lineage is incomprehensible. In the New World the prospects for assimilation would seem to be more propitious, though in fact the same resistance is also found. Thus upon independence from Britain, Canberra implemented its "White Australia" policy, denying too wide an extension of the assimilationist logic, while the guiding myth of the contemporary Canadian social structure is the "ethnic mosaic," the very denial that assimilation is feasible or advisable. It is in America where the commitment to assimilation seems most firmly grounded, and yet even here more needs to be said (and will be said in succeeding chapters). Neither the sense of political community nor the prospects for political consensus are advanced when ethnic minorities receive so little encouragement to assimilate.

Failing a solution to heterogeneity that keeps political rule intact, public officials may find it necessary to grant territorial autonomy to constituent social groups. If the various ethnic groups are geographically concentrated, several methods of political disaggregation may be pursued. The least extreme is the devolution of authority to subnational geographical units, a regionalization of political power that allows local autonomy to coexist with national territorial integrity. Separatism is the most drastic possibility, changing the character of the state by dismembering it.

The problem with this approach is, of course, that no state wishes to be torn asunder—nations go to war to prevent this very thing. But besides the resistance stemming from political hubris, there are very pragmatic reasons to avoid such a development. The resources required to confront the problems of a modern political economy point to more territorial integrity and national coordination, not less. The interdependence of the world economy suggests on a global scale what must happen on the national level. In this respect, territorial fragmentation is obstructionist, stripping government of the ability to tackle major issues of public policy. It is also the ultimate recognition that the problems of consensus and community in an ethnically divided state are intractable.

Conclusion

The argument against ethnic heterogeneity may now be stated in full. First, ethnic diversity makes more difficult the preservation of political community. Heterogeneity suggests competing political loyalties and the lack of emotional integration characteristic of a healthy polity. Additionally, because ethnic loyalties are often fierce, political conflict understood in ethnic terms will be intense and resistant to compromise. Within the context of a democratic political community, a community united by a commitment to the political equality of all its members, heterogeneity may be particularly troubling. The greater the number of ethnic groups to which political power must be distributed, the more difficult it is for democracy to proceed on the basis of equality. Democracy also articulates the right to self-determination, lending weight to the claims of ethnic groups for political autonomy; according to much democratic theory, ethnic homogeneity is not only a guarantor of stable democracy but its by-product. Second, ethnic heterogeneity is said to undermine the psychological foundations of the democratic order. On this view, the prospects for stable democracy depend on a citizenry that affirms an imposing catalog of values and dispositions in a carefully calibrated mix. Moreover, democratic theory cites the importance of consensus on the appropriate set of attitudes; individual members of the political community are expected to espouse the same general standards of political judgment. Ethnic identity is founded, in part, on specific systems of belief common to a distinct cultural grouping. Thus, in an ethnically heterogeneous social environment, the achievement of consensus may involve reconciling discrete, and perhaps opposed, sets of political attitudes. For this reason an ethnically homogeneous citizenry, socialized to common political orientations, may be a more promising circumstance for stable democracy. Finally, should ethnic heterogeneity be an accomplished fact, there is little that democratic governments can do to limit its supposedly debilitating consequences, little that is effective or does not impose unacceptable political costs. It is on the basis of this three-pronged analysis that theorists of democracy most often find ethnic heterogeneity wanting for democracy.

Democratic theory's approach to the subject of immigration is shaped by its perspective on ethnic heterogeneity. By implication, immigration poses a challenge to the integrity of the political community, and to the maintenance of political consensus necessary to the democratic order, because it is likely to produce the ethnic diversity that democratic theory views with apprehension. Moreover, as democratic governments have only a limited ability to reduce the political consequences of an ethnically heterogeneous population, it may be thought that the best way to deal with an ethnically diverse population is to avoid dealing with it; immigration restriction is a natural outgrowth of this perspective. Admittedly, this case against immigration is often latent, implicit in general observations concerning ethnic heterogeneity, but it is a case that is nonetheless real. It manifests itself most clearly when addressing countries where immigration has been the primary source of diversity. The United States is one such country.

Notes

1. As the examples cited—conscription and taxation—suggest, concern for national integration is in one sense a function of the expanding compass of state power. For that reason, a number of scholars date its appearance as a political issue of some urgency, at least in Europe and North America, from the middle of the nineteenth century. See E. J. Hobsbawm, *Nations and*

Nationalism Since 1780: Programme, Myth, Reality (Cambridge: Cambridge University Press, 1990), pp. 81–92; also Anthony H. Birch, *Nationalism and National Integration* (London: Unwin Hyman, 1989), pp. 8–9.

2. Quoted in David Bell and Lorne Tepperman, *The Roots of Disunity* (Toronto: McClelland and Stewart, 1979), p. 133.

3. Ernest Barker, *Reflections on Government* (Oxford: Oxford University, 1942), p. 62.

4. For a discussion of the relationship between ethnic homogeneity and majoritarian democracy see Arend Lijphart, *Democracies: Patterns of Majoritarian and Consensus Government in Twenty-One Countries* (New Haven: Yale University Press, 1984), pp. 21–45.

5. John Stuart Mill, *Considerations on Representative Government* (1867; rpt. London: J. M. Dent and Sons, 1972), p. 361.

6. Ibid., pp. 359–66.

7. Ibid., pp. 360–61.

8. Michael Walzer, "Pluralism in Political Perspective," in *The Politics of Ethnicity*, ed. Stephan Thernstrom (Cambridge: The Belknap Press of Harvard University Press, 1982), p. 5.

9. Robert A. Dahl, *Polyarchy: Participation and Opposition* (New Haven: Yale University Press, 1971), pp. 108—10.

10. Lijphart, *Democracies*, pp. 42–43.

11. G. Bingham Powell, *Contemporary Democracies: Participation, Stability, Violence* (Cambridge: Harvard University Press, 1982), pp. 42–45, 73–96.

12. Leslie Lipson, *The Democratic Civilization* (New York: Oxford University Press, 1964), p. 120.

13. Gabriel Almond and G. Bingham Powell, eds., *Comparative Politics Today: A World View* (Boston: Little, Brown, 1980), pp. 42–48.

14. See, for example, W. H. Morris-Jones, "In Defence of Apathy: Some Doubts on the Duty to Vote," *Political Studies*, II, No. 1 (1954), 36–37.

15. Ernest S. Griffiths, John Plamenatz, and J. Roland Pennock, "Cultural Prerequisites to a Successfully Functioning Democracy," *American Political Science Review*, L, No. 1 (1956), 130.

16. Ibid.

17. Gabriel Almond and Sidney Verba, *The Civic Culture: Political Attitudes and Democracy in Five Nations* (Boston: Little, Brown, 1965), pp. 29–30.

18. Ibid., pp. 19–30, 339–41, 479–83.

19. See, for instance, C. B. MacPherson, *The Real World of Democracy* (Toronto: Canadian Broadcasting Company, 1965), p. 58.

20. See, for example, Dahl, *Polyarchy*, pp. 144–49; Almond and Verba, *Civic Culture*, p. 488.

21. On this theme see Griffiths, Plamenatz, and Pennock, *Cultural Prerequisites*, pp. 119–21, 132; also Dorothy Pickles, *Democracy* (New York: Basic Books, 1970), pp. 151–54.

22. See, for example, J. Roland Pennock, *Democratic Political Theory* (Princeton: Princeton University Press, 1979), pp. 241–42; also Dahl, *Polyarchy*, pp. 150–52.

23. Alexis de Tocqueville, *Democracy in America,* trans. Henry Reeve, revised Francis Bowen, ed. Phillips Bradley (New York: Vintage, 1945), II, p. 9.

24. Seymour Martin Lipset, *The First New Nation: The United States in Historical and Comparative Perspective* (New York: Basic, 1963), pp. 3–16.

25. Griffiths, Plamenatz, and Pennock, *Cultural Prerequisites,* p. 132.

26. Ibid., p. 132.

27. William Ebenstein, *Today's Isms: Communism, Fascism, Capitalism, Socialism,* 8th ed. (Englewood Cliffs: Prentice-Hall, 1980), p. 83.

28. Joseph Schumpeter, *Capitalism, Socialism, and Democracy,* 3rd ed. (New York: Harper, 1950), pp. 294–96.

29. Herbert McClosky, "Consensus and Ideology in American Politics," *American Political Science Review,* LVIII (1964), 376–77.

30. Robert A. Dahl, *Who Governs? Democracy and Power in an American City* (New Haven: Yale University Press, 1961), p. 314.

31. Ralf Dahrendorf, *Class and Class Conflict in Industrial Society* (Stanford: Stanford University Press, 1959), pp. 207–08.

32. See Bernard Crick, *In Defense of Politics,* 2nd ed. (Harmondsworth: Pelican, 1964), p. 177.

33. McClosky, *Consensus and Ideology,* p. 376.

34. Ibid., pp. 378–79.

35. Dahl, *Who Governs?* p. 325.

36. Dahrendorf, *Class and Class Conflict,* p. 225.

37. See, for example, Henry W. Ehrmann, *Politics in France* (Boston: Little, Brown, 1983), pp. 1–17; William Safran, *The French Polity* (New York: Longman, 1977), pp. 35–50; Gordon Smith, *Democracy in Western Germany: Parties and Politics in the Federal Republic* (London: Heinemann, 1979), pp. 17–34; P. A. Allum, *Italy: Republic Without Government* (New York: Norton, 1974), pp. 20–45; also see Joseph LaPalombara, *Democracy Italian Style* (New Haven: Yale University Press, 1987), esp. chs. 2 and 5, although La Palombara argues that Italy is not as unstable as it might first appear.

38. See, for example, Francis Castles, "Scandinavia: The Politics of Stability," in *Modern Political Systems: Europe,* ed. Roy C. Macridis, 5th ed. (Englewood Cliffs: Prentice-Hall, 1983), pp. 401–07; M. D. Hancock, *Sweden: The Politics of Post-Industrial Change* (Hinsdale: Dryden, 1975), pp. 40–45; S. E. Finer, "Politics of Great Britain," in *Modern Political Systems: Europe,* ed. Roy C. Macridis, 5th ed. (Englewood Cliffs: Prentice-Hall, 1983), pp. 24–27; Richard Rose, *Politics in England,* 3rd ed. (Boston: Little, Brown, 1980), pp. 111–38.

39. Max Weber, *The Theory of Social and Economic Organization* (New York: Oxford University Press, 1947), pp. 324–29. Also see David Easton, *A Systems Analysis of Political Life* (New York: John Wiley and Sons, 1965), pp. 273–87.

40. Almond and Verba, *Civic Culture,* pp. 490–91.

41. Harry Eckstein, *Division and Cohesion in Democracy* (Princeton: Princeton University Press, 1966), pp. 30–31, 234–41.

42. Mill, *Considerations,* p. 363. Also see Mill's discussion on the difficulties of colonial rule, pp. 383ff.

43. Arend Lijphart, *Democracy in Plural Societies: A Comparative Exploration* (New Haven: Yale University Press, 1977), pp. 25ff.

44. See ibid., pp. 134–76.

45. Ibid., p. 54.

46. See Francis G. Castles, *Political Stability* (Milton Keynes: The Open University, 1974), pp. 66–68.

47. Raymond H. C. Teske and Bardin H. Nelson, "Acculturation and Assimilation: A Clarification," *American Ethnologist,* I (1974), 359–61.

3

Immigrants, Consensus, and America

He is an American, who, leaving behind him all his ancient prejudices and manners, receives new ones from the new mode of life he has embraced, the new government he obeys, and the new rank he holds. He becomes an American by being received into the broad lap of our great Alma Mater. Here individuals of all nations are melted into a new race of men, whose labor and posterity will one day cause great changes in the world.

—J. Hector St. John de Crevecouer,
Letters from an American Farmer

But are there no inconveniences to be thrown into the scale against the advantage expected from a multiplication of numbers by the importation of foreigners? . . . They will bring with them the principles of the governments they leave, imbibed in their early youth; or, if able to throw them off, it will be in exchange for an unbounded licentiousness, passing, as is usual, from one extreme to another. . . . In proportion to their numbers they will share with us the legislation. They will infuse into it their spirit, warp and bias its directions, and render it a heterogeneous, incoherent, distracted mass.

—Thomas Jefferson

In the literature of American democratic theory, discussions of immigration are marked by circumspection. Although the United States is widely acknowledged as the greatest of all settler societies,[1] a society whose nature and development cannot be understood apart from immigration, students of American politics, following the lead of conventional democratic theory, have often considered the foreign-born a potentially destabilizing political force.

This latter assertion seems curious at first, sullying traditional notions of American benevolence. It is Emma Lazarus's verse, "Give me your tired, your poor, your huddled masses yearning to breathe free," that provides the dominant understanding of America's treat-

34

ment of immigrants. Nor should this interpretation of history be cynically dismissed. American generosity has been motivated mostly by the demand for foreign labor and undoubtedly has been rewarded with economic benefits. Nevertheless, for the greater part of the nineteenth century and much of the twentieth, the "golden door" has been left open. Millions of immigrants have been permitted to disembark and take up permanent residence. And whatever the motivation of the United States government, the outcome has been that socially and economically oppressed peoples have found tangible freedoms and in many cases have achieved material success. Furthermore, and the significance of this must not be understated, America has extended an opportunity for immigrants to become American, to assume American identities. In some instances, particularly with regard to Asians, there has been a certain ambivalence about the latter, but all things considered, a good case can be made for American beneficence, especially when placed in comparative context.

That said, the American record on immigration is inescapably checkered. Indeed, by the time Lazarus's poem was celebrated at the Statue of Liberty's dedication (1886), the first in a series of immigration restriction acts had been passed that would culminate in the comprehensive limiting legislation of the 1920s. The juxtaposition of public sentiment is instructive—the American demeanor has been at once charitable and inhospitable, embracing immigrants yet wary of them. To be sure, the United States takes official pride in its immigrant roots, strength through ethnic diversity being an elementary lesson of civic education. But this positive assessment of the foreign-born and their progeny has never been thoroughgoing, as the enduring potency of nativist movements attest. Even when the animus of nativism has been absent, a generalized fear of the immigrant has often inspired widespread support for restrictionist political initiatives. If an intermittent affliction, this apparently collective amnesia concerning the republic's social origins points to a not so subtle American irony: a nation of immigrants in which immigrants have not always been welcome.

The present chapter suggests that one source of these restrictionist inclinations, though by no means the only source, has been a concern for immigrant-induced ideological diversity. In this respect, the practice of American politics has in some measure conformed to the cautionary approach of American democratic theory regarding immigration. Political theorists frequently observe that America is a highly consensual country, one whose stability is believed to rest on the extent of citizen attachment to a particular set of liberal-democratic values and whose identity is defined by those values. In terms of the distinctions drawn in the previous chapter, sentiments of community and consensus merge in the United States, intellectual allegiance to a set of political ideas simultaneously defining the affective boundaries of the American political community. Moreover, given that American society is extremely heterogeneous with respect to ethnicity, commitment to this shared political ethos serves to integrate the republic's political and social order. Consequently, students of American politics have reasoned that the foreign-born, socialized to alien norms not only unsettling to America's ideological equilibrium but also striking at its very sense of nationhood, threaten political disruption. The United States can accommodate ethnic idiosyncracies if all this means is the introduction of new cuisine, quaint folk rituals, or even alternative modes of worship. On the conventional theoretical wisdom, however, what cannot be so easily entertained is a political value system that is too pluralistic.

The challenge of American democracy, then, has been to find a means of reconciling immigrants to the central political creed on which the republic's identity and stability are said to rest. Historically, efforts to exorcise "deviant" immigrant attitudes via the proscriptions of law, or, more usually, to assimilate immigrants through ambitious programs of political socialization, have been motivated by this concern. And, in fact, the success of the American experiment in democracy is regularly credited to the immigrant's acceptance of the values in question. As will be related, students and practitioners of American politics have tended to believe that it is only by virtue of continual pressures to Americanize that a "polyglot boarding house" has been transformed into a consensual democracy. The underlying assumption, however, seems clear: immigrants qua immigrants are politically unreliable and must be recast in an American ideological mold.

The Nature of the American Consensus

Tocqueville encapsulates the consensus perspective on American society. His explanation of the American democratic order centers on the attitudinal characteristics of the citizenry. It is the "habits of the heart," the character of the mind, that are the preeminent reason for the success of the American polity. The entire moral and intellectual condition of a people determines their aptitude for certain forms of government. Tocqueville writes:

> The customs of the Americans of the United States are, then, the peculiar
> cause which renders the people the only one of the American nations

that is able to support a democratic government; and it is the influence of customs that produces the different degrees of order and prosperity which may be distinguished in the several Anglo-American democracies.[2]

But more than just the customs of the Americans, the pervasiveness of the dominant political ethos assures the status of democracy:

> In the United States the fundamental principle of the republic is the same which governs the greater part of human actions; republican notions insinuate themselves into all the ideas, opinions, and habits of the Americans and are formally recognized by the laws; and before the laws could be altered, the whole community must be revolutionized.[3]

In the view of many students of American democracy, these "republican notions" of which Tocqueville speaks are shaped by the values comprising Lockean liberalism and participatory democracy. To invoke the name of Locke is not to suggest that the Founding Fathers were necessarily mesmerized by the *Second Treatise* (although some of them certainly were). The substance of American political culture may be attributed to other things—revolutionary origins, the frontier, the absence of a feudal past, Puritanism, economic abundance, even immigration itself. But the philosophy of Locke, when given a heightened democratic profile, seems to capture prevailing political opinion in America.

This enriched variety of liberalism consists of several interrelated values. First, Locke celebrates the individual; society is brought into existence through the voluntary consent of independent agents seeking to maximize their self-interest. One of the earliest social historians of the American scene, Crevecouer, noted this Lockean impulse in the American "new man." Bursting the fetters of socially stratified Europe, the American was able to pursue the essence of his or her nature—self-interest—and create a nation based on personal initiative and self-reliance.[4] Certainly the heros of the national mythology are rugged individualists who tame the wild countryside or, through powers of self-assertion, fight against corruption and evil—the "Lone Ranger" is a modern fictional example of this persona; Davy Crockett and Daniel Boone are the traditional nonfictional ones.

Consonant with this perspective is the belief that society and government are merely the summation of the separate wills of individuals. Society and government exist to serve individual persons, to assist them in the attainment of individually determined goals, and to secure the preservation of their right to life, liberty, and happiness.

As Thomas Paine, in the opening lines of *Common Sense,* draws the distinction, "Society is produced by our wants and government by our wickedness; the former promotes our happiness positively by uniting our affections, the latter negatively by restraining our vices."[5] In this manner, government is more of a police officer defending the individual against unwarranted intrusions than a creative agency or a vehicle through which a common public life might be shared. It is precisely this "first language of American individualism" that several social commentators have taken to task for destroying the mutuality of American public life. On this view, individualist standards of judgment are so pervasive as to prevent Americans from developing a strong sense of an integrating public good, some common object of citizenship. In the United States the public good is simply another way of expressing the resolution of conflict among competing interests, while citizenship is largely understood in an instrumental fashion—a means of securing individual (or at least group-specific) satisfactions. Consequently, it is maintained, Americans lack a sense of belonging to something greater than themselves, a commitment to a community wider than their immediate families that might provide the meaning and security they seek but have difficulty finding.[6]

Lockean individualism touches on a further characteristic of the American value system—freedom. In terms of the conventional distinction between negative and positive notions of freedom, the American conception is highly negative. It is important to Locke that individuals retain as much autonomy as is consistent with the rudiments of civil society. Indeed, the purpose of government is to protect natural rights so that the exercise of freedom is more secure than in the state of nature. Any extension of political authority beyond the minimal provisions necessary for external security and internal order requires the consent of the citizenry. Locke is skeptical that a government left unchecked can be trusted to preserve the widest range of freedoms possible for the society it regulates. So too, Americans have generally been suspicious of political authority and quick to restrain the exercise of power. In part this outlook is a legacy of a nation born in rebellion against a perceived oppressor; in part it is a product of being a settler society with a relatively fluid frontier beyond the grasp of established authority. Accordingly, Americans have hedged government about with an impressive array of devices meant sharply to fragment its power: a bill of rights guaranteeing freedom of expression, assembly, and religion, redress of grievance, and due process of law; a written constitution specifying discrete powers relative to the various branches of government, which, under the rubric of an additional American commitment to the idea of checks and balances, is functionally a system of separate institutions with shared powers; a federal system of rule that, in principle, imposes the countervailing power of state against national government and, at the very least, inhibits the cohesion of the latter through a bicameral Congress in which the two legislative chambers are regarded as virtual equals. From the perspective of political theory, this lack of a single locus of political authority has also meant that in the United States the doctrines of sovereignty so familiar in Europe are absent. At best, Americans seem to entertain a somewhat amorphous belief in the concept of legal sovereignty, or the even more ambiguous (if not for that reason uncelebrated) popular sovereignty, but clearly are made uncomfortable by any statement of the legitimacy and superior authority of the state. Indeed, it has been pointed out that even American radicalism has shared this distinctly antistate cast. The history of the American labor movement, for instance, generally reveals a preference for syndicalism (e.g., the American Federation of Labor) or anarcho-syndicalism (e.g., the Industrial Workers of the World), unionists typically placing their confidence in worker voluntarism, not the state, as a vehicle of positive change. By contrast, in the electorate's eyes one of the major liabilities of the late-nineteenth–early-twentieth-century American socialist movement, and a reason for the meager support it received, was precisely its belief, imagined or otherwise, in the utility of state power.[7]

Americans have insisted that the benefits of personal freedom be extended to economic interaction so that the sphere of government authority in this area is also minimized. As the archetypical "possessive individualist," Locke once again provides the touchstone in these matters, arguing that insecurity of ownership is a major liability of the state of the nature and making the preservation of private property rights the prime function of civil society. Similarly, in *The Federalist* #10, Madison describes the "first object of government" as the protection of faculties through which men are led to possess different amounts of property. Although the practice of American political economy has long ago departed from such laissez-faire ideals, capitalist principles—the free market, private ownership, unlimited appropriation and the profit motive—remain firmly rooted in American soil. And just as Locke sanctions the right to unlimited accumulation, the spark igniting the capitalist engine, preoccupation with the acquisition of wealth does not offend the American sense of propriety. In fact, intense competition for material gain is a frequently noted aspect of American society.

Expressing the sentiments of numerous nineteenth-century contemporaries, Alexander Mackay writes:

> The love of money is regarded by many as a striking trait in the American character. I fear that this is a weakness to which humanity must universally plead guilty. But it is quite true that it is an absorbing passion with the Americans. This cannot be denied, but it may be explained. America is a country in which fortunes have yet to be made. Wealth gives great distinction, and wealth is, more or less, within the grasp of all. Hence, the universal scramble. All cannot be made wealthy, but all have a chance of securing a prize. This stimulates to the race, and hence the eagerness of the competition.[8]

On this reading, then, America's economic ambitiousness is not simply grounded in the Calvinist/Puritan legacy as described by Weber, but is also influenced by the leveling that takes place in postrevolutionary societies, the intensity of the drive for wealth tied to the fluidity of the social structure.[9] As the achievement of wealth is a major criterion of social success, the acquisitive impulse is vented not only for the comfort it can create but also for the status it may bring.

Persistent jostling for status and wealth seems to contradict another Lockean value, that of equality. But the betrayal is only superficial; commitment to equality is an entrenched feature of the American ethos.[10] Locke grounds his political philosophy on the essential equality of all men under the authority of natural law. Similarly, that all men are created equal, that they possess intrinsic worth and thereby are owed equal respect, is a first principle of the Declaration of Independence, reinforced by the philosophies of Jefferson and Jackson, and is revealed in the recurrent strength of American populist movements. This is not to claim, of course, that American practice furnishes a benchmark for egalitarianism in all its forms. The newly independent America acknowledged a commitment to the equal administration of the law, quite a different thing from ensuring that the law recognizes the equality of all, as the black American experience so clearly demonstrates. Yet although the principle of equality has often been honored in the breach, its persuasive power persists.

In comparative perspective the extent of social equality in America seems distinctive; in any event this was the considered opinion of foreign commentators who visited the United States in its adolescence. Tocqueville claimed that the preeminent characteristic of the American social condition was democracy, Americans owning a greater equality in fortune and intellect than the nationals of any other country on earth.[11] Similarly, Harriet Martineau said that nothing struck her, "so forcibly and so pleasurably as the invariable respect paid man to man" (save people of color).[12] Fanny Trollope observed the same social leveling but found in it the major defect of American society, believing that when social distinctions became more prominent, "then we shall say farewell to American equality and welcome to European fellowship one of the finest countries on earth."[13] All this was not to claim that Americans ignored status; these same individuals found Americans quite status hungry. But status achieved in open economic competition rather than through ascription did not entail relations of deference, a circumstance quite different from that obtaining in Europe.

The economic implications of equality in the United States are ambiguous. Certainly, neither Locke nor Madison countenanced the limitation of wealth in the interest of equality. In America equality of opportunity has been emphasized, not equality of outcome. Large material differences have been tolerated as long as all have had an equal chance to become successful, i.e., have had equal competitive advantages in the free market.[14] Indeed, Americans generally regard wealth as a sign of individual distinction, applauded not only for its own sake but also for the character of its possessor. The self-made man, the entrepreneur who "pulls himself up by his own bootstraps," is Alger's American hero. To be sure, there is an inescapable conflict between the demand for equality of opportunity and a capitalist economic system that by sanctioning considerable economic disparities undermines that equality, yet the majority of Americans have seemed willing to live with the tension. And if over the last quarter century the United States has appeared to give special economic consideration to the claims of ethnicity and gender, the justification for such treatment has been compensatory, the implicit assumption being that the effect of past discrimination must be put right so that all may take part in the race to prosperity on an even footing.[15]

It is in the political sphere where the mandate for equality spills over into another feature of the American creed: participatory democracy. If all men are created equal, possessing equal worth and equal rights, then the natural conclusion is that they should be able to partake in their own governance. Thus, ideally, all citizens must be allowed to share in the corporate decisionmaking process, and in equal measure. In ideological terms the American commitment to such an ideal may be termed *populism*, the belief that, minus the distorting effect of representative government, mainstream popular opinion can and should be directly translated into public policy.[16]

It is here, of course, that parallels between Locke and the American political ethos are strained. In the *Second Treatise* the logic of democracy is pushed only so far, Locke's Whiggism not permitting the amount of popular participation demanded by some of his contemporaries—notably the Levellers or the Diggers. But at a minimum he does set the tone for American democratic practice by insisting that the consent of the governed is necessary to legitimate political rule. Government, in Locke's view, is simply a trustee of the citizenry, the power of dissolution ultimately resting in the people's hands. *The Federalist* likewise affirms this popular criterion of political authority, Hamilton pointing out that a major defect of the Articles of Confederation was lack of provision for direct election of public officials.[17] Still, direct or "pure" democracy was no cure for the inevitable factionalism that would afflict the new nation. Instead, republican or representative government was the answer, representatives furnishing a buffer between popular immoderation and administrative autocracy.[18] The proposed structure of government reflected the ambiguity with which the Founding Fathers regarded the citizenry—the popularly elected House was to be tempered by the Senate elected from the state legislatures. Mistrust of government required democracy, but mistrust of the people deflected its full impact.

These initial reservations aside, the democratic impulse has readily asserted itself in the development of the American polity. The inclination has not only been confined to political behavior; Tocqueville was impressed by the penchant of Americans for associational life, believing it an important counterweight to the potential of majority tyranny, and Martineau discovered that democracy entered into American family life, affecting childraising practices.[19] But the participatory imprint on American political institutions is unmistakable. The early adoption of universal white male suffrage, and the establishment of broadly based political parties to mobilize the newly enfranchised voters, can both be pointed to as remarkably democratic gestures for their time. To these may be added the establishment of the direct primary, passage of the Seventeenth Amendment providing for direct election of the Senate, frequent use of the referendum and the initiative at state and local levels of government, or simply the sheer number of political offices open to public contestation—more than 500,000, or one for every 478 citizens, according to Bureau of the Census estimations.[20] Alternatively, from a sociological perspective, populism's persistent appeal may be recognized not only in the series of political movements embodying its norms (one of which explicitly bears its name), but also more broadly in the American conviction that the common person is as politically astute, if not more so, than elected officials. Doubtless, too, this championing of the "little man" gives American public debate its particular tenor, politicians being eager to identify themselves with the interests of the ordinary citizen and regularly proclaiming their desire for a government "as good as its people."[21]

To reiterate, these five values—individualism, negative liberty, capitalism, equality, participatory democracy—are most often cited as the constituent elements of the American creed. Others might, with some justification, lay claim to inclusion on the list. For instance, numerous commentaries note an impressive level of religious commitment in American society. Tocqueville wrote that American history was determined by the first Puritan who touched American soil, and that by regulating domestic life, religion was able to regulate the state itself.[22] Locke, too, evinced a certain sensitivity to the religious dimension of man's existence, making God the source of natural law to which man's behavior should conform and from which his rights are derived. But religious conviction seems more a source of the central political values of Americans than something that actually typifies their political behavior. It is the values just enumerated, as mutable as they may appear to be, that do the latter. And the notable thing about them is the extent to which they are accepted as definitive by scholarly opinion. Political scientists, sociologists, and historians, although operating from different disciplinary perspectives, expressing different academic concerns, and using different methodologies, tend to congregate around Lockean liberalism and participatory democracy as distinctive of the American political character.[23]

That is not to claim that Locke's status as ideological patriarch of the American polity has gone without challenge. In what is no small academic debate, many historians of American political thought point to the influence of classical republicanism on the Founding Fathers.[24] Such individuals contend that the republican ideal of political virtue—that is to say, of public service and community centeredness—was a particularly significant point of reference for the founders, one that may be contrasted with the liberal emphasis on private rights and economic industriousness. The merits of the historiographic case are difficult to assess, not the least because in several respects the concerns of republicanism and liberalism appear to overlap—for example, both ideologies affirm the covenantal basis of political authority, limited government, and negative freedom, albeit for slightly different reasons. Consequently, several students of American intellectual history have found it best to stake out a middle ground, seeing the late eighteenth century as a transitional period of political evolution in which both liberal and republican ideas had currency.[25]

Yet if classical republicanism contributed to the intellectual ferment surrounding the denouement of colonial America, its continued influence on the theory and practice of an independent United States is more doubtful—proponents of the republican thesis often admit as much.[26] The arguments that carried the day at the Constitutional Convention focused on individual rights, the inviolability of private property, and government as created and legitimated by the consent of moral equals in pursuit of self-interest—elementary propositions of a distinctly liberal perspective.[27] And even though the Constitution itself is not unmitigatedly liberal in inspiration—of the foundational documents, the Declaration is the quintessential Lockean text—it does suggest that the founders placed their hopes for good government more in the institutional mechanisms of the separation of powers than in the selfless citizenry required by republicanism. To the extent that aspects of republican thought have survived into the nineteenth century and beyond, they have commanded only minority appeal. Certainly the Jacksonian era, with its broadly based partisan organizations and its open employment of interest-specific patronage politics, would seem to have sharply reduced any enduring affinities for republican conceptions of political virtue.[28] Furthermore, given that the South was the primary antebellum repository of republican values, the defeat of the Confederacy served to marginalize republicanism all the more.[29] At least since then, it would appear that liberalism has constituted America's public philosophy nonpareil.[30]

But not only does Lockeanism with a democratic cast characterize the American political temperament; to a remarkable degree Americans appear united in their commitment to these ideals. Analyses of American society typically conclude that the United States is an extraordinarily consensual political system, one defined by its citizens' fidelity to a particular interpretation of democratic practice. This consensus is further understood to function as the cement of the polity, furnishing the unity in diversity instrumental to the maintenance of an ethnically heterogeneous political order. Perhaps the classic statement occurs in *The Federalist* #2 by Jay:

> Providence has been pleased to give this one connected country, to one united people, a people descended from the same ancestors, speaking the same language, professing the same religion, attached to the same principle of government, very similar in manners and customs, and who, by their joint counsels, arms and efforts, fighting side by side throughout a long and bloody war, have nobly established their general Liberty and Independence.[31]

Clearly, Jay exaggerates the ethnic uniformity existing at the time of his essay; sizable populations of blacks, Germans, Scotch-Irish, Dutch, Huguenots (Jay himself was of French ancestry), and others resided within the confines of the newly independent nation. But given his conviction that homogeneity, sociological and ideological, was the key to the success of the revolutionary effort, the error may well have been intended. From Jay's point of view, the health of the American polity was to be guaranteed by the essential unity of its people, including their agreement on the "same principles of government."

This perspective, both descriptive and normative, is consistently seized upon by analysts of American society and politics. It is apparent, for instance, in the commentaries of European visitors to the United States, individuals whose observations are particularly instructive given the comparative context in which they are formed. Tocqueville is the archetypical example, but his views are not unique. Writing toward the end of the nineteenth century, James Bryce observes that Americans

> have an unbounded faith in what they call the People and in a democratic system of government. The great states of the European continent are distracted by the contests of Republicans and Monarchists, and of rich and poor, contests which go down to the foundations of government, and in France are further embittered by religious passions. Even in England the ancient Constitution is always under repair, and while many think it is being ruined by changes, others hold that still greater changes are needed to make it tolerable. No such questions trouble native American minds, for nearly everybody believes, and everybody declares, that the frame of government is in its main lines so excellent that such reforms as seem called for need not touch those lines, but are required only to protect the Constitution from being perverted by the parties.[32]

Half a century later, Harold Laski reflects that the "uniformity of values which has been the outcome of the American conquest of the continent is far more startling than even that remarkable observer, Tocqueville, predicted it would be."[33] And commenting on the "basic homogeneity and stability of [America's] valuations," Gunnar Myrdal writes:

> America, compared to every other country in Western civilization, large or small, has *the most explicitly expressed* system of general ideals in reference to human interrelations. This body of ideals is more widely understood and appreciated than similar ideals are anywhere else. The American Creed is not merely—as in some countries—the implicit background of the nation's political and judicial order as it functions. To be sure, the political creed of America is not very satisfactorily effectuated in actual social life. But as principles

which *ought* to rule, the Creed has been made conscious to everyone
in American society.[34]

The most eminent American students of politics likewise acknowledge the descriptive validity of the consensus thesis. Robert Dahl
asserts that "Americans are a highly ideological people. It is only that
one does not ordinarily notice their ideology because they are, to an
astounding extent, all agreed on the same ideology."[35] Samuel
Huntington cites with approval Tocqueville's statement that Americans
are "unanimous upon the general principles that ought to rule human
society."[36] "In contrast to most European societies," Huntington
comments, "a broad consensus exists and has existed in the United
States on basic political values and beliefs."[37] Richard Hofstadter writes
of the "common ground," the "unity of cultural and political tradition"
that prevents severe disagreements from afflicting the American
political system.[38] And Daniel Boorstin celebrates the "givenness" of
the American creed, an organic political theory with roots in the beliefs
of the colonial fathers, the experience of the physical environment,
and the continuity of American political evolution.[39] That liberal values
in America are assumed is born out in political dialogue: "Much of
what passes for public debate," writes Boorstin, "is . . . less an attempt
to tell the people what to do than to state what everybody already
thinks."[40]

But perhaps the most ardent proponent of the consensus perspective,
whose work has done the most to promote it, is Louis Hartz. Hartz's
The Liberal Tradition in America puts the consensus case in its
strongest terms. Hartz's central thesis is that the American political
experience can be interpreted only in light of a pervasive Lockean
liberalism. This, plus recognition of the import of the absence of a
feudal tradition, should be the common denominator of all political
analyses of the United States, according to Hartz. Lockeanism, with
its belief in the autonomy of the individual, is the "master assumption"
of American political life and the wellspring of its cultural phenomena.[41] The power of this central creed, Hartz argues, is revealed by
America's resistance to ideological diversification:

> [A] society which begins with Locke, and thus transforms him, stays
> with Locke, by virtue of an absolute and irrational attachment it
> develops for him, and becomes as indifferent to the challenge of
> socialism in the later era as it was with the heritage of feudalism in
> the earlier one. It has within it, as it were, a kind of self-completing
> mechanism, which insures the universality of the liberal idea.[42]

In Hartz's view, so comprehensive is the American commitment to Lockeanism that Americans have difficulty recognizing the highly ideological nature of their thought. Hartz believes that American liberalism has a "quiet, matter of fact quality, it does not understand the meaning of sovereign power, the bourgeois class passion is scarcely present, the sense of the past is altered, and there is about it all . . . a vast and almost charming innocence of mind."[43] In the United States, the commitment to liberalism is so complete that it is not seen for what it is. Instead there is an acknowledgment of a common "American Way of Life," a facade for the foundational ethos.

To be fair, even though a considerable amount of empirical evidence has been adduced in support of the consensus thesis,[44] not all social scientists share this reading of the American political system. In the first instance, survey data generated in the mid- to late 1950s have been used to cast doubt on the pervasiveness of the liberal-democratic ethos.[45] Such data reveal that while Americans agree on the propriety of abstract democratic principles, when these are translated into specific propositions, consensus on the creed evaporates. It is the political activists (those having greater than average political involvement) who are the carriers of the democratic value system and who display a more thorough fidelity to it. Yet, even though consensus among the "political strata" is stronger than that of the general citizenry, it too is far from perfect. In brief, the depth of consensus is found to be highly restricted in the case of the electorate and not overwhelming in the case of civic activists.[46]

It must be pointed out, however, that the research on which this particular argument against consensus is based has not gone without criticism. Many rebuttals have centered on the methodological inadequacies of the various research projects.[47] Particularly indicting, however, are the results of more recently conducted surveys. Noteworthy in this regard is the work of Herbert McClosky, if only because his earlier research lent support to the anticonsensus position. In *The American Ethos*, published in 1984 and based on survey data of mid- to late 1970s vintage, McClosky claims that ideological conflict in America operates "within a broad framework of almost universal public support for the basic values of capitalism and democracy."[48] Opinion leaders still demonstrate high levels of support for the American creed, but the support of the general public does not lag far behind on most issues. Furthermore, those individuals possessing an incomplete attachment to the creed are not expressly antagonistic; they simply lack the sophistication to fully comprehend it.[49] On this basis even McClosky, a former adversary, concedes to the descriptive validity of the consensus thesis.

Nevertheless, the consensus thesis does not furnish the only viable paradigm of American politics. At least two other major schools of interpretation have captured the favor of political scientists: pluralism and what has been called the progressive, or more lately New Left, rendition of the American political process. On the pluralist view, the characteristic feature of American politics is competition among interest groups over public goods and services, including political power. In the words of Arthur F. Bentley, a pioneer of the pluralist approach (Madison's allusions in *Federalist* #10 excepted), "All phenomena of government are phenomena of groups pressing one another, forming one another, and pushing out new groups and group representatives (the organs or agencies of government) to mediate their adjustments. It is only as we isolate these group activities, determine their respective values, and get the whole process stated in terms of them, that we approach to a satisfactory knowledge of government."[50] Refined and promoted by Robert Dahl, Theodore Lowi, and David Truman, among others, pluralism is likely the explanatory framework most widely employed by contemporary students of American politics.[51] It is not, however, an approach antithetical to a consensus perspective on American public life. Indeed, if competition is not to become so intense as to make the formulation and implementation of a cohesive public policy impossible, interest groups must operate under a canopy of shared values determining the rules and objectives of political contestation. In America, one may argue, it is the liberal creed that fixes the boundaries of pluralist politics. Thus Dahl, while advocating the utility of the pluralist approach, also emphasizes the consensual quality of the American political process. Competition among interest groups for influence over public policy does not result in a politically debilitating free-for-all; compromise is possible because of a "massive convergence of attitudes" regarding the norms that should regulate political behavior.[52]

Pluralism in this sense, it should be added, is not to be confused with cultural pluralism, a concept that is more at home among sociologists and anthropologists than political theorists and that signifies—and often commends—a national community marked by considerable ethnic diversity. First popularized in the 1920s by the social philosopher, Horace Kallen, who used it as a rejoinder to Anglo conformity and melting pot perspectives on American identity, cultural pluralism has become over the last fifty years a favored interpretation of American society.[53] Its relationship to the political variety of pluralism, however, remains ambiguous; certainly those social scientists employing the concept are more interested in the persistence of ethnic attachments, and by extension the limits of assimilation, than in politics per se. Yet to the degree that cultural pluralists have turned to broader questions concerning the integration and preservation of an ethnically diverse society, they, too, have concluded that shared political convictions—Kallen called it common commitment to the "American Idea"—are essential.[54] Thus if cultural pluralism and political pluralism have a common denominator, it may be that each is inclined to regard consensus as the adhesive of an otherwise fissile community.[55]

Progressivism, on the other hand, is more difficult to square with the consensus model of politics, taking as its point of departure conflict in American public life. Reacting against a naively harmonious reading of American political history dominant in late-nineteenth century historiography, the earliest advocates of the progressive approach— most famously James Allen Smith, Charles A. Beard, and Vernon L. Parrington (all of whom claimed inspiration from *Federalist* #10)— sought to reorient the study of American politics in the direction of elementary material interests.[56] The progressive case has rested on the conviction that political behavior can best be explained by underlying economic motives—or as a recent book in the progressive mode would have it, "the politics of America, at whatever level, is mostly business in one form or another."[57] Specifically, progressivists have regarded conflict of interest between a well-propertied minority and a relatively impoverished majority as the dominant motif of American political history. Parrington puts the perspective succinctly:

> From the first we have been divided into two main parties. . . . On one side has been the party of the current aristocracy—of church, of gentry, of merchant, of slave holder, of manufacturer—and on the other the party of the commonality—the farmer, villager, small tradesman, mechanic, proletariat. The one has persistently sought to check and limit the popular power, to keep the control of the government in the hands of the few in order to serve special interest, whereas the other has sought to augment the popular power, to make government more responsible to the will of the majority, to further the democratic rather than the republican ideal.[58]

On the progressive interpretation, the partisans of privilege scored their greatest triumph at the Philadelphia Convention, gaining constitutional sanction for private property rights and legal protection for the holdings of the well-to-do.[59] All major subsequent episodes of the American political drama have been marked by a struggle between the forces of economic affluence and the forces of the "commonality," a struggle in which the former—wrapped in a cloak of constitutional legitimacy and able to translate economic into political power—have usually proved victorious. Despite the persistence of a still small democratic voice, according to the progressivists the history of the republic confirms that "those who control the means of production in reality control the rest."[60]

Appearances to the contrary, it is possible to reconcile the consensus and progressive/New Left paradigms. Certainly the consensus approach can accommodate the progressivist assertion that American politics is marked by a conflict of economic interest between rich and poor, provided this is not regarded as the sole theme of American public life. Of course in comparative perspective, an outlook near and dear to the hearts of consensualists, the extent of class-based strife in the United States may appear relatively limited. The most explicit institutional manifestations of such confrontation in other liberal democracies are found in ideologically heterogeneous party systems and robust trade union movements, neither of which, more arguably in the latter instance, have taken deep root in American soil. Even so, the consensualist does not need to deny the reality of class conflict in America—in view of recent historical scholarship it would be foolish to do so.[61] The consensualist need only maintain that class conflict takes place within the confines of a regulating and moderating, some might say suffocating, political ethos. Relatedly, it may well be true, as the progressivists observe, that the pursuit of economic gain characterizes the behavior of the American citizenry. But on the wisdom of the consensus thesis this is to be expected: possessive individualism, the acquisitive impulse at the core of capitalism, is part and parcel of the Lockean creed. Symptomatic of the power of the creed, then, the "class struggle" in America assumes a peculiarly egalitarian form. The objective of the underclass is not to replace those who are economically and politically dominant but to join them. For better or worse, equal opportunity, not equal distribution, has been the rallying cry of the disadvantaged in America. It is this almost universal belief in the virtues of a meritocratic society that accounts for what Max Lerner has called the "Great Paradox" of the American class system:

> First, although political and economic attitudes differ sharply between the upper and lower classes, those below reject the notion that they are there permanently; second, despite the often big gap between the encouraged claims of each class, especially the lower ones, and the limited fulfillment possible in any one generation, there is neither great class tension nor loss of cultural hope. . . . The term "social partnership"

elides the elements of class difference and class struggle, but it is true that the struggle is carried on within a framework of mobility and hope.[62]

Given the tenacity and pervasiveness of capitalist norms among the American citizenry, even committed progressivists, albeit grudgingly, acknowledge the descriptive validity of the consensus paradigm. Thus Ira Katznelson, in an attempt to reconcile class-based and consensus orientations to American politics, argues that although the politics of class has often been in evidence in the workplace, outside the factory gate consensus politics has been the rule.[63] To the same end, if on a different note, Gabriel Kolko, a historian of New Left persuasion, writes, "A system that rules with the consent of the oppressed, who strive only to be counted in at the top also, thereby reconciles the notion of consensus with the structural reality of class."[64] Kolko's salvo aside, undoubtedly the meritocratic emphasis of the American creed has legitimated what progressivists contend are the privileges of wealth. As Laski remarks of America, "Nowhere, in any society of any major importance have . . . 'the underprivileged' so fully accepted the assumptions upon which successful men have made their way to power."[65] Understood in this way, the American consensus operates conservatively, entrenching the authority of political and economic elites. For Kolko and like-minded others, the valuational unity of Americans is a function of the superior coercive abilities of a ruling class and is largely irrelevant to the warp and woof of power politics.[66] The merits of that case need not be assessed here, though it seems unlikely the creed is merely an epiphenomenon of economic, hence political, predominance—after all, equality and participatory democracy have been enduring aspects of the creed, values that are frequently in tension with the capitalist component of the ethos and that challenge the suzerainty of any ruling class.[67] What the argument does suggest, however, is that the consensus and progressive approaches to American politics are not necessarily incommensurable; vis-à-vis present concerns, that is the theoretically significant point.

Immigrants in the
Theory and Practice of American Politics

That the United States is a politically consensual country may be a fair interpretation of the sociological evidence, but vis-à-vis the disposition of immigrants, it suggests an important corollary: in order to maintain the republic's stability, deviations from the political norm need to be discouraged. With respect to the American environment, it is not difficult to understand why ideological uniformity might appeal. Political orthodoxy is the United States' response to the ethnic diversity virtually unavoidable in settler societies; commitment to common political values is the cement joining the political and social systems. Noting this integrative function of the national ethos, Myrdal observes:

> The "Old Americans," all those who have thoroughly come to identify themselves with the nation—which are many more than the Sons and Daughters of the Revolution—adhere to the Creed as the faith of their ancestors. The others—the Negroes, the new immigrants, the Jews, and other disadvantaged and unpopular groups—could not possibly have invented a system of political ideals which better corresponded to their interests. So, by the logic of the unique American history, it has developed that the rich and secure, out of pride and conservativism, and the poor and insecure, out of dire need, have come to possess the same social ideals. The reflecting observer comes to feel that this spiritual convergence . . . is what makes the nation great and what promises a still greater future. Behind it all is the historical reality which makes it possible for the President to appeal to all in the nation in this way: "Let us not forget that we are all descendants from revolutionaries and immigrants."[68]

In this manner, an ideological, rather than a more broadly cultural, version of nationhood has come to characterize the American, one tailor-made to absorb distinct immigrant populations. In fact, such a concept of nationality may be taken as both cause and effect of the United States' ethnically heterogeneous population: cause, in that membership in the American political community is awarded on the basis of political conviction as opposed to birth or lineage, an attraction to immigrants of various ethnic origins; effect, in that American identity must be drawn in ideological, as opposed to more narrowly cultural, terms because its population, largely on account of immigration, is too ethnically diverse to permit otherwise. Because of this politically grounded concept of national identity, discrete ethnic groups have not been forced to relinquish the majority of their cultural inheritance, nor, with a few notable exceptions, has cultural dissimilarity been a major criterion of immigration restriction in the United States. But in order that the tessellation of society not be reproduced in the political system, America has required the political conformity of its citizenry.

And this requirement points to a tension intrinsic to America's relationship with the foreign-born. In the United States, a national identity based on ideological consensus encourages the immigration of culturally diverse individuals who, to the extent they carry alien ideological baggage, knowingly or not threaten the very consensus facilitating immigration. Or, to put it another way, while immigration is stimulated by what Herbert Croly called the "promise" of American life,[69] it simultaneously places the political foundations of that promise at risk. It is true, as Myrdal indicates, that immigrant origin per se is not sufficient reason for exclusion from the national community; one need not be born American to become American—acceptance of the liberal political faith is the litmus test of national identity. Yet at least initially, it is not to be expected that immigrants will be committed liberals in the American mold. Given both the complexity of the creed and its flowering in a specifically American social context, the majority of the foreign-born are unlikely to possess the appropriate convictions. Consequently, in principle, immigration presages political disruption.

Considering the United States' relatively enviable record of stability, then, what accounts for the failure of immigration to have the anticipated result? Among theorists inclined to the preceding mode of analysis, the favored answer, of course, is assimilation—the deus ex machina of the American political system. By means of political socialization, a process directly and indirectly mediated by the native-born (as well as foreign-born "converts"), immigrants, it is claimed, are brought to affirm the values integrating the American political order. Indeed, according to Boorstin, because American ideals are "in the air . . . they are readily acquired; actually, it is almost impossible for an immigrant to avoid acquiring them."[70]

Thus, in a consideration of the issue with relevance extending beyond the United States, Hartz has argued for the palliative effect of assimilation. On Hartz's view, settler societies are ideological fragments of Europe. The ideology in vogue at the time of the new society's foundation becomes its normative belief system as well as the essence of its national identity. Given the inextricable relationship between a country's dominant ideology and its estimation of the national welfare, every attempt is made to insulate this unifying creed from external contamination, including that brought on by immigration. Restrictionism is a natural outcome of this perspective, although, as Hartz attests, it is not necessarily the most compelling one:

> There is no doubt that societies like the Afrikaner, or the French-Canadian, which have tended to renew themselves from within, have presented us with the purest case of fragment traditionalism. But the power of that traditionalism is better illustrated in its proven capacity,

despite all fear, to meet the immigrant challenge. And here the new nationalism plays a part. By consciously articulating the fragment ethic, it provides an instrument for absorbing the immigrant into it. This takes place regardless of the substance of the ethic, and works in the case of Australia and Brazil as it does in the case of the United States. But the United States, not only the greatest of all the immigrant fragments, but with a genius for transparent terminology, has coined a word for the process. Together with Americanism there is "Americanization."[71]

If Hartz's approach to the immigrant question is in some respects idiosyncratic, his conclusions are not. Writing toward the end of the last century, Lord Bryce remarks that

> any one can see how severe a strain is put on democratic institutions by the influx every year of half a million of untrained Europeans. . . . Being in most States admitted to full civic rights before they have come to shake off European notions and habits, these strangers enjoy political power before they either share or are amenable to American opinion. . . . But the younger sort, when, if they be foreigners, they have learnt English, and when, dispersed among Americans so as to be able to learn from them, they have imbibed the sentiments and ideas of the country, are thenceforth scarcely to be distinguished from the native population. They are more American than the Americans in their desire to put on the character of their new country. This peculiar gift which the Republic possesses, of quickly dissolving and assimilating the foreign bodies that are poured into her, imparting to them her own qualities of orderliness, good sense, self-restraint, a willingness to bow to the will of the majority, is mainly due to the all-pervading force of opinion, which the new-comer, so soon as he has found social and business relations with the natives, breathes in daily till it insensibly transmutes him.[72]

More than seventy years later, Dahl makes a similar assessment, maintaining that the process whereby immigrants have been politically acculturated has been as important to the shape of the American political character as the frontier, industrialization or urbanization. Commenting on the pivotal role of publicly sponsored civic education programs in sustaining the democratic order, he writes:

> The result was as astonishing an act of voluntary political and cultural assimilation and speedy elimination of regional, ethnic, and cultural dissimilarities as history can provide. The extent to which Americans agree today on the key propositions about democracy is a measure of the almost unbelievable success of this deliberate attempt to create a seemingly uncoerced nation-wide consensus.[73]

And more recently still, Huntington expresses like wonderment at the power of assimilation. While concerned that contemporary immigration from Latin America and the Caribbean might introduce alien and disruptive ideas into America's public discourse, he, too, trusts the time-tested assimilative capacity of the national creed:

> Defined vaguely and abstractly, these ideals have been relatively easily adopted to the needs of successive generations. The constant social change in the United States, indeed, underlies their permanence. Rising social, economic, and ethnic groups need to reinvoke and reinvigorate those values in order to promote their own access to the rewards of American society. . . . The more culturally pluralistic the nation becomes, particularly if cultural pluralism encompasses linguistic pluralism, the more essential the political values of the Creed become in defining what it is that Americans have in common.[74]

In short, among students of American democracy the process of Americanization, largely voluntary but nonetheless obliging, is widely regarded as precluding immigration from taking its political toll.

The American political experience demonstrates that this theoretical understanding of immigration and immigrants is not simply the product of scholarly fancy. Clearly the Founding Fathers were not immune to the fear of political dissonance stemming from immigration. Concerned in some measure with the political sympathies of Pennsylvania's German community, Franklin warned of the "Palatine Boors" who threatened to "establish their language and Manners, to the Exclusion of ours" and make Pennsylvania into a "colony of aliens."[75] Washington maintained that with respect to immigration "there is no need of encouragement," as the foreign-born are inclined "to retain the Language, habits, and principles (good or bad) which they bring with them."[76] Based on his reading of political theory, Hamilton argued that "the safety of a republic depends essentially on the energy of a common national sentiment; on a uniformity of principles and habits; on the exemption of citizens from foreign bias and prejudice; and on that love of country which will almost invariably be found to be closely connected with birth, education, and family."[77] On those grounds, he reasoned,

> the influx of foreigners must . . . tend to produce a heterogeneous compound; to change and corrupt the national spirit; to complicate and confound public opinion; to introduce foreign propensities. In the composition of society, the harmony of the ingredients is all-important, and whatever tends to a discordant intermixture must have an injurious

tendency. . . . To admit foreigners indiscriminately to the rights of citizens, the moment they put foot in our country . . . would be nothing less than to admit the Grecian horse into the citadel of our liberty and sovereignty.[78]

And even though, ultimately, Jefferson's administration pursued a relatively generous policy toward immigrants, he, too, worried about their politically disruptive potential:

> Civil government being the sole object of forming societies, its administration must be conducted by common consent. Every species of government has its specific principles. Ours perhaps is more peculiar than those of any other in the universe. . . . To these nothing can be more opposed than the maxims of absolute monarchies. Yet from such we are to expect the greatest number of immigrants. . . . It would be a miracle were they to stop at the point of temperate liberty.[79]

Consequently, that citizenship should be characterized partly in ideological terms was an idea established early in the history of the republic. Even before a national government had crystallized via the Constitution, most of the state governments had passed legislation specifying residence requirements for prospective citizens in the belief that the exercise of political rights required familiarity with and devotion to American civic norms—presumably an uncertainty among aliens.[80] The first federal naturalization statute (1790) stipulated only that a candidate for citizenship be a resident of two years, be of good character, and swear to uphold the principles of the Constitution—the tangible legal expression of American political beliefs. But as the naturalization law evolved, concerns about allegiance to the liberal creed increased. Thus in the congressional debate over the Second Naturalization Act (1795), legislation raising the minimum period of residence for citizenship to five years, Samuel Smith of Maryland voiced the majority rationale that "the prejudices which the aliens had imbibed under the Government from whence they came might be effaced, and that they might by communication and observance of our laws and government, have just ideas of our Constitution and the excellence of its institutions before they were admitted to the rights of a citizen."[81] Institutionalizing similar anxieties, the Adams administration a few years later introduced harsher measures to limit the political impact of the foreign-born: the Naturalization Act (1798) raised the residency requirement for citizenship from five to fourteen years; the Aliens Act (1798) gave the president power to arrest and deport resident aliens suspected of subversive (i.e., pro-French) activities; and the Sedition Act (1798), while not explicitly pertaining to foreigners, was aimed at foreign-born journalists and pamphleteers critical of the Federalists. All of this legislation was enacted for partisan as much as for expressly ideological reasons, with the Federalists hoping that such restrictions might quiet some of the Democratic Republican's most vocal immigrant supporters, and Jefferson repealed the restrictionist legislation soon after he assumed the presidency. But the tone of American thought and practice on the issue of immigration was set—the American political ethos was to be kept free of foreign contaminants. To that end, sufficient knowledge of and support for the institutions and principles of American government continue to be the central criteria of naturalization, long after gender and racially based qualifications have been invalidated.[82] So too, because of a lack of affinity with those principles, various anarchists, communists, unionists (e.g., members of the Industrial Workers of the World), and pacifists have during the course of the twentieth century been deemed unsuitable for American citizenship and in certain cases subject to denaturalization.[83]

The legal significance of America's consensus does not stop with considerations of citizenship, however; the United States has also made the political convictions of immigrants grounds for exclusion and deportation. Throughout most of the nineteenth century the government adopted a laissez-faire attitude toward immigration policy, the need for labor being considered of greater importance than political orthodoxy. But by the turn of the century, America had begun to display a greater fear of imported political radicalism; the Haymarket riot, the assassinations of McKinley and the Austrian archduke, the Russian Revolution, and increased labor militancy focused the authorities' attention. The Anarchist Act of 1903, the first in an explicitly ideological category of legislation, denied entry to individuals advocating the overthrow of governments and the assassination of public officials. Succeeding statutes painted the criteria of exclusion with broader strokes: a revised Aliens Act (1918) made it easier to exclude "politically undesirable aliens advocating radical theories"; the Nationality Act of 1940 prevented from becoming naturalized aliens who within ten years of arriving in America had been affiliated with organizations promoting revolution or had championed such causes in print, and the act allowed immigrant radicals to be denaturalized; the Internal Security Act of 1950 specified that communist immigrants could be excluded from the United States or could be prevented from becoming naturalized and established the Subversive Activities Control Board to monitor the movements of potential radicals, domestic or foreign-born; and the Immigration and Nationality Act of 1952—commonly known as the McCarran-Walter Act—restated the ban on communist and anarchist sympathizers and required only reasonable suspicion of an immigrant's subversive proclivities to bar him or her from the United States (the political proscriptions of this act were finally voided in 1988).[84] Furthermore, these statutes not only established political grounds for exclusion but also used the same criteria to threaten immigrant radicals with deportation.[85] In neither case has the judiciary readily come to the immigrant's rescue, the courts tending to maintain a distinction between the civil rights of citizens and those of aliens.[86]

Even the United States' humanitarian impulses, as signified in its refugee policy, have seemed to be regulated by ideological commitments. For most of the post–World War II period until 1980, the American government defined a refugee primarily as someone fleeing a communist country, grants of asylum following ideological suit. It is only by virtue of the 1980 Refugee Act that American usage has been brought into line with the "depoliticized" definition employed by the United Nations, according to which a refugee is anyone with a well-founded fear of political, racial, ethnic, or religious persecution. Nevertheless, there are considerable indications that congressional intent notwithstanding, during the 1980s the United States remained far more disposed to accept refugees from communist states than from those governed by right-wing dictatorships.[87]

Evidence that the question of consensus looms large in American political practice is not exhausted by investigation of the specific activities of government. The popular outbursts of nativism that impugn the American historical record also have, in part, an ideological character. This is not to claim that the source of nativism per se is ideology or that nativism in all instances expresses itself in ideological terms. Nativism is best understood as a reaction by native-born Americans to the threatened loss of traditional status positions, a predicament for which immigrants are held responsible.[88] Thus, nativist sentiments are readily cultivated among native-born workers who believe their security of employment is jeopardized by cheap immigrant labor. The way in which nativism manifests itself, however, is a consideration distinct from the forces that produce it, and although nativists may castigate immigrants on economic grounds, nativist condemnations are drawn more broadly than this. As John Higham points out, the essence of nativism is nationalism, "the intense opposition to an internal minority on the ground of its foreign (i.e., 'un-American') connections."[89] To the degree that the "American way of life" is understood as essentially Anglo-Saxon and Protestant, nativism is couched in terms of the cultural unacceptability of immigrants lacking such credentials. Catholic immigrants have long been subject to nativist disapprobation, an animosity that was particularly virulent during the public/parochial school controversies of the last century and that has been given institutional form by various political organizations, perhaps most famously the Know-Nothing party of the 1850s (an organization that advocated raising the naturalization period from five to twenty-one years), the American Protective Association of the 1880s and 1890s, and, of course, the Ku Klux Klan. Similarly, nativism has been vented in an explicitly racist manner, as it was at the turn of the century when the pseudo-science of eugenics attempted to collect evidence of the superiority of northern European genetic stock. Economic pressure may provide an impetus to nativism, but a diffuse ethnocentrism has often been its favored mode of communication.[90]

Nevertheless, the specifically political aspects of nativism must not be overlooked. The American nation is first and foremost an ideological, not an ethnic, entity. And this suggests that when the nativist levels the charge of "un-Americanism," it may well be the political convictions of immigrants that are at issue. To be sure, the fear of economic competition and an intolerance of cultural diversity are the most common elements of nativist movements. Nevertheless, there is a decidedly ideological strain in nativist thought. Since the early years of the republic, nativists have claimed that immigrants infrequently possess the attitudes required for the preservation of American democracy and that they are the major proponents of, or are at least highly susceptible to, radical ideologies—Jacobinism, socialism, anarchism, communism—incompatible with the liberal creed. Even the nativist desire to maintain America's ethnic homogeneity has often been accompanied by related political considerations. Given that American political values are often understood to be of British vintage, and that for many years America's social identity was regarded as essentially Anglo-Saxon and Protestant, cultural and ideological arguments are readily conflated. From this perspective, individuals of Nordic lineage are presumed to have a special affinity for democratic government, whereas less enlightened peoples lack the sophistication for self-rule.[91] In this vein, one of the best known of the eugenicists, Madison Grant, wrote of southern and eastern Europeans that "the whole tone of American life, social, moral, and political, has been vulgarized by them."[92] Similarly, Catholics have been thought ill-suited for democracy because of the authoritarian structure of their church, while Judaism has been linked with Bolshevism and Zionism.[93] Spokespeople for immigration restriction have recognized that arguments supporting ideological and ethnic (or, as early restrictionists would have termed it, racial) homogeneity are not mutually exclusive. Albert Johnson, representative from Washington and chief architect of the 1920s quota legislation, used both to advantage:

> Today, instead of a well-knit homogeneous citizenry, we have a body politic made up of all and every diverse element. Today, instead of a nation descended from generations of freemen bred to a knowledge of the principles and practices of self-government, of liberty under law, we have a heterogeneous population no small proportion of which is sprung from races that, throughout the centuries, have known no liberty at all, and no law save the decrees of overlords and princes. In other words, our capacity to maintain our cherished institutions stands diluted by a stream of alien blood with all its inherited misconceptions respecting the relationship of the governing power to the governed.[94]

The most serious of the nativist's political charges has been that immigrants are prone to divided loyalties. This is the attribution of un-Americanism taken to a different level: the claim is made that immigrants not only threaten the political consensus that stabilizes the American republic but also actively support the interests of a foreign country. Rather than unwittingly undermining American political homogeneity by simple ignorance, the immigrant who identifies himself or herself with the fortunes of a foreign power does so as a matter of conscious choice; premeditation makes the sin all the more grievous. At this point, the native-born's regard for consensus seems to recede into the background and is replaced by a more emotive concern for the integrity of the American political community. But because community and consensus are so closely related in the American context, the issue of consensus does not completely disappear. The loyalty of immigrants to the American political community is questioned, in part, because non-American ideological perspectives retain their hold on the immigrant community. In fact, attributions of domestic political deviance and national infidelity can intersect so that immigrants may be criticized not only for their insufficient liberalism but also for their insufficient Americanism.

It is during a time of war that the issue of divided loyalty is addressed with special fervency. It is then that the immigrant's tie to the homeland is thought to preclude throwing full support behind the American war effort. Any American who wishes the United States to refrain from military involvement in foreign conflicts risks being branded un-American, especially if his or her perspective contradicts the public's prevailing mood. But the foreign-born and their progeny are particularly vulnerable, all the more so if their country of ancestry is a military opponent of the United States. Thus, during World War I, German-Americans were the object of nativist diatribes. Influenced by the considerable size of the German ethnic contingent, the American government interpreted any German-American political agitation, even if it was to petition for American neutrality in the European conflict, as evidence of disloyalty and a threat to political stability. German-Americans were thought to support the political ambitions of the kaiser; true Americans had a patriotic duty to suppress all vestiges of German political and cultural influence.[95] In World War II, the accusation of disloyalty fell most heavily upon the Japanese-American community. Racial prejudice against the Japanese had been a permanent fixture since their immigration to the West Coast in the late nineteenth century; the surprise attack on Pearl Harbor simply confirmed what the nativists had claimed to know all along—that not only were the Japanese genetically inferior, but they were treacherous as well. Executive Order 9066 (1942), authorizing the enforced removal of over one hundred thousand Japanese to detention camps, is the most poignant and infamous example of America's belief in the divided loyalty of immigrants.

A persistent claim of nativists, but one extending beyond the nativist camp, concerns the manner in which immigrants have conducted their politics. Public officials and concerned citizens alike have chided immigrants for their susceptibility to corruption and political fraud. Certainly, the historical record reveals evidence of immigrant complicity. During the nineteenth century and into the early part of the twentieth, it was not exceptional for aliens to register and vote soon after arriving in the United States. Although the federal government had authority to grant citizenship, individual states possessed the ability to assign the positive rights associated with naturalization. In some states, particularly those in the South and West, the granting of suffrage was permitted to precede the formal bestowal of citizenship, requiring only that a declaration of intent to become a citizen was dutifully filed. In other states, particularly those on the eastern seaboard, aliens voted as a matter of course, the letter of the law notwithstanding. Recognizing an imminent political resource, party officials eagerly processed these prospective voters, escorting them to the ballot box on election day. As immigrants and their children grew more politically sophisticated, flexing their political muscle without such external prompting, certain ethnic political institutions became the target of native-born disapprobation. The city machine, frequently under the dominance of Irish-Americans, drew the most fire. High-minded reformers rued the debasement of American politics by an organization maintaining itself on quid pro quos—securing jobs, food, shelter, recreation, and status in return for votes. Whether it was the immigrant's use of the ballot or the city treasury, the essence of the complaint was the same: lacking commitment to the American political value system, immigrants disrupt the democratic order.[96] Indeed, it is instructive that many turn-of-the-century municipal reform leaders were members of the Immigration Restriction League; presumably, the most effective way of stopping the foreign-born from acquiring political power was to prevent them from coming to America in the first place.

But exclusion has not been the primary means by which the United States has dealt with its fear of immigrant-induced dissensus. Instead, as already suggested, conscious programs of Americanization have been the favored mode of response, explicit attempts to impart American cultural values in general and American political norms in particular. Concerted efforts to teach those values to immigrants and their children were perhaps most prevalent in the first decades of the present century when, responding to heightened concern about the political affinities and economic capabilities of an increasingly diverse population, one recently altered by a massive influx of immigrants from southern and eastern Europe, federal and local governments, voluntary agencies, businesses, and unions sponsored thousands of civics courses to ensure the political and social conformity of the foreign-born.[97] But it is the American public school system that consistently has been regarded as the preeminent evangelist of the American political creed and hence a primary instrument of national integration. From the first years of the republic, the common school has been charged with producing a politically unified and responsible citizenry, or as the Pennsylvanian physician and statesman, Benjamin Rush, put it, with educating Americans as "republican machines."[98] By the middle of the nineteenth century, such a transformational concept of education had become widely accepted as foundational to the burgeoning public school system—an especially timely emphasis in the view of many, given the unprecedented waves of Irish and German immigrants then reaching American shores.[99] In that spirit, in 1850 a Midwestern newspaper observed, "As the child of the foreigner plays with his school fellow he learns to whistle 'Yankee Doodle' and sing 'Hail Columbia,' and before he leaves the school-desk for the plough, the anvil, or the trowel,

he is as sturdy a little republican as can be found in the land."[100] The
report of a superintendent of schools in 1919 is equally illuminating:

> The public school is the greatest and most effective of all Americani-
> zation agencies. This is the one place where all children in a community
> or district, regardless of nationality, religion, politics, or social status,
> meet and work together in a cooperative and harmonious spirit. . . .
> The children work and play together, they catch the school spirit, they
> live the democratic life, American heroes become their own, American
> history wins their loyalty, the Stars and Stripes always before their
> eyes in the school room, receives their daily salute. Not only are these
> immigrant children Americanized through the public school, but they,
> in turn, Americanize their parents carrying into the home the many
> lessons of democracy learned at school.[101]

For the same reason, educational issues in the United States often
acquire a peculiarly political flavor. Conflict over the language of
instruction and public aid for parochial institutions, facets of the
American educational debate for at least 150 years, are cases in point.
To anxious Americanizers, control of the schools by sectarian or
linguistic interests has implied the inculcation of culturally specific
systems of belief, perspectives potentially at odds with the American
public ethos. Thus it has not been simply that German, or lately
Spanish, might be a medium of instruction co-equal with English, or
(though this no longer seems so controversial), that a curriculum might
incorporate Catholic religious understandings, but that "un-American"
worldviews may be perpetuated among children who are members of
the American republic and who must become politically assimilated.[102]
That the public school system has guarded the American civic culture
so jealously points, once again, to the concern for consensus in
American political practice.

Conclusion

The various threads of the antiheterogeneity argument may now
be drawn together. The American case against ethnic diversity, and
by extension immigration, builds on the preexisting foundation of
general democratic theory. On the wisdom of conventional political
theory, ethnic heterogeneity threatens the preservation of stable
democracy. First, a sense of political community, the shared national
identity necessary to the maintenance of the political order, may well
be undermined in conditions of ethnic diversity. Heterogeneity
introduces the prospect of competing political loyalties, which may
end at the boundaries of ethnicity. As such loyalties are often intense,

commitment to a political entity larger than the ethnic group may be difficult to effect. Additionally, ethnic heterogeneity complicates the search for equality that informs a distinctly democratic notion of political community and promotes the right to self-determination that may dismember that community. Second, ethnic heterogeneity threatens to disrupt the attitudinal consensus securing the political order. On this view, ethnic diversity suggests a plurality of political orientations particularly worrisome to democratic states that rely on such an exacting configuration of citizen attitudes to assure stability.

In certain respects, scholarship on American politics magnifies the antiheterogeneity bias found in conventional democratic theory. At issue is the extraordinarily consensual nature of the American polity. Analyses of American political culture most often indicate that Americans are highly agreed on the merits of a central political value system. This common ethos, whose parameters are defined by Lockean liberalism and participatory democracy, integrates the republic's political and social order, enabling the United States to be politically stable despite its ethnic diversity. It is out of concern to preserve this political equilibrium that theorists of American democracy have tended to be wary of immigration. The literature of American democratic theory typically argues that without tutelage in the national creed, immigrants threaten political disruption. That they have rarely been disruptive in fact is a circumstance normally attributed to the irresistible force of political assimilation, immigrants coming to affirm the values believed central to American stability.

The record of American political history testifies to the explanatory power of this thesis. A regard for consensus has been readily apparent in the approach of the American government to immigration. Public officials have chosen to deal with the political liabilities of immigration in three ways: restricting the entry of politically unacceptable immigrants, excising them from the body politic by means of deportation, or converting them to the dominant value system. The manner in which the government has defined the essence of citizenship, the criteria it has used to determine the basis for exclusion and deportation from the United States, its method of implementing refugee policy, and its concern for civic education as administered by the public school system are all evidence of regard for the political characteristics of immigrants. Moreover, this desire for consensus is not only expressed by the government but is also revealed in the more diffuse constituency of nativism. For the nativist an immigrant's race or religion is most often the point of contention, but political values have also been at issue. Immigrants have been charged with radicalism, disloyalty, or corruption, held unfit for participation in

American public life by virtue of their foreign political sensibilities. Even when the maliciousness of the nativist attack has been lacking, well-intentioned citizens—the settlement house worker or the public school superintendent—may yet share the assumption that immigrants undermine the essential unity of the political system; for these individuals, however, salvation lies in assimilation, not exclusion.

The remainder of the present essay will argue that such apprehension—theoretical and otherwise—of the political attributes of immigrants is misguided, that far from being disruptive, by nature immigrants are a positive factor making for stability and this apart from the influence of assimilation. The literature of democratic theory, American democratic theory included, regularly fails to distinguish between different sources of diversity, an oversight causing immigration-induced diversity to be tarred with the same brush as all other sorts. But in fact, diversity can be produced by either the voluntary or the involuntary incorporation of ethnic groups, a distinction of critical importance. When heterogeneity is founded on coercion—the legacy of state-building processes that forcibly unite geographically discrete cultural communities—a political system may well be confronted with recalcitrant and resentful ethnic contingents unlikely to share the sentiments of political community necessary to stability or the attitudes characteristic of political consensus. Alternatively, when immigration is the major cause of heterogeneity, as it is in the United States, the political dynamics may be expected to be entirely different. In this instance, individuals freely place themselves under the authority of a given state and thus are more apt to identify with the political community that that state encompasses and more receptive to accepting the political norms of the community as their own. In brief, because America is a nation of immigrants, it has been able to avoid the ill-effects of heterogeneity that theorists of democracy predict; that is the "counterthesis" of the next chapter.

Notes

1. "Greatest" in this instance should be understood in terms of aggregate and not proportional measures of immigration. Since the middle of the last century, there have been settler societies—Canada, Argentina, Australia, for example—where in certain decades immigration has been of greater proportional significance relative to the native-born population. None of these, however, can rival the United States with respect to the total number of immigrants received or in the ethnic diversity conveyed by that immigration. For a comparative consideration of American immigration, see Frank Thistlethwaite, "Migration from Europe Overseas in the Nineteenth and

Twentieth Centuries," in *Population Movements in Modern European History,* ed. Herbert Moller (New York: Macmillan, 1964), pp. 73–80; also Roger Daniels, *Coming to America: A History of Immigration and Ethnicity in American Life* (New York: Harper Collins, 1990), pp. 23–25.

2. Alexis De Tocqueville, *Democracy in America,* trans. Henry Reeve, revised Francis Bowen, ed. Phillips Bradley (New York: Vintage, 1945), I, p. 334.

3. Ibid., p. 436.

4. "Here the rewards of [the Americans'] industry follow with equal steps the progress of his labour, his labour is founded on the basis of nature, self-interest; can it want a stronger allurement?" Hector St. John de Crevecouer, *Letters from an American Farmer* (1782; rpt. London: J. M. Dent, 1912), p. 44.

5. Thomas Paine, *Common Sense and Other Political Writings,* ed. Nelson F. Adkins (New York: The Liberal Arts Press, 1953), p. 3.

6. See, for example, Robert N. Bellah et al. *Habits of the Heart: Individualism in American Life* (Berkeley: University of California Press, 1985); John Patrick Diggins, *The Lost Soul of American Politics: Virtue, Self-Interest, and the Foundations of Liberalism* (New York: Basic Books, 1984); Ralph Ketcham, *Individualism and Public Life: A Moral Dilemma* (Oxford: Basil Blackwell, 1987). Also see Rupert Wilkinson, *The Pursuit of American Character* (New York: Harper and Row, 1988), esp. pp. 27–38.

7. Seymour Martin Lipset, *Continental Divide: The Values and Institutions of the United States and Canada* (New York: Routledge, 1990), pp. 27–30, 164–65. Lipset also notes the aversion to the state of the New Left movement of the 1960s, another indication of the anarchist strain in American radicalism.

8. Alexander Mackay, *The Western World* (1849; rpt. New York: Negro University Press, 1968), III, p. 339.

9. Seymour Martin Lipset, *The First New Nation: The United States in Historical and Comparative Perspective* (New York: Basic Books, 1963), p. 213.

10. For a good general discussion of the place of equality in the American civic culture, see Kenneth L. Karst, *Belonging to America: Equal Citizenship and the Constitution* (New Haven: Yale University Press, 1989), esp. chapter 3.

11. Tocqueville, *Democracy,* vol. I, pp. 49–55.

12. Harriet Martineau, *Society in America,* ed. Seymour Martin Lipset (Garden City: Anchor-Doubleday, 1962), p. 259.

13. Fanny Trollope, *Domestic Manners of the Americans,* ed. Richard Mullen (1839; rpt. Oxford: Oxford University Press, 1984), p. 363.

14. On this theme see David Potter, *People of Plenty: Economic Abundance and the American Character* (Chicago: University of Chicago Press, 1954).

15. Lipset, *Continental Divide,* pp. 37–39.

16. On the character of populism, see Byron Shafer, "'Exceptionalism' in American Politics?" *Political Science and Politics,* 22, no. 3, (1989), 592–94.

17. Alexander Hamilton, James Madison, and John Jay, *The Federalist* (1778; rpt. New York: Tudor Publishing Co., 1947), p. 99.

18. Madison in *The Federalist,* No. 10, pp. 67–69.

19. Tocqueville, *Democracy,* vol. I, pp. 96–98, 198–205; vol. II, pp. 114—18, 123—28; Martineau, *Society in America,* pp. 309–14.

20. Lipset, *Continental Divide,* p. 32.

21. For quantitative evidence of the American disposition to participate see Gabriel Almond and Sidney Verba, *The Civic Culture: Political Attitudes and Democracy in Five Nations* (Boston: Little, Brown, 1965), pp. 313–14; also see Donald J. Devine, *The Political Culture of the United States: The Influence of Member Values in Regime Maintenance* (Boston: Little, Brown, 1972), pp. 146–49; Warren E. Miller and Teresa E. Levitin, *Leadership and Change: The New Politics and the American Electorate* (Cambridge: Winthrop, 1976), pp. 219–21; Alan I. Abramowitz, "The United States: Political Culture Under Stress," in *The Civic Culture Revisited,* ed. Gabriel A. Almond and Sidney Verba (Boston: Little, Brown, 1980), pp. 196–99; G. Bingham Powell, Jr., "American Voter Turnout in Comparative Perspective," *American Political Science Review,* 80, no. 1 (1986), pp. 17–43.

22. Tocqueville, *Democracy,* vol. I, pp. 310–19.

23. See, for example, Abramowitz, "The United States: Political Culture Under Stress"; Almond and Verba, *The Civic Culture;* Bellah et al., *Habits of the Heart;* Devine, *The Political Culture of the United States;* Richard Hofstadter, *The American Political Tradition And the Men Who Made It* (New York: Alfred A. Knopf, 1948), Samuel Huntington, *American Politics: The Promise of Disharmony* (Cambridge: Belknap, 1981); Herbert McClosky and John Zaller, *The American Ethos: Public Attitudes Toward Capitalism and Democracy* (Cambridge: Harvard University Press, 1984).

24. See, for example, Bernard Bailyn, *The Ideological Origins of the American Revolution* (Cambridge: Harvard University Press, 1967); Russell L. Hanson, *The Democratic Imagination in America: Conversations with Our Past* (Princeton: Princeton University Press, 1985); J.G.A. Pocock, *The Machiavellian Moment: Florentine Political Thought and the Atlantic Republican Tradition* (Princeton: Princeton University Press, 1975); Gordon S. Wood, *The Creation of the American Republic, 1776–1787* (Chapel Hill: University of North Carolina Press, 1969).

25. See Michael Lienesch, *New Order of the Ages: Time, the Constitution, and the Making of Modern American Political Thought* (Princeton: Princeton University Press, 1988); also Steven M. Dworetz, *The Unvarnished Doctrine: Locke, Liberalism, and the American Revolution* (Durham: Duke University Press, 1990).

26. Wood, *Creation,* pp. 562 *ff.,* pp. 594 *ff.;* Hanson, *Democratic Imagination,* pp. 121 *ff.*

27. Forrest McDonald, *Novus Ordum Seclorum: The Intellectual Origins of the Constitution* (Lawrence: University Press of Kansas, 1985), pp. 7–10; Thomas L. Pangle, *The Spirit of Modern Republicanism: The Moral Vision of the American Founders and the Philosophy of Locke* (Chicago: University of Chicago Press, 1988), pp. 124 *ff.*

28. Hanson, *Democratic Imagination,* pp. 121–52.

29. See, for example, Anne Norton, *Alternative Americas: A Reading of Antebellum Political Culture* (Chicago: University of Chicago Press, 1986). On

republicanism's durability, see Rogers M. Smith, "The 'American Creed' and American Identity: The Limits of Liberal Citizenship in the United States," *The Western Political Quarterly*, 41 (1988), 225–52.

30. On liberalism's dominance of American political culture, see Terence Ball and Richard Dagger, "The 'L-Word': A Short History of Liberalism," *The Political Science Teacher*, 3, no. 1 (1990), 1–6.

31. Hamilton, Madison, and Jay, *The Federalist*, p. 15.

32. James Bryce, *The American Commonwealth* (London: Macmillan and Co., 1895), II, p. 283. Bryce's caveat notwithstanding, even the American party system suggests the dominance of the liberal ethos. An outstanding feature of American parties is the narrow range of the ideological spectrum within which they operate. Partisan differences are masked by an electoral system prejudicial to the chances of third parties, but the character of the American electorate must be considered as well. Other countries—Britain and Canada, for instance—also have single member plurality systems of voting, yet the gamut of parties and party positions represented in their legislatures is greater. One suspects that American parties congregate around the ideological midpoint, at least in part, because in so doing they reflect the disposition of the great majority of their constituents. Even when alternative parties have made a breakthrough, in the name of Populism or Progressivism, they have tended to call the nation back to its traditional political creed, not to introduce a new one.

33. Harold J. Laski, *The American Democracy: A Commentary and Interpretation* (New York: Viking, 1948), p. 50.

34. Gunnar Myrdal, *An American Dilemma: The Negro Problem and Modern Democracy* (New York: Harper and Brothers, 1944), p. 3.

35. Robert A. Dahl, *Pluralist Democracy in the United States: Conflict and Consent* (Chicago: Rand McNally, 1967), p. 357.

36. Huntington, *American Politics*, p. 4.

37. Ibid., p. 17.

38. Hofstadter, *American Political Tradition*, pp. viii–x.

39. Daniel Boorstin, *The Genius of American Politics* (Chicago: University of Chicago Press, 1953), pp. 1–33.

40. Ibid., p. 157.

41. Louis Hartz, *The Liberal Tradition in America: An Interpretation of American Political Thought Since the Revolution* (New York: Harcourt, Brace, 1955), p. 62.

42. Ibid., p. 1.

43. Ibid., p. 7.

44. See, for example, Donald J. Devine, *The Political Culture of the United States: The Influence of Member Values on Regime Maintenance* (Boston: Little, Brown, 1972).

45. Herbert McClosky, "Consensus and Ideology in American Politics," *American Political Science Review*, LVIII (1964), 361–82; James W. Prothro and Charles M. Grigg, "Fundamental Principles of Democracy: Bases of Agreement and Disagreement," *Journal of Politics*, 22 (1960), 276–94; Samuel

A. Stouffer, *Communism, Conformity, and Civil Liberties* (Gloucester: Peter Smith, 1963). For a similar perspective based on early 1970s vintage data see Lawrence J. P. Herson and C. Richard Hofstetter, "Tolerance, Consensus and the Democratic Creed: A Contextual Interpretation," *Journal of Politics*, 37 (1975), 1007–32.

46. McClosky, "Consensus and Ideology," p. 375; Prothro and Grigg, "Fundamental Principles," p. 291.

47. See Joseph V. Femia, "Elites, Participation and the Democratic Creed," *Political Studies*, 27 (1979), 1–20; Robert W. Jackman, "Political Elites, Mass Publics and Support for Democratic Principles," *Journal of Politics*, 34 (1972), 753–73.

48. McClosky and Zaller, *American Ethos*, p. 233.

49. Ibid., p. 261.

50. Arthur F. Bentley, *The Process of Government: A Study of Social Pressures* (1908; rpt. Bloomington: Principia, 1935), p. 269.

51. Robert A. Dahl, *Pluralist Democracy in the United States: Conflict and Consent* (Chicago: Rand McNally, 1967); Theodore Lowi, *The End of Liberalism: Ideology, Policy, and the Crisis of Public Authority* (New York: W. W. Norton, 1969); David B. Truman, *The Governmental Process: Political Interests and Public Opinion* (New York: Alfred A. Knopf, 1965).

52. Dahl, *Pluralist Democracy*, pp. 326 ff. Also see Truman, *Governmental Process*, pp. 512 ff.

53. On the history of the cultural pluralist concept, see Philip Gleason, "Americans All: World War II and the Shaping of American Identity," *The Review of Politics*, 43, no. 4 (1981), 483–518.

54. See Horace M. Kallen, *Cultural Pluralism and the American Idea* (Philadelphia: University of Pennsylvania Press, 1956); Allan Smith, "National Images and National Maintenance: The Ascendancy of the Ethnic Idea in North America," *Canadian Journal of Political Science*, 14, no. 2 (1981), 249–53; Gleason, "Americans All," pp. 502–11. Also see Lawrence H. Fuchs, *The American Kaleidoscope: Race, Ethnicity, and the American Civic Culture* (Hanover: University Press of New England, 1990), esp. pp. 1–75.

55. It has been suggested to the author that pluralist democratic theory—particularly the American version of that theory as specified, for instance, in Madison's *Federalist Papers* #10 and #51—is more solicitous of ethnic diversity than the present thesis might indicate. On this view, maximum ethnic heterogeneity is to be encouraged as a further means of ensuring that within any governing majority, power checks power.

In response, although in fact pluralism may be (and in the United States, has been) reconciled with ethnic diversity precisely along these lines, with few exceptions (perhaps Lord Acton?) theorists of political pluralism have not conceived of the concept in this way. Clearly, in *Federalist* #10 and #51 the type of social diversity that Madison has in mind stems from differences in region and class, not ethnicity. That cultural heterogeneity may well promote the limitation of authority political pluralists desire is not to be doubted, but such seems incidental to a political theory typically constructed on other grounds. More than this, if, in comparison to other varieties of democratic theory, pluralism is potentially more accommodating to social diversity, theorists of pluralism yet maintain that agreement on common values is crucial to the effective functioning of the political process. For that reason, even within pluralist democratic theory, there appears to be an inescapable tension between ethnic heterogeneity and democratic stability.

56. James Allen Smith, *The Spirit of American Government, A Study of the Constitution: Its Origin, Influence and Relation to Democracy* (1907; rpt. New York: Macmillan, 1911); Charles A. Beard, *An Economic Interpretation of the Constitution of the United States* (1913; rpt. New York: Macmillan, 1935); Vernon L. Parrington, *Main Currents in American Thought: An Interpretation of American Literature from the Beginnings to 1920* (New York: Harcourt, Brace, 1927).

57. G. William Domhoff, *Who Rules America Now? A View for the '80s* (Englewood Cliffs: Prentice-Hall, 1983), p. 197.

58. Quoted in Richard Hofstadter, *The Progressive Historians: Turner, Beard, Parrington* (New York: Alfred A. Knopf, 1968), p. 438. For a current statement of the progressivist case, though one not specifically assuming the progressivist label, see Michael Parenti, *Democracy for the Few*, 5th ed. (New York: St. Martin's Press, 1988).

59. See Beard, *Economic Interpretation*; Parrington, *Main Currents*; Smith, *Spirit of American Government*, also Merril Jensen, *The Making of the American Constitution* (Princeton: D. Van Nostrand, 1964), and *The Articles of Confederation: An Interpretation of the Social-Constitutional History of the American Revolution, 1774–1781* (Madison: University of Wisconsin Press, 1959).

60. J. A. Smith, *Spirit of American Government*, p. 389.

61. See, for example, Sean Wilentz, *Chants Democratic: New York and the Rise of the American Working Class, 1788–1850* (New York: Oxford University Press, 1984); and Ira Katznelson, *City Trenches: Urban Politics and the Politics of Class in the United States* (Chicago: University of Chicago Press, 1981).

62. Max Lerner, *America as a Civilization: Life and Thought in the United States Today*, 2nd ed. (New York: Henry Holt, 1987), p. 539.

63. See Katznelson, *City Trenches*, especially ch. 1.

64. Gabriel Kolko, *Main Currents in American History* (New York: Harper and Row, 1976), p. 271.

65. Laski, *American Democracy*, pp. 50–51.

66. Kolko, *Main Currents*, pp. 273 ff.

67. Acknowledging this point, Parrington writes, "The humanitarian idealism of the Declaration has always been echoed as a battle cry in the hearts of those who dream of an America dedicated to democratic ends. It cannot be long ignored or repudiated, for sooner or later it returns to plague the councils of practical politics. . . . Without its freshening influence our political history would have been much more sordid and materialistic." Parrington, *Main Currents*, vol. III, p. 285.

68. Myrdal, *American Dilemma*, p. 13.

69. Herbert Croly, *The Promise of American Life* (1909; rpt. Cambridge: The Belknap Press of Harvard University Press, 1965).

70. Boorstin, *American Politics*, p. 28.

71. Louis Hartz, *The Founding of New Societies* (New York: Harcourt, Brace, and World, 1964), p. 14.

72. Bryce, *American Commonwealth*, vol. II, pp. 367–68.

73. Dahl, *Who Governs?*, p. 318. Cf. Dahl, *Democracy and Its Critics* (New Haven: Yale University Press, 1989), pp. 259–60.

74. Huntington, *American Politics*, pp. 230–31.

75. Cited in Madison Grant and Charles Stewart Davison, *The Founders of the Republic on Immigration, Naturalization and Aliens* (New York: Charles Scribner's Sons, 1928), p. 26. Clearly, Grant's and Davison's volume was intended to provide further ammunition for the forces of immigration restriction; that does not, however, diminish its utility as a partial record of the founders' views on immigration.

76. Ibid., p. 90.

77. Ibid., p. 49.

78. Ibid., pp. 50–51.

79. Cited in Edith Abbot, *Historical Aspects of the Immigration Problem: Select Documents* (Chicago: University of Chicago Press, 1926), pp. 704–705.

80. James H. Kettner, *The Development of American Citizenship, 1608–1870* (Chapel Hill: University of North Carolina Press, 1978), pp. 213–19.

81. Quoted in ibid., p. 242.

82. The United States is not alone in expecting that candidates for citizenship should show conversance with and support for the political institutions of their country of adoption. Canada and Germany, for example, have similar naturalization provisions. See William Rogers Brubaker, "Citizenship and Naturalization: Policies and Politics," in *Immigration and the Politics of Citizenship in Europe and North America*, ed. William Rogers Brubaker (Lanham: University Press of America, 1989), pp. 109–12.

83. Rudolph J. Vecoli, "Immigration, Naturalization and the Constitution," *News for Teachers of Political Science*, No. 50 (1986), 12–13.

84. Steven R. Shapiro, "Ideological Exclusions Closing the Border to Political Dissidents," *Harvard Law Review*, 100 (1987), 931–34; Vecoli, "Immigration," pp. 9–10.

85. Vecoli, "Immigration," pp. 10–11.

86. Shapiro, "Ideological Exclusions," pp. 935–38; Vecoli, "Immigration," pp. 10–13.

87. See Pastora San Juan Cafferty et al., *The Dilemma of American Immigration: Beyond the Golden Door* (New Brunswick: Transaction, 1983), pp. 43–45; Norman L. Zucker and Naomi Flink Zucker, *The Guarded Gate: The Reality of American Refugee Policy* (New York: Harcourt Brace Jovanovich, 1987), esp. chs. 4–5; Gil Loescher and John A. Scanlon, *Calculated Kindness: Refugees and America's Half-Open Door: 1945 to the Present* (New York: The Free Press, 1986); Barbara M. Yarnold, *Refugees Without Refuge:*

Formation and Failed Implementation of U.S. Political Asylum Policy in the 1980's (Lanham: University Press of America, 1990).

88. Seymour Martin Lipset and Earl Raab, *The Politics of Unreason: Right-Wing Extremism in America, 1790–1970* (New York: Harper and Row, 1970), pp. 47–60. Also see David H. Bennett, *The Party of Fear: From Nativist Movements to the New Right in American History* (Chapel Hill: University of North Carolina Press, 1988), pp. 4–7.

89. John Higham, *Strangers in the Land: Patterns of American Nativism, 1860–1925,* revised ed. (New York: Atheneum, 1978), p. 4.

90. On the ethno-cultural basis of American national identity, see R. M. Smith, *American Creed.*

91. Higham, *Strangers,* p. 11.

92. Madison Grant, *The Passing of the Great Race* (New York: Charles Scribner's Sons, 1916), p. 90.

93. Higham, *Strangers,* pp. 277–81.

94. Johnson in Roy L. Garis, *Immigration Restriction* (New York: Macmillan, 1927), p. vii.

95. See Frederick C. Luebke, *Bonds of Loyalty: German-Americans and World War I* (DeKalb: Northern Illinois University Press, 1974).

96. On this theme see, for instance, Richard Hofstadter, *The Age of Reform: From Bryan to F.D.R.* (New York: Vintage Press, 1955), pp. 174–84.

97. For a discussion of how political and industrial concerns often intersected in the agenda of the Americanizers, see Steven Meyer, "Adapting the Immigrant to the Line: Americanization in the Ford Factory, 1914–1921," *Journal of Social History,* 14 (1980), 67–82; also Oliver Zunz, *The Changing Face of Inequality: Urbanization, Industrial Development, and Immigrants in Detroit, 1880–1920* (Chicago: University of Chicago Press, 1982), pp. 309–18. On the role of the federal government in the movement, see John F. McClymer, "The Americanization Movement and the Education of the Foreign-Born Adult, 1914–1925," in *American Education and the European Immigrant: 1840–1940,* ed. Bernard J. Weiss (Urbana: University of Illinois Press, 1982), pp. 96–116.

98. Robert A. Carlson, *The Quest for Conformity: Americanization Through Education* (New York: John Wiley and Sons, 1975), p. 42.

99. Oscar Handlin, "Education and the European Immigrant, 1820–1920," in *American Education and the European Immigrant: 1840–1940,* ed. Bernard J. Weiss (Urbana: University of Illinois Press, 1982), pp. 6–8.

100. Quoted in Leonard Dinnerstein, Roger L. Nichols, and David M. Reimers, *Natives and Strangers: Ethnic Groups and the Building of America* (New York: Oxford University Press, 1979), p. 115.

101. Dahl, *Who Governs?* pp. 319–20.

102. See, for example, the argument set forth by Georges Fauriol, "U.S. Immigration Policy and the National Interest," *The Humanist,* 44, no. 5 (1984), 5–26.

4

The Counterthesis:
Immigrants Enhance the
Political Stability of the United States

Immigrants constitute a potentially disruptive force in democratic political systems in general and that of the United States in particular; that is the conventional wisdom the present chapter will challenge. The contention will be that immigrants tend to be supportive and quiescent citizens notwithstanding the influence of assimilation. This is true for solid and predictable reasons. It is precisely their status as guests that makes immigrants relatively undemanding politically, while their desire to prove themselves worthy members of the American republic tends to make them patriotic. These characteristics help to explain what, from the viewpoint of most political theory, is a paradox: despite the cultural heterogeneity of its citizenry, America is a democratic but stable nation with a high level of political integration. It is not territorial amalgamation but immigration that has produced most of the heterogeneity in America, and the difference is crucial. The former process creates resentment; the latter, loyal citizens.

The current chapter proceeds in three stages: (1) immigrant political value systems are examined, (2) immigrant orientations toward political participation are investigated, and (3) the claim that immigrants have been susceptible to political radicalism, civic corruption, and labor militancy is evaluated. In this manner, the central assumptions of the case against immigrants will be assessed: that immigrants arrive in America with political beliefs antipathetic to the dominant liberal creed and that they are prepared to put those beliefs into practice. The inquiry reveals that both claims are flawed.

In place of the anti-immigrant argument a counterthesis will be offered. It will be maintained that immigrants do not threaten the American democratic order and may make it more secure. This counterthesis is simply a hypothesis, forwarded tentatively and resting on data that are only suggestive. Nevertheless, if in its specific applications this counterthesis exaggerates, prima facie evidence indicates that its general outlines are correct. Such evidence acknowledges that even though immigrants do not necessarily embrace all elements of the American creed, they compensate for this by displaying an earnest patriotism. Furthermore, they have little inclination to participate in American politics, let alone give much encouragement to "unsavory" political movements.

Immigrants and the American Creed

What do immigrants believe about politics? Do the values and attitudes they bring to the political process disqualify them from being virtuous citizens? Students of American politics as well as spokespersons for restrictionism frequently contend that immigrants lack political beliefs consonant with the American political culture. And in a country that understands its national identity in terms of a political creed, such a deficiency, it may be ventured, not only prevents immigrants from functioning as worthy participants in a democracy but also prevents them from becoming American. It is necessary to ask, therefore, just what it is that immigrants think about the political process and, in particular, to what extent they understand and accept the essentials of America's liberal ethos.

Given both the subtlety of the creed (as has been pointed out, not even the native-born are completely conversant with its assumptions) and the wide variety of immigrant groups in America—possessing different cultures, produced by different circumstances, and experiencing the United States in different ways—only the greatest of optimists would expect the ideological convergence of the foreign-born. Acceptance of the creed depends on the particular immigrant group in question and the time at which various members of the group migrated to the United States. Some ethnic groups seem to reflect the foundational liberal belief system better than others, and even within a specific group, contingents arriving in separate periods of history may possess distinct ideological affinities.[1]

Furthermore, concrete data with which to assess immigrant orientations are difficult to come by; few opinion polls or surveys are available to furnish the relevant information. Instead, political attitudes must be deduced from discrete sources: the history of immigrants in their homelands, the behavior of immigrants in America, and the testimony of immigrants themselves. Such evidence indicates little uniformity of belief. But several observations concerning the manner in which immigrant sensibilities in general compare with the central elements of the American political value system—individualism, equality, participatory democracy, negative freedom, capitalism—can be offered.

If individualism means acknowledging that a person must make his or her own way in America without much assistance from the public authorities, then most immigrants have been individualists. Presently, welfare programs embrace even the foreign-born who, in many cases, are eager recipients of government support.[2] Yet for the greater part of America's history that has not been the case, nor is it clear that immigrants would necessarily have welcomed public intervention. Immigrants have been individualists in this sense—that they set out on their own in order to pursue their self-interest, particularly economic interests. For those immigrants circa the 1920s and before, public intervention would have suggested the restriction of individual achievement rather than its promotion; surely the homeland experience would often have led them to this conclusion. America was the land of opportunity, of self-fulfillment, precisely because the government was loathe to intervene. In fact, a source of tension between more contemporary immigrant groups—say, post-1965, the end of the national quota system—and their predecessors is that the latter often take exception to the way in which the newer groups avail themselves of the public largesse. The older contingents are frequently great expositors of the "bootstraps" philosophy of social and economic advancement: since we had to make good by fending for ourselves, they seem to argue, so too must the recent arrivals. Yet what may separate the two groups is less that their motivations are opposed than that the government has become more activist.

In other respects, however, it is less clear that immigrants embrace individualism. Immigrants generally have not championed individualism if it means the promotion of self-interest to the exclusion of broader social obligations. In the nineteenth and early twentieth centuries at least, the majority of immigrants emerged from social systems strongly influenced by feudalism and manorialism. And although the psychological consequences of this are somewhat speculative in nature, it would not be surprising if the communitarian side of the immigrant personality was more highly developed than that of native-born Americans who have no heritage of feudalism and its corporate ethos.[3]

The behavior of the foreign-born in America lends support to this thesis. Even among those who arrive in America alone, emigration may be undertaken primarily as a means of meeting family obligations in the homeland. In the middle of the last century, for instance, one of the factors sending thousands of Chinese laborers to the United

States, frequently destined to live the solitary life for the duration of their working years, was a sense of familial responsibility. The parlous state of the southeastern Chinese economy meant that many Chinese families relied on foreign remittances for survival. In this manner Chinese immigrants came to America, not to escape traditional obligations, but to fulfill them.[4]

Yet more than an acute family consciousness prevents the immigrant from an unqualified individualism. Immigrants also construct ethnic communities in the New World, self-contained sets of social institutions around which an individual's life may revolve. That community might encompass both Old World social organizations transferred to the New World and institutions having a distinctly American genesis. In either instance the immigrant community provides the security longed for in the midst of an alien culture, a buffer against the harsher discontinuities of American life. Without question, one of the greatest comforts to a prospective emigrant has been the knowledge that compatriots stand in ready welcome at the opposite end of the journey. Few immigrants have been willing to seek individual satisfaction at the expense of ostracism from this support of compatriots, a condition requiring the suppression of a certain amount of individual ambition lest involvement in the wider American social milieu risk attenuating ties with an immediate circle of friends.

Individualism in a more restricted political sense likewise has held little appeal. That the individual stands at the center of the political system, that the system exists to promote self-interest, that the common person possesses inalienable rights, and is the ultimate arbiter of political right and wrong—such concepts appear contrary to the experiences of the majority of immigrants and uncharacteristic of their outlook. This was surely the situation before the limiting legislation of the 1920s, when most of the largest sending countries—Germany, Ireland, Italy, Austro-Hungary, Russia—would not have had much experience with liberal-democratic forms and would not have given encouragement to ideas, such as individualism, that are part of the democratic ethos (Britain, Scandinavia, and Canada arguably being the exceptions). But neither does it seem that the major new sources of emigration to America—Korea, Cuba, Mexico, the Philippines, Southeast Asia—have any greater facility for democratic individualism, notwithstanding that the ideals and structures of democracy are now more widely disseminated. Of course, a handful of immigrants have come to America with preformed affinities for the liberal-democratic ethos—the German Forty-Eighters, for instance. Yet many, perhaps most, of the foreign-born have been tutored in submission and obedience to political authority, not the virtues of individual political autonomy. Even in the United States this conservative approach to politics might be perpetuated within the immigrant community. Churches, especially those following an episcopal form of organization, such as the Catholic church and various Lutheran synods, in their theology, decisionmaking practices, and counsel to parishioners have often fostered an outlook contrary to the American emphasis on individualism.[5] And given that the church has been for many immigrants a primary instrument of solace, its teachings and example have not been lightly regarded. That said, as will be argued, politics has rarely been of sufficient interest to the majority of immigrants for them to challenge these antidemocratic admonitions.

If immigrants are unlikely to be wholehearted individualists, neither are they fully conversant with the egalitarian component of the American creed. To be sure, equality of respect, equal administration of the law, and the equal opportunity to achieve are among the most attractive of America's offerings to the foreign-born. Immigrants have usually come from class-riven societies in which status gradations are maintained and promoted. This rigidity of the social hierarchy, and the limited possibilities for economic advancement open to those at its lower levels, has certainly been a factor in many decisions to emigrate. In the mid-nineteenth century, an Irish immigrant wrote of the difference between his country of birth and America:

> Poeple that Cuts a great dash at home, when they come here the[y] tink it strange for the humble Class of poeple to get as much respect as themselves [but] when they come here it wont do to say i had such and was such and such at home [for] strangers here the[y] must gain respect by there conduct and nut by there tongue. . . . I know poeple here from [Ireland] that would not speak to me [there] if the[y] met me on the public road [but] here i can laugh in there face when i see them.[6]

Moreover, for those immigrants who have experienced ethnic persecution in their countries of nativity, the prospect of equality in the United States is especially welcome. Whether it be Jews fleeing Russian domination, Slavs escaping Magyarization, Armenians seeking relief from Turkish autocracy, or Chinese taking refuge from Vietnamese oppression, the American creed promises equal dignity and equal treatment.

Nevertheless, it is unclear just how deeply this affinity for equality runs. For many emigrants the decision to relocate to the United States has been prompted less by a desire that all social distinctions be abolished than from fear that their status in the Old World is precarious.[7] These "middling" groups have been among the best candidates for emigration; wealthier individuals have often had little incentive to leave, while in the short-term those most impoverished may have lacked the means to do so. Immigration thus becomes the solution for those whose grip on the status ladder is slipping, an opportunity to shore up social standing or, better still, to enhance it. Comparatively, the United States' advantage is that it does not impose cultural impediments to accumulating wealth—the major criterion of social distinction in America—and moving up the ranks of success and status. Many immigrants have recognized this and are eager to come to the United States because of it; it would be difficult to call their interest in emigrating a commitment to social equality.[8]

Although the initial contingent of immigrants from a given country has usually been drawn from this middle class, their less fortunate compatriots eventually have made their way to the United States as well. Particularly since the late nineteenth century, decreasing transportation costs have done much to place the act of emigration within reach of a broader population, and remittances from compatriots already in America (not to mention government efforts to expedite the settlement of refugees) can furnish the necessary wherewithal—it is the latter that helped the destitute Irish famine refugees to emigrate, for example. But even these immigrants have not been immune to the belief that social distinctions are normative. The weight of Old World practice frequently shapes attitudes in the New World, and many of the foreign-born, regardless of social station, accept an inequality of social relations. Of the nineteenth-century Boston Irish, Oscar Handlin writes:

> In America, too, the Irish agreed that everyone should "mate with their equals, high as well as low," and the [Boston] *Pilot* pointed out that the poor Irish family was "much more happy and contented in its place on life" than the American. But Judith O'Rourke expressed this acceptance of class most clearly when, scoffing at the possibility of educating her children, she hoped that her sons would "grow up honest good men, like them that's gone afore them, not ashamed of their station, or honest toil," while her daughter " 'll be the same lady her mother is . . . an' that's good enough. . . . She'd look purty I'm thinkin' wid her music in one corner an' I wid my wash tub in another."[9]

This is not to imply, of course, that the virtue of social equality has never been accepted by immigrant-stock Americans.[10] Indeed a major source of conflict between first- and second-generation immigrants often turns on the disregard of children for the social conventions of their parents. But the inegalitarianism of Old World traditions are only slowly eroded over time. Nor may the immigrant's reception in America do much to increase confidence in equality: found in the lowest tiers of the work force, and periodically the target of nativist outrage, immigrants may quickly become disillusioned with the ideal of equality in America.

A third component of the American creed is participatory democracy. Concerning the participatory urge among immigrants more will be said later. At present, suffice it to note that the disposition to participate in politics has not been very strong among the great majority of immigrants. Even so, contrary cases may be cited. Immigrants in the forefront of the liberal European revolutions of 1830 and 1848, for instance, came to America already convinced of the virtues of participation. German Forty-Eighters—the "Greens" as they came to be called—chided their "Gray" compatriots who had lived in America for a number of decades, appalled at their passivity in American politics and especially their failure to take up the cause of abolitionism.[11] But perhaps the most outstanding departure from the nonparticipatory norm was made by the Irish immigrants, a group whose inclination to take part in American politics was forged by historical experience. By the time the Irish began to arrive in America in sizable numbers, they had been engaged in a struggle for the common rights of citizenship for generations. Indeed, the demands of Irish nationalists for political equality within the British Empire, if not complete independence, had a certain cohesiveness with the values that Americans held dear. As Thomas Brown observes, the nationalist possessed a "conviction that he was acting in the name of certain values common to all Americans and worthy of all men. . . . He was asking Americans to live up to their highest ideals."[12] The right to self-governance was one of these ideals.

Yet the Irish passion for American politics is without parallel. The language barrier is one circumstance distinguishing other groups from the Irish. But beyond this, little in the history of most immigrant groups familiarizes them with the virtues of civic participation, at least not on the liberal-democratic understanding of that term. As already noted, in the homeland, immigrants are most often acted upon rather than play a vital role in political decisionmaking. And in those cases where immigrants are relatively well acquainted with participatory norms, familiarity does not necessarily translate into political activism in the United States. In fact, the participatory demands of homeland regimes may have caused the foreign-born to emigrate in the first place. Even the most authoritarian governments often expect ritualistic expressions of popular support, participation that, even if hollow, is nonetheless time-consuming and tedious. So, for example, Russian Jewish immigrants have been known to express a weariness with politics: Komsomol meetings, political discussion sessions at work, and compulsory voting (compulsory at least in the sense that it is a cultural expectation) have all been aspects of Soviet practice threatening to overpoliticize the immigrant and diminish any enthusiasm for participation in America.[13] Alternatively, it may be the oppressive character of politics in the country of birth that dissuades the immigrant from participation; here government is treated as an institution best avoided. In either instance the effect is the same—tepid commitment to the principle of participatory democracy. On this score, from the immigrant's perspective the appeal of American life may be the diminution of the political.

By contrast, the dedication of immigrants to the fourth feature of the creed—freedom—is strong. As Marcus Hansen has written, immigrants soon learn the "magic charm of this confession of faith."[14] Doubtless such a confession pleases their hosts. Nevertheless, immigrants do seem to have a genuine affection for the theory and practice of American freedom—the freedom from government. Handlin notes that for many immigrants government is "simply a taskmaster, a tax collector, a crime punisher, over which they had no control and from which they wanted most of the favor of being left alone."[15] Both the strength and the weakness of what the United States offers are just that freedom of autonomy. Jews of Eastern European immigrant stock furnish an excellent example of the general point, their heritage helping to determine their staunch commitment to liberalism.[16] Geographically confined to the Pale of Settlement, restricted in educational and employment opportunities, the target of special taxes, and periodically subject to state-sponsored pogroms, Jewish immigrants and their descendants have known the value of being left alone, Nazism providing a horrific reminder. But historically, countless other groups have benefited as well: Italians of the Mezzogiorno have escaped the burden of oppressive taxation, Irish immigrants have been relieved from the payment of tithes to the Anglican church, Russian-German Mennonites have been freed from military obligations, and assorted dissenters have found the opportunity to worship without fearing the vindictiveness of an established church. All such freedoms are tangible, and their importance to various immigrant contingents must not be underestimated.

Accordingly, when immigrants have championed social causes, those causes have often been connected with issues of personal liberty. Controversies over native tongue instruction in public schools and Sabbatarianism can be interpreted in this light. Prohibition has been the greatest among such causes, if only because of its national import. Admittedly, not all immigrant-stock groups opposed the temperance movement; most notably Scandinavians of pietistic religious inclination did not (A.J. Volstead, who sponsored the famous act instituting the Eighteenth Amendment, was of Norwegian descent). But the majority of ethnic groups, including the largest—the Irish and the Germans—were absolutely opposed, seeing Prohibition as a public attempt to undermine their cultural freedom. For like reason, to the degree that political parties have affirmed the cause of personal liberty and cultural autonomy, immigrant partisanship has been greatly determined; the traditional, though by no means exclusive, Democratic advantage among immigrant-stock voters of non-British lineage, especially those of liturgical religious persuasion, may be partially explained in this manner.[17]

Perhaps the most precious freedom of all from the immigrants' point of view, and the feature of the American creed for which they express the greatest attraction, is the freedom of economic interaction—the liberty to accumulate the wealth animating capitalism. The majority of immigrants are unmitigated capitalists in the simple sense that they come to the United States driven by a desire to become materially successful. Plainly, America offers land, or money, or sustenance that the immigrant's country of birth cannot. Through legislation such as the Public Land Act of 1796 and its amendments, the Preemption Act of 1841, and to lesser effect, the Homestead Act of 1862, the United States government smoothed the way for early immigrants to achieve a level of welfare open to only a few in the old country. And although the possibility of significant holdings in land was diminished by the late nineteenth century, immigrants of that era and beyond have been no less drawn to America by the prospect of economic gain. In the United States a budding entrepreneur is unfettered by the public proscriptions and social conventions that often exist in the home country. Moreover, a capitalist ethos lends support to the acquisitive urge; the pursuit of wealth is not regarded as improper, nor is it thought to require much regulation. As a turn-of-the-century Italian immigrant testifies:

> If I am to be frank, then I shall say that I left Italy and came to America for the sole purpose of making money. Neither the laws of Italy nor the laws of America, neither the government of one nor the government of the other, influenced me in any way. I suffered no political oppression in Italy. I was not seeking political ideals: as a matter of fact I was quite satisfied with those of my native land. If I could have worked my way up in my chosen profession in Italy, I would have stayed in

Italy. But repeated efforts showed me that I could not. America was the
land of opportunity, and so I came, intending to make money and then
return to Italy. This is true of most Italian emigrants to America.[18]

That the promise of wealth alone attracts many immigrants is
revealed by the numbers of people who have come to the United
States exclusively for that purpose, having no inclination to become
permanent residents. "Birds of passage" have been plentiful at various
periods of America's history, particularly so between the advent of
steam transportation, which made seasonal migration feasible, and the
quota legislation of the 1920s, which made it virtually impossible—for
Europeans at any rate. Southern Italians are generally recognized as
the first and greatest of these temporary migrants. This status is
reflected both in that three-quarters of Italian immigrants between
1899 and 1910 were male (family roots were not transplanted) and
that rates of return were high: 31% between 1897 and 1901; 38%
between 1902 and 1906; and 72.6% between 1907 and 1912.[19] Other
nationalities were equally eager to return to their countries of origin:
from 1900 to 1913, perhaps 50–60% of non-Jewish Poles moved back
to the homeland, whereas between 1908 and 1923, more than 50% of
all Russian, Slovak, and Balkan states' immigrants did the same. The
economic motive of such individuals is further suggested by the fact
that return migration was at its highest during periods of depression
in the American economy.[20] Nor has this phenomenon been solely
European: at one time or another Chinese, Japanese, and Mexican
immigrants have followed a similar pattern (many of these having
been contract laborers).[21] And even though in the postwar era
immigrants have tended to remain in greater numbers, it is estimated
that more than 15% of those arriving since 1960 leave the United
States within ten years, with an even higher percentage of returnees
among individuals thirty years of age and older.[22] Though these
statistics do not identify multiple migrants—that is to say, individuals
who leave and return more than once (among the Italians, for example,
regular seasonal migration was well developed)—they do indicate the
transiency of a sizable portion of America's immigrant population, a
group understanding America purely as a means to material gain.[23]

What the foregoing discussion suggests, then, is that immigrants
do not necessarily embrace the whole of the American political creed;
certain features, specifically the American value of freedom, both in
its political and economic aspect, are easier for them to accept than
others. But as to the supposed prerequisites of a stable American
polity—that citizens must achieve consensus on a central political
belief system—immigrants would seem to be wanting. They simply

do not show evidence of a uniform commitment to the values integrating the American political system. Again, given the precision of the creed that immigrants are expected to comprehend, this is understandable. Nevertheless, if part of the assessment of immigration's political effect in America turns on discovering what immigrant political values are, and those values do not cohere with the stabilizing core of American beliefs, then it might be argued that immigration is in fact a disruptive political force.

Drawing that conclusion, however, would be premature. To begin with, though immigrants may not display a natural affection for all elements of the creed, neither do they indicate conscious animosity toward them. For this reason it is altogether possible that immigrants can be convinced of the merits of the American political value system; in fact they already are supportive of at least two of its props. Because the creed is the substance of American identity and enables immigrants actually to become American through confessing the political orthodoxy, immigrants who wish to experience fully the advantages of life as an American will voluntarily accept it; it is their ticket to economic opportunity and social acceptance in the New World. Thus, when asked questions concerning political values, immigrants often parrot the wisdom of their citizenship courses—immigrants are receptive students.

But fear of immigrant disruptiveness is misplaced for another reason, too: the range of immigrant political beliefs is not exhausted by an inventory of their views about the creed. By focusing on the immigrant's lack of fit with the American political value system, and consequently on the means by which those values have been imparted to newcomers of diverse national origin, standard interpretations of the immigrant political experience tend to overlook the manner in which the foreign-born have promoted democratic stability quite apart from any affinity for America's liberal political norms. Granted, upon arrival in the United States immigrants are unlikely to be good Lockeans. It does not follow, however, that, save rapid political assimilation, they are liable to be disruptive. Immigrants have all sorts of convictions regarding the United States, many less precise than those pertaining to the specifically liberal dimensions of America's political culture but no less crucial to the evaluation of immigration's political consequences. And prime among these additional attitudes, it would seem, are an inclination to political quiescence—a factor insulating the political system from the ideological dissonance that immigration portends—and an earnest patriotism toward their adopted country that goes far toward compensating for any lack of ideological orthodoxy. So, even though assimilation to a particular set of political values may ultimately guarantee the integrity of the American democratic order, at least in the short term the allegiance of the foreign-born may be secured by forces inherent to the process of immigration itself.

The Politics of the Lifeboat

From the perspective of many immigrants, America is a lifeboat, a vehicle of deliverance from the difficulties of the homeland. In the United States, millions of immigrants have sought relief from economic, political, or religious distress, a fact that has greatly determined their political loyalties and solidified their commitment to the republic.

Immigrant allegiance is founded on the offer of American sanctuary. Reservations concerning the commensurability of immigrant values with America's liberal creed must be assessed in this light. It is not that the theoretical arguments concerning the attitudinal requisites of stable democracy are wrong; rather, they are incomplete. Certainly, Lockean liberalism with a participatory democratic twist defines the central political value system of the United States, a creed against which there must not be deep-seated opposition if the political order is to endure. Stability requires that there be both general acceptance of the outputs of the political process and agreement on the rules regulating that process. If common values inform both the procedures of decisionmaking and the decisions themselves, the political system will be to that degree more secure. But the benefits of simple patriotism to the sustenance of the political order cannot be underestimated. Even if common values are absent, and the processes and outputs of government have slight resonance among the citizenry, an affective relationship between the governed and the government may yet buttress political authority. Although specific political decisions might be ill-received, or the political process might remain largely unintelligible, patriotism can foster legitimacy on other grounds. In part for cause of gratitude alone, immigrants are inclined to be highly allegiant; for them, however, the emotional commitment of political community precedes the intellectual commitment of consensus. Thus, in the short term at least, support for the liberal-democratic system need not rely on the immigrants' possession of a discrete set of carefully arranged attitudinal variables—nothing so elaborate is required. Patriotism is an elementary substitute, and patriotism is a quality that immigrants possess in considerable measure, a function of lifeboat politics.

That said, undoubtedly the political system cannot rely forever on loyalties created by the immigrant experience. As the years pass and memories of life in the Old World become less vivid, America will be evaluated less and less on comparative grounds. Given that fidelity to the liberal ideological consensus preserves, ultimately, the integrity of the American political community, understanding and acceptance of the core values of American democracy will gradually become more important as guarantors of stability. Yet because the act of migration is so psychologically compelling, it is likely that remembrances will endure—perhaps two or more generations will pass before the legacy of the lifeboat completely vanishes. And at a minimum this buys time for processes of political assimilation to bring immigrants and their progeny to an affirmation of the creed on which American stability may finally depend. Indeed, given that among students of ethnicity assimilation is increasingly seen, not as a direct and inexorable progression toward a dominant national culture, but as mutable process, varying among different immigrant groups pursuant to their time of arrival in the United States, the economic, political, and social context of the sending and receiving communities, and the tenacity of Old World traditions transplanted to the new, the lifeboat thesis as an explanation of American democratic stability may be especially apposite.[24]

Fear furnishes a general motivation for much immigration, whether it be the gentler fear of loss of status and economic opportunity or the more brutal fear of physical and mental persecution. For that reason, in terms of present theoretical concerns, conventional and legal distinctions between refugees and immigrants are difficult to sustain.[25] It might seem that emotional attachment to the country of immigration would be most highly developed among refugees than among immigrants per se, the difference turning on the subjective sense of desperation impelling the move to the New World. Immigrants who are not refugees are as likely to be pulled by the attraction of the country of adoption as they are to be pushed by developments in the homeland. There is an element of calculation in their decision to move, a weighing up of the pros and cons of migration. Refugees do not have this luxury. They are forced from their country of nativity, outcasts for reasons of nationality, religion, or politics. As victims of persecution they search for a host society that can offer asylum and may not have had the opportunity to evaluate the merits of such a place in a more thorough fashion. There is an immediacy to their flight distinguishing them from other migrants. For refugees, America is quite literally the lifeboat, as their physical existence is jeopardized in the country of birth.

And yet, this characterization is too neatly drawn. For one thing, it is immigrants who ultimately may develop the more lasting bond with the country of adoption because, unlike refugees, they choose it. But beyond this, all immigrants confront the anxieties and insecurities that grip refugees to a greater or lesser degree, and thus all carry with them some concept of immigration to America as the remedy for their difficulties. As Fernando Ainsa writes of the lure of immigration:

> No matter how difficult the voyage seems, the Utopia that "already exists in another place" has had an enormous attraction for man. It has always been easier to conceive of a voyage, a form of escapism, than to assume the risks or confront the impossibility of radically changing the customs and institutions in the place where one lives. Immigration is a form of escapism—sometimes the only one—from a predetermined destiny, and access to the hoped for Utopia, without passing through the painful and arduous task of demolishing the existing one.[26]

America affords solace to many immigrants; it is simply that the lifeboat image is more immediately compelling with respect to refugees from oppression.

Certainly, there are costs involved in the act of emigration. From compatriots can come the charge of political disloyalty or condemnation for abandoning the corporate struggle for a better life.[27] In fact for the greater part of the nineteenth century, no emigrants from the European continent could lawfully leave their parishes until they had signed at least a dozen documents, thereby renouncing any claims on his country and community.[28] Emigration can also rend the extended family, perhaps permanently should it become impossible for the émigré to return. In the early decades of mass immigration, for instance, returnees who desired to go back to America had to resubmit to a complete immigration check and could be refused reentry. But it is the very willingness to bear such risks that gives the act of emigration its import and suggests how captivating is the vision of a better life in the United States. On this theme William Shannon writes:

> Irish life in America begins from a sharp and tragic rejection. To "come out" to the new country meant thrusting behind the old, usually forever, unless in a few instances success brought enough money to visit the old country once more. Even then, however, many who could financially afford the return visit to Ireland never made the trip. It would be a journey back in more than one sense, a journey back into the house of their father, into the womb of old memories and long forgotten sadnesses. To return would be to reconsider the crucial decision that it would be no use to reconsider. The pleasures of nostalgia would not be worth the pain.

Why did they leave and what did they seek?
The answer is that most did not leave willingly. They were hurled
out by forces larger and more complex than they could fully understand
or cope with. They made the decision to go, of course; the responsibility
was theirs and they could not deny it . . . but the range of choice was
narrow. To the question What did they seek? the answer is the same
for them as for all men. They sought a door that would open and give
them access to hope. . . . Ireland was beautiful and damned. There was
no life for them there. They had to go.[29]

For some immigrants the hope of the New World has been political;
in the activity of government lies the reason for their departure.
Indirectly, the government of the country of nativity is always
involved in a citizen's decision to emigrate in the sense that its laws
can encourage or discourage the process. Until the latter part of the
nineteenth century, many European governments sought to inhibit
emigration, viewing it as a drain on a precious national resource—labor
power. By century's end, however, legal proscriptions against emigration had been dropped everywhere in Europe, save Turkey and Russia,
regardless of whether government attitudes had changed as well. There
have been instances, however, when governments have positively
promoted emigration as a form of "bloodletting" of inconvenient
populations. To that end, in 1827 Great Britain removed restrictions
on Irish emigration, a parliamentary committee maintaining that if
the Irish were not allowed to go to the New World they would "deluge
Great Britain with their poverty and wretchedness."[30] In the nineteenth
century, several German and Swiss local governments subsidized the
emigration of their more impoverished citizens to the same purpose.[31]
Elsewhere, emigration was encouraged for the more positive aim of
increasing national prosperity via remittances; Austria, Hungary,
Denmark, Croatia, and Japan are among those that attempted to
sponsor and regulate emigration for the tangible benefits it might
bring.[32]

Yet the strongest political motivation for emigrating has probably
been fear of violence. Although political exiles in the strictest sense
have been relatively few, every period of American immigration has
included those arriving in response to revolution and war. At times,
America has been a haven for failed insurgents—the Irish, German,
Hungarian, and Italian leaders of unsuccessful liberal revolts in 1830
and 1848, for instance, or their Canadian counterparts defeated in 1837
and 1838. Alternatively, the United States has received the victims of
revolution: those fleeing the disorder and impoverishment of southern
and eastern China during the third quarter of the nineteenth century
consequent to the Taiping Rebellion, the displaced persons created by

the Mexican Revolution in the early 1910s, or more recently those individuals seeking relief from the upheavals in Indochina. Finally, emigration has been resorted to in order to escape intergovernmental hostilities, Jewish refugees from the atrocities of World War II being a tragic example. In still other cases, conscription itself has been found objectionable and has furnished the impetus for emigration, particularly so when loyalty to the government commanding obedience has been weak: thus Slovaks left Europe prior to World War I in order to avoid imminent recruitment into the imperial army of Austro-Hungary; similarly did Russian Poles refuse to enlist, their conviction compounded by the prospect of combat against their fellow Poles in the German and Austrian armies in World War I; neither have Vietnamese of Chinese extraction been willing to fight in border wars against China nor participate in the occupation of Kampuchea.

Just what is it that America can offer these exiles from armed conflict? Physical safety is first and foremost among the advantages to be had. For failed revolutionaries in particular, the United States provides an opportunity to regroup, possibly to plan another attempt at seizing power in the home country; such was the attraction for various European nationalists in the nineteenth century. But more than this, America not only allows political exiles to find sanctuary but also positively welcomes those exiles, at least in theory. Whatever the motivation, the United States has wished to cultivate the image of a place where the oppressed, perhaps the politically oppressed most of all, might find relief; the importance given to the Statue of Liberty in America's iconography testifies to this desire. Americans are generally sympathetic to casualties in the struggle for self-government—especially in the name of those democratic virtues that the United States believes its own political system to encompass—be they French émigrés in the eighteenth century, Italian and Irish in the nineteenth, or Vietnamese and Afghani in the twentieth (some of whom already take inspiration from the American Revolution). So, too, has America been relatively open to individuals displaced by war or victimized by political persecution. Doubtless such immigrants are welcomed in part because they reinforce America's self-identity and provide, on the nationalist view, confirmation of the superiority of the host polity; should the immigrant group in question be victimized by one of the United States' ideological antagonists, Cubans a prominent example, so much the better. But estimations of altruism notwithstanding, to pursue the lifeboat analogy a bit more, America does not simply throw political exiles a lifeline; it rolls down the gangplank to welcome them aboard.

Granted, American munificence is not without limit. The American response to immigrants has been double-sided—a humane impulse struggling against a nativist one. Thus political refugees have sometimes been denied entry during restrictionist episodes in American history. The anti-Asian legislation passed in the late nineteenth and early twentieth centuries, as well as the quota-based legislation of the 1920s, applied to all immigrants regardless of the circumstances of their migration. Abiding by the letter of such laws, American authorities could turn away boatloads of Jewish refugees fleeing Nazism. Furthermore, to the extent that the United States has defined its ideological antagonist as Soviet-style communism, it has seemed reluctant to accommodate refugees from governments that, while not liberal-democratic, are staunchly anticommunist; in the postwar era, tyrannies of the Right have often not been regarded as oppressive as those of the Left.

But these caveats aside, the record of America's magnanimity is comparatively impressive. Over the past two hundred years the United States has far outdistanced any competitor in the sheer number of immigrants received. And though it is impossible to determine precisely how many of these qualify as political refugees, it is estimated that the United States has accommodated more than two million such individuals since 1945, accepting as many refugees as the rest of the world combined between 1975 and 1980.[33] Moreover, since World War II, political refugees have been the beneficiaries of special legislation: the Displaced Persons Act of 1948 and the Refugee Relief Act of 1953 were instrumental in receiving victims of war—concentration camp survivors, forced laborers, and evacuees from Eastern Europe anticipating the consolidation of the region under Soviet hegemony.[34] And these acts have been succeeded by other pieces of legislation giving financial support to Hungarian, Cuban, and Indochinese exiles. Even the cold war priorities that have dictated refugee policy over the past few decades are being moved away from in principle, if not in fact: the 1980 Refugee Assistance Act has broadened the definition of refugee to comply with that of the United Nations, a definition according to which ideological persuasions are of no significance.[35] In short, the American lifeboat is no fiction.

That lifeboat has been available to refugees not only from political unrest but also from social hardships more generally conceived. For some immigrants, religious convictions—membership in minority denominations and the concomitant ostracism and impediments to worship stemming from that membership—have prompted the move to the United States. In fact, if often observed in the breach, religious toleration is one of America's officially recognized virtues; a central national myth, duly commemorated each Thanksgiving holiday, recalls the flight from Europe, the hardship and eventual victory of the Protestant dissenters. Furthermore, America lacks an established church, both the effect and cause of its religious diversity. This is not to say that religion makes no difference to social status in America— Protestantism is still.a plus in this regard. But it does mean that neither religious practice nor sectarian affiliation is grounds for public persecution. Pressure may be brought to bear by private citizens concerned with encouraging orthodoxy, but the federal government cannot play religious favorites. And for many groups this represents an immense improvement on the environment of the old country, where the power of the religious majority might be enhanced by government patronage.

Ethnic minorities emigrate to the United States for reasons other than religion, of course. Cultural differences, religion being only one of these, make certain minority groups targets of majority antipathy. As already noted, most governments only grudgingly tolerate ethnic heterogeneity when confronted with it. The tendency is to equate political strength with national homogeneity; sociocultural pluralism is widely regarded as detrimental to unity of political purpose. So it is that governments have engaged in the forced assimilation of their ethnic minorities or, failing that, physical persecution. A Russian Jewish immigrant recalls:

> But every night the pogroms were all around. I hate to tell you. They were chasing us out. They were chasing after us, to kill everyone. I remember the pogroms . . . how they frightened us to death. One night we were hidden in a basement with a two-or-three-month-old baby. And we had to "shush, shh, shh" the baby. We said, "Keep still! Maybe somebody is going to hear us!" This I remember very well. We had working for us a girl, a Gentile girl—she had brought up my father yet. While we were hidden in the basement, she gave us food through a little crack. I'll never forget it.
>
> One day there was a rumor that they are coming to us, the pogrommers. What are we going to do? My father took all the knives and the scissors and everything, and he buried them someplace, so they can't kill us. . . .
>
> [My] father said, "That's going to be the end of it. We're going to get out. Let's get out while we're still alive." He sold the house as soon as I'm talking to you—it didn't take two hours. The house was only a couple of months built. We had just got into it, but my father said, "I don't want to own anything. I want my family alive."

We left the same night.[36]

In this manner, oppressed ethnic groups—Russian Jews, Armenian Turks, Vietnamese Chinese, to name but a few—have understood the United States as a place of social emancipation. That is not to imply that America is free of ethnic prejudice, only that it may not be as intense and durable as that found in other culturally pluralist societies. In the United States, political conformity is required; apart from politics, cultural differences in lifestyle, language, or religion are generally tolerated, especially if their political significance is deemed minimal. Certainly there is an American culture, defined by distinctive material goods, outlooks, and patterns of behavior, and just as certainly a great deal of social pressure is placed on those who depart from the cultural norms. But such pressure is applied, in the main, independently of the auspices of government. Acceptance of the dominant cultural trappings is voluntary, no matter how strong the persuasive power of the majority. In truth, America makes few attempts to hide its ethnic diversity, quite the opposite. Ethnic festivals, including folk dances, ethnic crafts, and cuisine, are a common occurrence and represent celebrations of diversity without fear of reprisal or hostility from the majority. All of this may make America a much more amiable place in which to live than is the homeland of many immigrants, where even seemingly nonthreatening cultural displays might be fair game for legal proscription or at least public condemnation. In the United States, if ideological unity is secured, cultural pluralism is no vice.

But immigrants who come to America as a result of cultural prejudice and persecution gain more than simply the opportunity to practice a lifestyle. In the United States immigrants also have the opportunity to become full-fledged Americans, the consequence of a nationality defined in terms of political belief. Provided that the political orthodoxy is affirmed, the chance exists for immigrants to become American, in principle to belong fully to the national community within their own lifetime. And this may differ sharply from the situation in the country of origin, where, simply due to an accident of birth, a given individual may be permanently excluded from full incorporation into the life of the polity. By contrast, becoming an American is an act of will contingent on an appropriate political confession of faith—cultural distinctions are not adequate criteria for disqualification. As Philip Gleason writes:

> To be or not to become an American, a person did not have to be of any particular national, linguistic, religious, or ethnic background. All

he had to do was to commit himself to the political ideology centered
on the abstract ideals of liberty, equality, and republicanism. Thus the
universalist ideological character of American nationality meant that it
was open to anyone who willed to become an American.[37]

Clearly, the offer of full legal status to people for whom this has been
previously denied is a further attraction of the American lifeboat and
an encouragement to immigrant patriotism.

Yet a majority of immigrants do not come to America because of
political or sociocultural distress but rather for economic gain and,
more fundamentally, economic security. In this manner America can
be an economic lifeboat, emigration a solution to the fear of a lost
livelihood. Indeed, it can make perfect sense to speak of economic
refugees, those for whom material welfare in the homeland is so slim
that they must leave or face imminent death. Such economically
induced fears may be matters of personal perception, but they are not
for that reason any less real than the anxieties produced by cultural
or political persecution.

The famine Irish are, perhaps, the most outstanding example of
emigrants in such a predicament—their motive for coming to the
United States was survival, pure and simple. Thus they were willing
to make the move despite warnings concerning economic hardship in
America, despite having little with which to stake a claim in the new
world, despite the prospect of traveling in midwinter on ill-regulated
ships, and despite the impending fragmentation of traditional family
structures. Undoubtedly the Irish are an extreme case. Even though
famines have sparked other emigrations—in Germany in the 1850s
and in Scandinavia in the 1860s, for instance—most economic migrants
have not been as impoverished as the Irish. But fear of falling into
the ranks of the destitute has motivated many to make the voyage.

Historically, concern for being landless in the country of origin,
and thus without means of physical sustenance, has been an impetus
for emigration cutting across national boundaries. Population pressure
usually plays a part. Unless national resources—food, shelter, employment—can keep pace, population growth portends an ominous future
for the lower ranks of the social order. Depending on inheritance
patterns, ownership of land can become so splintered that farms are
not large enough to meet subsistence-level needs.[38] Making things all
the more difficult is the commercialization of agriculture. Frequently
coinciding with population pressures, the introduction of industrial
capitalism reshapes agricultural traditions. Landownership is rational-
ized to produce specialized goods for an industrial, urban, and

sometimes foreign market. Smallholdings cannot be encouraged as they are uneconomic, so the trend is toward centralization of ownership, eventually capital-intensive farming, and consequently the reduction of small-scale farming and even the need for the agrarian laborer. If a country's industrial development is sufficiently advanced to coopt those pushed off the land, impoverishment may be avoided. But should economic development not be so advanced, the alternative may be either bare subsistence as an agrarian tenant/laborer or emigration.

To immigrants coming from such circumstances, as well as for those in not so desperate straits, the United States promises material sustenance and an opportunity for economic betterment. Since the middle of the nineteenth century, America's attraction has been that it offers the largest, most dynamic, and most prosperous economy among competitors for the immigrant's attentions—that and its dedication to a philosophy of capitalism applauding the achievement of wealth. At a minimum, economic migrants require that the United States meet their most basic physical needs; for many, America does so. A Czech immigrant (c. 1914) recalls:

> There was absolutely no chance for the common man over there to get ahead. You just lived, and you finally died, and probably the country had to bury you.
> We'd have meat about once a year. We had goats and we had a cow, but most of the time we were brought up on goats' milk, me and my three younger sisters. And once in a while, Mother would buy one of those short bolognas, cut it up, put it in the soup, and everybody would get a little piece. I used to think, "If I would get enough of that to fill my stomach!"
> Well, when we came to America, for a few cents we ate like kings compared with what we had over there. Oh, it was really heaven![39]

Here is the economic aspect of the lifeboat brought down to its most elementary level. As Crevecouer remarks, *Ubi panis ibi patria* is the motto of all immigrants.[40]

This is not to depreciate the very real hardships that many immigrants encounter upon their arrival in America. Although current immigration law tries to discriminate against the unskilled laborer through preference categories, and thus contemporary immigration includes a considerable number of professionals and specialized technical workers (25% of the total among immigrants finding employment in the 1980s), the occupational profile of the majority of the foreign-born has remained relatively constant over time.[41] Initially, immigrants tend to swell the ranks of the lowest tiers of the economic order, finding jobs as agricultural laborers, unskilled or semiskilled industrial labor, or more recently as lower-level service workers—dishwashers, taxicab drivers, maintenance and clerical workers, and so on.[42] This should come as little surprise. Higher-status occupations most often demand facility in the English language, advanced and specialized education, and some understanding of American business practices and culture. Thus, even if immigrants were not taken advantage of by padrones or coyotes (the Mexican equivalent), or exploited by cynical employers, or subject to restrictive legislation, even if a perfectly free and equitable labor market existed, many immigrants would lack the qualifications to assume more than menial jobs in any event. Moreover, low-status jobs are most often accompanied by low wages, long hours, and harsh living conditions.[43] Such circumstances have contributed to the periodically high incidence of violent crime among certain of the foreign-born, economically disadvantaged immigrants being the primary victims as well as the perpetrators of that violence.[44] So too, in pursuit of the social mobility seemingly denied via more reputable channels, members of various immigrant groups have become involved in organized vice—illicit activity, to be sure, even if an avenue of advancement that Daniel Bell and others have argued is solidly American in character.[45] In any event, the immigrant's immediate experience in the American economy has frequently been rugged, a circumstance no less true for those taking up farms in the Great Lakes Basin than for those entering the mines and factories of the era of industrialization or for those working in the kitchens of the service economy.

Yet despite the very real adversity that confronts many immigrants, they rarely seem to question the integrity of the American dream or lose a belief in their ability to accomplish it. It is not that immigrants are unaffected by hardship. But in a very real sense they seem willing to accept America despite its obvious imperfections. Even if impressionistic evidence, testimony describing the economic benefits of life in America is plentiful. Writing to his countrymen in Europe, a nineteenth-century Norwegian-American remarks:

> Every poor person who will work diligently and faithfully, can become a well-to-do man here in a short time, and the rich man on the other hand, has even better prospects, for he can work out his career with less drudgery and fewer burdens and thus have a much more peaceful life here than in Norway. You may take as an example myself, for all my money—twenty-eight dollars in silver—was stolen from me in the city of Albany, so that I was able to ward off starvation for me and my family only with great difficulty. . . . Despite the fact that I come here empty-handed and sick, I have nevertheless acquired the following property: one cow, a year-old pig, one calf, two-year-old oxen (which

are necessary to everyone for work), and forty acres of land, though I owe eighteen days of work on this land.

This will show what advantages there are for everyone who can come to work here. Though I have been sick almost half a year and have a family to take care of, still I have achieved much more than a worker can in Norway.[46]

Such sentiments are not confined to pioneer farmers. Equally revealing is the reminiscence of a Sicilian immigrant:

Regarding my final impressions about the immigrant experience I can say this is the greatest country in the world. There are no words to describe it. I came from Europe without much money, with no friends and with no knowledge of the language, as a kid. Eight years later I was a lawyer. I would say to these critics who vilify this country that they could not succeed like that elsewhere and certainly not in Italy. In Italy, if you wanted to become a lawyer or doctor your father had to be a millionaire. Those from humble backgrounds could never rise to such heights in that society. Here, however, it could and did happen. . . . "Only in America." I am only one small example but there are millions of others.[47]

Nor does this optimism concerning material gain seem any less powerful among the most recent immigrants. Remarking on the success of a countryman, a Korean immigrant expounds on the attractions of America:

One fellow I know was so poor in Korea that he went to join the Korean army and fought in Vietnam for the few dollars it gained him. He made friends with some American GI's and came to the United States. South Koreans who imported wigs gave him a box-full to sell. He went to Harlem—this was in the early seventies—and stood on the streets, hawking, really. On some days he cleared three hundred to five hundred dollars. A day. No taxes. He took the money and opened a fruit stand in the Stuyvesant Town area. It did well. Rich Koreans bought him out and he used the money to invest in real estate. You can't buy this guy today. That could never have happened in Korea.[48]

Accounts such as these are at best suggestive. In the first instance, such testimony might well be drawn from the unrepresentative sample of the minority of economically successful immigrants. Alternatively, it may be the case that immigrants are inclined to exaggerate the benefits of life in America; to do otherwise would be to cast doubt on whether the momentous decision to emigrate was well advised—an especially painful exercise in second-guessing. But it need not be argued that all immigrants in America actually achieve their dreams of wealth, only that a significant number do, and that these inspire many others.

Moreover, the benchmark against which the immigrant measures economic satisfaction is not necessarily an American one. Real adversity notwithstanding, the immigrant may yet feel better off than he or she would be in the country of birth. As Stephan Thernstrom writes in his classic study of the working class in Newburyport, Massachusetts, 1850–1880:

> Most of the social gains registered by laborers and their sons during these years were decidedly modest—a move one notch up the occupational scale, the acquisition of a small amount of property. Yet *in their eyes* these accomplishments must have loomed large. The contradiction between an ideology of limitless opportunity and the realities of working class existence is unlikely to have dismayed men whose aspirations and expectations were shaped in the Irish village or the New England subsistence farm. The "dream of success" certainly affected these laboring families, but the personal measure of success was modest. By this measure, the great majority of them had indeed "gotten ahead."[49]

In fact, satisfaction with life in America may be greater for those coming with less. It has been suggested, for example, that Vietnamese refugees of the first migratory wave (c. 1975) are much less content with their lives in America than are those of the second wave—the "boat people" (c. 1978–1979)—and this despite having higher income and employment levels. The explanation may lie in the two groups' relative situation in Vietnam: the 1975 contingent is drawn from what was the elite of Vietnamese society, well educated, well represented in the higher socio-economic categories, and less exposed to life under communist rule; the boat people cover a much wider socioeconomic spectrum and have had at least a minimum of experience with the discontinuities of communist rule. For this reason the expectations of the 1975 immigrants are likely to be higher than those of the boat people; downward mobility comes as more of a shock because there is farther to fall, and without the sobering experience of life under Hanoi the difficulties of American life appear all the less tolerable.[50] A similar pattern has been noted among Cuban immigrants, contentment in the United States being inversely proportional to socioeconomic status and level of satisfaction in Cuba.[51] In short, it is the immigrant's psychology that matters as much as the facts of his or her economic situation.

Certainly, however, many immigrants believe success can be theirs because America not only promises a better material life but often delivers on that promise. One indication of enhanced prosperity has been the size of remittances that immigrants have sent back home. For example, despite their relative impoverishment, between 1848 and 1864 Irish immigrants transferred $65 million of their American earnings to Ireland. In the mid-1890s, Danish-Americans sent between $800,000 and $1.6 million to Denmark, an amount that increased to $2.4 million by the time of World War I. Between 1900 and 1906, immigrants from Eastern and Central Europe transmitted as much as $69 million by money order alone to relatives and friends in Russia and the Austro-Hungarian Empire—villages in the region reported receiving remittances of between $120 and $554 per emigrant, considerable sums in a period when a cow might cost $16–$24, a pair of oxen $50–100, and a hectare of land $200–$500. The average remittance received by citizens of Hiroshima prefecture in Japan in the late nineteenth century was over twice as much as the average worker in Japan could hope to earn in a given year; indeed in 1891 over $230,000 were received—more than 54 percent of the operating budget of the prefectural government.[52] Such sums bear witness to the comparative affluence of the United States, and themselves have stimulated emigration. No doubt if potential earnings were not higher in America, there would be little reason to emigrate in the first place. Even seemingly low pay might be welcomed: thousands of Mexican immigrants came to the United States from the 1940s through the 1960s; though America offered wages as low as 20 cents an hour, living conditions were even worse in Mexico.[53]

Moreover, for much of America's history, property ownership has been within the reach of immigrants of modest means. For the first one hundred years or so of the republic, free or relatively cheap land was available to prospective farmers among immigrants. But apart from this, urban immigrants, too, have realistically aspired to homeownership. In his study of Slavic immigrants in Steelton, Pennsylvania, for instance, John Bodnar notes that in 1905 immigrants constituted 18% of all property owners in the city's immigrant wards but that ten years later this figure had increased to 35%—slow but steady growth among a population group comparatively new to America, one that by no means could be considered well-to-do.[54] Ewa Morawska, in an analysis of Eastern and Central European immigrants in Johnstown, Pennsylvania, observes the same halting progress: the percentage of homeowners among immigrants recorded in the 1900 census who were still in Johnstown by 1915 increased from 4.5% to 19%; by 1930, 35% of such immigrant "persisters" had their own homes (though, as Morawska points out, the aggregate data mask the extent to which a number of individuals actually lost their homes during the period under consideration and do not speak to the quality of accommodation).[55]

Additionally, there is a considerable body of scholarship concerning upward occupational mobility among immigrants. In truth, the findings are mixed,[56] but a good case can be made that immigrant groups have generally been able to move up the socioeconomic ladder, although—due to such factors as premigration work skills and the health of the local or national economy at a given historical period—at different rates. Of those immigrants coming to the United States since the late nineteenth century, Eastern European Jews are often cited as the greatest success story. In a study of the Jewish immigrant community in New York City, Thomas Kessner notes that between 1880 and 1915, 39% of his sample of blue-collar workers advanced to the white-collar ranks. Subjecting Italian immigrants to the same test over the same period of time, Kessner finds comparable results: 31% of blue-collar workers showing upward mobility.[57] Based on this and further aggregate data, Kessner maintains that the upward mobility of immigrants is a "fair interpretation of American reality."[58] Other scholars confirm this rendition of the immigrant experience. Gordon Kirk, investigating nineteenth-century Dutch immigrants, discovers that those at the bottom of the occupational structure experienced the highest rates of upward mobility and concludes that the United States offered "substantial opportunity for advancement."[59] Josef Barton indicates that immigrant-stock Rumanians in Cleveland, 1890–1950, realized significant occupational progress, especially when compared to the more limited gains of their Italian and Slovak counterparts.[60] Bodnar et al.'s investigation of immigrant workers in Pittsburgh, 1900–1920, reveals protracted, yet sustained mobility among Italian and Russian-Polish immigrant-stock laborers.[61] In an analysis based on 1970 census data, Barry R. Chiswick observes that the upward mobility of economic immigrants in toto (i.e., all those whose migration has been sparked by economic causes) is impressive: within ten to twenty years immigrants were found to have higher earnings than native-born coethnics, the pattern holding for white, Asian, and Hispanic immigrants, though there are marked differences among ethnic groups.[62] And Guillermina Jasso and Mark R. Rosenzweig, drawing on 1960, 1970, and 1980 census returns, observe that the rise in earnings of 1960 and 1970 "recent entrant cohorts" for the decades 1960–1970 and 1970–1980, respectively, exceeded that of identically aged native-born residents. Jasso and Rosenzweig note as well that the average earnings of foreign-born and native-born workers over the twenty-year period tended to move in tandem, albeit with the average earnings of the foreign-born remaining at a slightly lower level.[63] Although immigrant life is by no means uniformly rosy, the evidence does suggest that many immigrants have reason to believe America's powers of preservation are not only political and cultural but economic as well.

It should also be remembered that the United States has often been quite literally the endpoint of a harrowing journey and thus may serve as a lifeboat in the most immediate sense. Much has been written of the danger and discomfort surrounding nineteenth- and early-twentieth-century Atlantic crossings. Before the transportation revolution made steam the primary means of ocean travel, prospective emigrants from the European continent faced two to three months at sea. They also confronted inadequate berths, usually located on the steerage level of ships primarily equipped as commercial vessels; primitive sanitary facilities; and minimal provisions for cooking and ventilation. This, plus the lack of fresh food and water, made the voyage disagreeable at best and fatal at worst. Even after the transition to steam and greater efforts at government regulation, the journey to America was not always amiable or safe. Travel to the port of embarkation might be fraught with its own difficulties. In some cases, reams of bureaucratic red tape had to be cut through, or well-placed bribes had to be paid; in other cases, dangerous overland expeditions were undertaken, requiring the evasion of uncooperative and hostile police or border guards. When the port of debarkation was finally reached, worries were not yet over; there was always the chance that entry might be refused for reasons of disease or pauperism. Furthermore, once having completed processing by immigration officials, the new arrivals might be promptly set upon by runners, innkeepers, peddlers, porters, and cab drivers, all with less than honorable intentions. In cases where immigration could be planned, other concerns might be added to these: which route to follow, what season to go in, how much money to take, and how to raise it. Contemporary emigrants confront a process of migration no less frightening: thus Cubans and Haitians strike out for America in vessels barely seaworthy, and Vietnamese boat people risk brutalization by pirates in the South China Sea or, if they are among the more fortunate, find their way to refugee camps where, provided they are not turned away by unaccommodating host governments, they can expect several years of confinement. Final settlement in the United States provides relief from some of these concerns; at least it represents the completion of an anxiety-producing adventure.

In sum, for reason of the circumstances surrounding their migration as well as the reception extended to them in the new world, immigrants will tend to be devoted Americans. Evaluating their country of adoption from a comparative perspective—what life was like in the homeland—and consequently susceptible to the influence of what may be termed a *cult of gratitude*,[64] immigrant allegiances may be even more tenacious, and more uncritical, than those of native-born citizens. Indeed, immigrants may be so dedicated to the United States' supposed virtues that they come to feel more American than the native-born. So, for instance, a Russian immigrant maintains, "I am more 100 percent American than some of the born Americans. I resent some losses of freedom more quickly. I mean I want to be proud of my country, I think more than a born American does."[65] For immigrants of this type, understanding and promotion of the values of the American creed are of secondary importance. The possession of an unqualified patriotism gives time for the American creed to percolate into immigrant attitudes and behavior, gradually orienting them to the core beliefs defining American identity. And immigrants are usually willing communicants, eager to assume the full trappings of loyal Americans. Yet for them, patriotism precedes assimilation of the dominant political culture; the American political community is embraced before the valuational consensus that defines the community is internalized.

The tragedy is that despite such "natural" patriotism, the immigrant is under a cloud of suspicion. The native-born always have nagging questions concerning where the immigrant's true loyalties lie, an attitude for which immigrants must compensate by placing commitment to the country of adoption beyond all doubt, making special efforts to demonstrate allegiance. Indeed, if immigrants have at all been susceptible to political extremism, it has been a peculiarly centrist (and it should be said, American) variety of extremism. Given their concern for acceptance into the host society, immigrants may tend to overidentify with American values, promoting an orthodoxy that can be turned against those, both immigrant and native-born, thought to lack the appropriate convictions—the support for McCarthyism among certain immigrant-stock groups has been explained in this manner.[66]

Suspicions have been most salient during America's involvement in war. Yet it is precisely during such periods that most immigrant institutions—churches, newspapers, ethnic associations—have encouraged their charges to demonstrate their patriotism most fervently. As Frederick Luebke writes of German-Americans during World War I:

[M]ost German-American leaders were temperate in their reactions to the new circumstances. They understood that their task was to prepare their constituencies for the likelihood of war and to urge them to appropriate behavior. War would mean many difficulties for German-speaking citizens. The only way to combat intolerance and suspicions, moderate voices cautioned, was for German-Americans to avoid anything that could cause the least offense, and at the same time, they should perform willingly every duty imposed by citizenship. Their dread of war with Germany was conditioned by fear for their own status in America, not by solicitude for the Kaiser and his government.[67]

With few exceptions immigrant constituencies have given overwhelming support to the American war effort, whether serving in the military, contributing money to war bond campaigns, or laboring in factories producing war matériel. The claim of divided loyalty has largely been without foundation—immigrants have been eager to acknowledge their political commitments to the United States. In fact, a major consequence of America's mobilization for war has been to undermine ethnic exclusivity, the foreign-born and the native-born joining together against a mutual enemy.

Of course even if America is not on a war footing, any instance of immigrant nationalism can be regarded as revealing uncertain loyalties. Two things may be pointed out in response. First, as Maldwyn Jones observes, immigrant nationalism is usually cultural rather than political. On this account, ethnic assertion may be more a response to the American situation of immigrant groups—an affirmation of self-worth in the face of the host society's bigotry—than to political events in the homeland.[68] Second, immigrant nationalists seem to make exceptional efforts to define themselves as superpatriotic Americans. The most aggressive of immigrant nationalists—the Irish—are a prime example. Leaders of the movement took care to applaud America's political values, expressing a wish to duplicate the civic norms of the United States in an independent Ireland. In fact it was suggested that the history of the two countries might have been parallel if Ireland, as America, had successfully rebelled against British authority.[69]

Once in the American lifeboat, immigrants have had little disposition to capsize it; as recipients of the benefits of the host society, the last thing they wish to do is to be critical or disruptive. They quickly understand that acceptance in the United States is contingent on assuming a low political profile, at least until their participation is completely grounded in the American creed and they are regarded as fully assimilated members of the American national community. Given that immigrants are under considerable social pressure to demonstrate that they are not a malevolent political force, it is likely that their political inclination is to be America's loudest supporters but also to refrain from engaging in political action of a more controversial nature.

And this suggests a further aspect of immigrant political sensibilities requiring consideration: their disposition to be politically active. Even though immigrants arrive in America with political values often noncongruent with the national creed, they are not apt to operationalize such values. Apart from avid expressions of patriotism, immigrants are generally politically quiescent residents of the republic. This, too, reduces the likelihood of immigrants being a destabilizing political force. Simply put, left to their own devices they are rarely a political force at all.

Immigrants and Political Participation

In the main, immigrants do not seek to be active in politics. That is not to say, of course, that immigrants do not participate in politics at all. Indeed, at certain points in the history of the United States immigrant groups have been quite aggressive politically; Irish anti-conscription riots during the Civil War, especially those of New York City in 1863, are one of the most outstanding examples of direct immigrant confrontation with American political authority.[70] Yet such extraordinary episodes aside (and in terms of the specific instance cited, what could be more extraordinary than the circumstances of the republic during the Civil War?), the inclination of the great majority of immigrants—especially when it comes to matters of American national government—is toward political passivity. Such activism as exists is most often prompted by extraneous factors, particularly the mobilizing efforts of native-born party politicians. But when immigrants do participate, an action entered into with the greatest caution, they tend to do so in a manner characterized by simple patriotism, with participation itself viewed as a vehicle for being a "good" American.

As voting is the most basic of all democratic political actions, rates of turnout are a rudimentary indicator of the immigrant's participatory dispositions. Unfortunately, most information on turnout concerns the participation of ethnic groups rather than immigrants per se, and what data there are on immigrant turnout are thin—little published information pertains to voting rates before the late nineteenth century, for example. A few investigations do reveal that certain immigrant groups have voted at levels equal to or exceeding that of the general American population;[71] Cuban-Americans seem stellar in this regard.[72] But at least as frequent are assertions that immigrants vote at levels lower than the American population at large.[73] For instance, in a recent book on voter turnout, Paul Kleppner notes that between 1876 and 1892, in congressional and presidential elections, the largest differences in turnout were between foreign-stock and native-born voters, the conditions of immigrant life being responsible for an inability to participate even among the second generation.[74] Kleppner maintains that increases in general turnout between 1932 and 1960 were in large measure due to the successful mobilization of immigrant-stock nonvoters, though he observes that immigrant parentage remains a factor depressing contemporary turnout.[75]

The import of studies such as these is limited, however, unless rates of naturalization are also taken into account. Presently, of course, immigrants are not permitted to vote without becoming naturalized citizens. That has not always been the case. Beginning in the mid-nineteenth century, several states allowed aliens to vote provided they had filed a declaration of intent to become a citizen and had resided in a given state for a stipulated period of time (usually between one and two years). By the turn of the century, however, this practice had fallen out of favor and by the 1920s had been everywhere revoked. Thus, at least for the last hundred years or so, rates of naturalization should provide a rough indicator, if only a rough one, of immigrant participation in American politics. Claims that immigrant turnout equals or exceeds that of the native-born population must be assessed in this light. In some instances the proportion of immigrants eligible to vote who actually do so might be relatively impressive but as a percentage of the total number of immigrants—naturalized and nonnaturalized—in fact might be quite small.

Fortunately, when it comes to rates of naturalization the evidence is more plentiful than in the case of voting. Table 4.1, constructed from United States Census Bureau information, suggests that a considerable proportion of foreign-born residents, the majority in certain decades, do not transfer their citizenship. Independent inquiries reinforce this finding. Survey data reveal that immigrants in the early twentieth century took a long time to gain citizenship, between ten and twenty years for some of the "newer" groups from southern and eastern Europe.[76] Certain national groups have seemed especially reticent. Italian immigrants were particularly slow to gain citizenship papers: by 1920 only 35% of Italian adults had been naturalized, a proportion rivaled by Poles, Greeks, and Yugoslavs, among others.[77]

TABLE 4.1 Non-Naturalized Inhabitants in the United
States, 1890-1980

Year	Adult Foreign-Born Inhabitants	Percentage of Non-Naturalized
1890	4,348,459^m	42%
1900	5,010,286^m	43%
1910	6,780,214^m	55%
1920	12,086,393	53%
1930	13,336,353	42%
1940	11,292,821	36%
1950	10,020,450	25%
1960	N.A.	N.A.
1970	8,520,398	31%
1980*	14,079,900	49.5%

Sources: U.S. Bureau of the Census, Historical Statistics of
the United States, Colonial Time to 1970 (Washington, D.C.,
G.P.O., 1975) 116; U.S. Bureau of the Census, Statistical
Abstract of the United States: 1986 (Washington, D.C., G.P.O.,
1985), p. 87.

m: Includes only male foreign-born. Prior to 1920, the
citizenship inquiry of the Census was confined to males 21
and over.

*: Includes foreign-born of all ages. However, if the pattern
in previous decades is any indication, the inclusion of those
under the age of 21 should increase the number of non-
naturalized residents by only a few percentage points at most.

Even the most recent census data indicate that a large majority of immigrants of non-European origin are not naturalized citizens of the United States.[78] Hence, a sizable number of immigrants have not been able to participate in American electoral politics even if they have so desired.

For immigrants who do acquire the political privilege of citizenship, and the even smaller number who choose to vote, the decision to become naturalized and to cast a ballot on election day is not necessarily an indication of participatory orientations. Historically there have been a number of reasons why an immigrant might take up citizenship papers apart from a desire to be eligible to vote and hold office. Writing in the 1920s, Harold F. Gosnell listed several motivations behind the decision to naturalize: (1) citizenship carries certain economic benefits—citizenship is usually mandatory for employment in the public sector, though preferential hiring practices are not unknown in the private sector as well; (2) citizenship makes an immigrant's family situation easier—for instance, spouses or parents of native-born residents are under some pressure to naturalize so that all family members might have the same legal status (under the quota legislation of the 1920s a further advantage of a husband being naturalized was that his wife and unmarried children could be regarded as nonquota immigrants, making it easier for them to come to America); and (3) naturalization guarantees reentry to the United States should the immigrant wish to leave the country for a time. On the basis of interview data, Gosnell concluded that the primary reasons for acquiring citizenship were economic.[79]

But Gosnell noted a further motivation to begin the naturalization process—a "desire to become identified with the community."[80] A plurality of those he interviewed cited this as the primary reason they declared an intention to become citizens, a conviction that America should serve as the focus of national affection. In this lies an alternative explanation of an immigrant's act of voting. Some immigrants participate in elections, not from a conviction about candidates or issues, but from a belief that it is proper behavior for a good American. The process of naturalization works as a self-selection mechanism in this regard. Those immigrants willing to meet the qualifications necessary for the granting of citizenship make a considerable commitment to the American polity. Beyond a five-year residency requirement and the foresight to file a declaration of intent between two and seven years before a final hearing, immigrants must demonstrate minimum facility in speaking, reading, and writing English as well as having knowledge of American history and civics. For many immigrants this is no small chore, and the undertaking itself suggests a commitment to America. Once citizenship is granted it would not be surprising to see its privileges exercised in a most sincere fashion.

Thus the voting act may take on symbolic significance for immigrants, a manifestation of their political allegiance. Charles Merriam and Gosnell drew this conclusion in light of their findings that naturalized citizens were less likely to regard voting as a futile gesture than were native-born Americans.[81] More recently, Andrew Greeley et al. have interpreted the impressive level of turnout among Polish voters in this regard, voting being an important sign of Americanism.[82] And in a different vein, though with similar implications, Raymond Wolfinger and Steven Rosenstone have explained higher levels of Mexican than Puerto Rican turnout by virtue of the Mexicans' naturalization, an experience that Puerto Ricans need not undergo.[83] (Levels of naturalization among Mexican immigrants, however, remain relatively low.)[84] In all these cases voting is not so much an indicator of an activist disposition as it is an end in itself, a vehicle of Americanization and a function of immigrant patriotism. As Michael Parenti expresses it, the "tendency to view ethnic politics as a function of the ward machine or some narrow group interest may have obscured the fact that much of the impetus for participation stems from this desire to share directly in the activities of the American world, to acquire the accoutrements of the non-marginal man, in short, to Americanize."[85] For immigrants of whom this is true, casting a vote is another feature of the politics of the lifeboat.

Yet even those immigrants who do vote are not always self-starters. Frequently, the impetus to cast a ballot has been supplied by political parties. Conveniently concentrated in certain wards, perhaps possessing a sense of group identity that might be politicized in support of a given slate of candidates, in the view of local party bosses immigrants have presented a rich electoral resource; urban, and eventually national, electoral strategies have been predicated accordingly. At the very least, prior to the development of more precise polling techniques immigrant ethnicity furnished an expedient means of classifying the citizenry, imposing a certain coherence on electoral calculations.[86] (On the other hand, when the foreign-born were of no positive political help, as was the case with Chinese and Japanese immigrants, who for many years were prohibited from voting, local politicians paid them little attention.) Thus because of politicians (most often Democratic) solicitous of immigrant votes as well as opposing electoral coalitions (most often Whig or Republican) to some degree based on antipathy to the newcomers, immigrant groups and immigrant-related issues have been important variables in the American party system and, in the view of several scholars, catalysts of partisan realignment.[87] That, however, may say as much about the tactics of American political parties as it does about the participatory inclinations of the majority of the foreign-born.

As part of their attempt to mobilize the immigrant, parties have engaged in concerted efforts at naturalization and voter registration. In these activities Tammany Hall was the archetypal partisan organization. While Tammany was still under native control (until the 1870s), it made a sustained effort to politicize the largest immigrant group in New York City: the Irish. To that end, naturalization headquarters were established in virtually all the city's wards, often in the saloons providing a focal point for Irish socializing. Judges, at Tammany's behest, expedited the process. At the apex of the naturalization effort, in 1868, 41,000 Irish received their citizenship papers, immediately becoming a potent political force in the interests of the Democratic Party that nurtured them.[88] In this manner, the Irish of New York were introduced to American politics through the auspices of native-born politicians. And this sequence of events has been reproduced in numerous cities and counties across America, though after the turn of the century it has often been Irish-dominated machines introducing American politics to the newest immigrants, if not necessarily giving them like opportunities for economic and political mobility.[89]

But in order to assure the loyalty of the immigrant voter, the local party had to offer something of value, something apart from the abstract appeals of political rhetoric. Patronage was the answer. Immigrants might be attracted to the ballot box because it was recompense for material welfare that the local party provided. The machine could directly tend to the most basic of immigrant needs: food, housing, heat, employment. Even if they did not work for the city per se, immigrants might still benefit from the party's largesse by being directed to private employers with city contracts or by being able to disregard certain city ordinances pertaining to small businesses they owned. In this manner the local party could function as a rudimentary welfare agency trading physical sustenance for votes. In fact the reduction in opportunities for patronage may be one reason recent immigrant groups may show even less concerted interest in politics than their predecessors.[90]

Material gain has not been the only motivation for immigrant political participation—there has also been the symbolic gratification of the politics of recognition. In an effort to consolidate power, political parties have appealed to the immigrant's desire for status and acceptance. In some instances this has meant the establishment of and support for various ethnic and social clubs or sponsorship of cultural events. In other cases, even modest patronage jobs—employment in the police force, for example—might have the same effect. But perhaps the most outstanding means of granting recognition to an immigrant group has been appointing a member of that group to public or party office.

To be sure, parties have elevated immigrants in this manner for reasons other than to promote a favorable response in the immigrant community; city politicians need conduits to immigrant constituencies, and kindred middlepersons have admirably suited this purpose. Yet by the same token, political appointments suggest a commitment of the party to immigrant-stock advancement, something that is not lost on immigrant voters. Promotion of an ethnically balanced ticket is, perhaps, the ultimate sign of recognition. Immigrants do in fact give special weight to the political directives of one of their kind who "makes it," and thus the tie between ethnic group and political party is further solidified.

Moreover, granting political recognition to immigrants is not only a shrewd gesture on the part of political parties activating normally passive citizens; but it likewise enhances immigrant identification with America. Carter Harrison II, a five-term mayor of Chicago (1897–1905; 1911–1915), and a beneficiary of immigrant support, pointed out this effect:

> I have seen enough of the resulting encouragement, of the pride fellow racials feel therein, of the stimulus given thereby to an entire nationality, to feel the firm conviction that nothing makes more surely for good citizenship, for true Americanism among these peoples, than the assurance that they are held worthy of a place in our public life.
>
> Ours is a strange country to them, ours a strange language. The habits, the customs of their adopted surroundings are new and startling. At best they do not know whether they are welcome or not. With a timid heart they enter into citizenship. They realize the greatness of this citizenship, indeed it weighs upon them, it almost overwhelms them. Not certain that they are really welcome among us, they are fearful that in some way, by some mishap they may lose this citizenship. . . .
>
> Then comes an appointment of one of their very own to some place, perhaps of a most trivial character.
>
> Instantly everything is changed. Certainty, security has come to them; now and hereafter they are part, parcel, and fibre of the government under whose flag they work and live.[91]

Admittedly the passage is prone to hyperbole, but its political lesson is genuine: the politics of recognition fosters patriotism.

That said, the politics of recognition has been employed sparingly, especially when high-level municipal, state, or national office is at stake. By the standard of most analyses of ethnic politics, according to which the emergence of such candidates and their successful attainment of public or partisan office mark an ethnic contingent's coming of age, the majority of immigrant groups have been late to mature politically—a further indication of their limited participation in American politics. This is true even of the Irish, who took to politics like no other immigrant group. After the mass migrations of the mid-nineteenth century, at least one generation passed before the Irish were able to assert control over the politics of a major American city. If the mayoralty is considered a symbol of ethnic success, such success was not soon in coming: Irish mayors were not elected in New York until 1880, Boston until 1884, and Chicago until 1893.[92] In similar fashion, Irish control of the party organizations of major American cities was not immediate: the Irish did not dominate Tammany until the 1870s or the Democratic Party in Chicago until the 1880s. Nor were the Irish very well represented in federal politics until considerably after the middle twentieth century; not until the New Deal did Irish politicians find much national success.[93] And the experience of the Irish is magnified in other immigrant groups lacking the Irish's political advantages—political experience and facility with the language. Thus Italians, Russian Jews, Poles, French-Canadians, Mexicans and many other groups have had long to wait before ethnic representatives filled significant political offices.[94]

Much immigrant interest in politics is what might be termed *the politics of reaction*. That is to say, immigrants may come to participate politically in response to the behavior of other ethnic or native-born groups and to certain issues that are thereby raised.[95] This is most obvious in the case of an immigrant's partisan preferences. For instance, French-Canadians and Italians in New England have often supported the Republican party, largely because their rivals, the Irish, permeate the Democrats. But immigrant involvement in politics has also frequently been a product of perceived native-born hostility. Policies and laws intended to secure the political and cultural hegemony of traditionally advantaged groups, most often Anglo-Saxon and Protestant in heritage, may provoke a political reaction from formerly passive immigrants, even more so among the second generation.[96] Thus, historically, issues pertaining to cultural freedom—language, public support for parochial education, proper use of the Sabbath, prohibition—have been the focus of considerable political efforts within the immigrant community. Yet such has not been the normal orientation of the foreign-born, but in a sense it has been forced upon them in defense of their ethnic identity.

There is, however, one aspect of the political world to which many immigrants pay attention without inducement: the politics of the homeland. In some cases, homeland governments themselves have attempted to take an active role in the affairs of expatriate communities. The intervention of the South Korean government through its consulates and the Korean Central Intelligence Agency is a well-known facet of Korean-American life; similarly the Taiwanese government has attempted to supervise the activities of Chinese-Americans.[97] Yet for the most part, immigrants' regard for homeland politics is not of this nature; instead it is sparked by a continuing interest in the welfare of former compatriots. Examples are plentiful: Irish concern for independence from Great Britain and presently for a satisfactory resolution of the Northern Ireland conflict; Polish interest in the creation of an independent Poland subsequent to World War I and more recently in autonomy from Moscow, including the success of the Solidarity movement; Greek fear of Turkish influence in Cyprus and elsewhere; Cuban promotion of a Castro-free Cuba. These issues and more have been of great significance to immigrant communities, a fact not lost on partisan politicians who have wooed ethnic voters by couching their appeals in such terms—"twisting the British lion's tail" as it has been called vis-à-vis the Irish voter.

Nevertheless, not all immigrants are equally passionate when it comes to an interest in their countries of birth. For this reason immigrants may be separated into two groups. The first consists of the nationalists proper, whose political attentions are consumed by events in the homeland. This group represents the small minority of all immigrants to America. Such individuals have little identification with America, most seeing themselves as only temporary residents until a more politically propitious time to return to the homeland can be arranged. In general, these hard-core nationalists show only limited adaptiveness to life in America, nor are they much inclined to do so as their sights are set elsewhere.[98]

The great majority of immigrants are ethnic nationalists in only a weak sense, however; they are concerned with political distress in their countries of birth for reason of cultural sympathy rather than political loyalty. It is frequently war or the cause of homeland independence that motivates them to display support for their compatriots. This is rarely symptomatic of divided allegiance. Lingering patriotism for the Old World is not an issue for most immigrants, both because of the circumstances of migration that wed them to America, and because the majority of immigrants have typically been excluded from nationalist movements while still in the homeland. Traditionally, nationalism finds adherents in the upper classes, which also furnish leadership for the movement; most immigrants are not from that social stratum.[99] Thus political activism in the interest of homeland causes is sporadic, linked to extraordinary historical events rather than expressing a fundamental political attraction to the Old World. For this reason, too, ethnic political organizations oriented to the country of origin are usually short-lived: wars end, independence is gained, or simply time spent in America dulls enthusiasm for the cause.[100] Even then, the limit of immigrant activism tends to be lobbying efforts in the interest of the homeland, participatory efforts for which most of the foreign-born show only sporadic enthusiasm and which in any event are often (though not always) directed to issues tangential to mainstream American politics.

In general, then, immigrants have little inclination to participate actively in American politics. Of course most citizens, foreign-born or not, are no more than intermittently active in the political process, but among immigrants the tendency to passivity should be even greater. And this is because immigrants lack many of the prerequisites that make citizens amenable to political participation. First and foremost, immigrants frequently do not have the appropriate psychological dispositions making participation likely. To reiterate, many immigrants arrive in the United States with an aversion to politics, one readily transferable to their country of adoption; indeed it may have been politics—in the form of war, revolution, or ideological persecution—that motivated their migration. Similarly, immigrants may lack tutelage in the norms of democratic participation, their experience of government in the Old World giving slight indication that the wishes of common citizens should make a difference in the policies of state. As Richard Hofstadter has written with respect to those immigrants, largely from Southern and Eastern Europe, who entered the United States in the late nineteenth and early twentieth centuries:

> The immigrant . . . coming as a rule from a peasant environment and from autocratic societies with strong feudal survivals, was totally unaccustomed to the active citizen's role. He expected to be acted on by government, but not to be a political agent himself. To him government meant restriction of personal movement, the arbitrary regulation of life, the inaccessibility of the law, and the conscription of the able-bodied. To him government was the instrument of the ruling classes, characteristically acting in their interests, which were indifferent or opposed to his own.[101]

Given such a frame of political reference, immigrants may well doubt that their participation has any particular significance in the United States.

The more sophisticated knowledge an individual has concerning the political process, the greater the probability of participation. On this score as well, many immigrants have been disadvantaged. Not only may knowledge of the American political scene be difficult to grasp, the United States surely possessing one of the most complex and idiosyncratic systems of government in the world, but in the immigrant's case access to that knowledge is often limited by a language barrier.[102] Sources of political information on which English-speakers most frequently rely—schools, the media, the family unit, and peer groups—are all restricted by lack of fluency in English. Nor are immigrants necessarily given to pursue an education compensating for some of these deficiencies. Knowledge of English and civics is the product of a school system most likely to affect the second generation, though at that, immigrant parents have often placed more emphasis on their children's wage-earning potential than their formal education.[103]

To the degree that socioeconomic status—commonly measured by occupational prestige and income—is positively related to participation,[104] it is a further factor diminishing immigrant political interest. To begin with, the sense of individual efficacy that the literature of political science finds central to the decision to participate will probably be lacking among immigrant populations.[105] It has already been noted that immigrants are typically found at the lower rungs of the occupational and income ladder, having scarce capital or specialized skills to permit otherwise. From this position they are unlikely to procure the political resources, time and knowledge first among them, required for successful redress of grievance. But in addition, politics is a time-consuming business; immigrants have more immediate interests—carving out an acceptable living in a new environment. Upward mobility may be possible in the United States, but the road to more prestigious and lucrative jobs is often long and arduous. In the event, immigrants are likely to devote themselves, not to politics, but to more pressing economic concerns. Unless a direct connection between specific policies and material well-being can be drawn, politics is liable to remain of peripheral interest. The perspective of a recent Jamaican immigrant to New York City seems representative:

Most of the city remains as removed from her thoughts as if she were a tourist. Of politics she knows nothing beyond the current mayor's name. She has never voted and does not see why she should. Of changes in the city's population, its tax structure, its transportation, she cares little beyond what directly affects her. If the A train gets new cars she is pleased, but when the television newscaster hints at a possible fare increase she is angry. Matching the Transit Authority's revenues and expenditures, either now or in the future, does not concern her. She will think only of her own checkbook.[106]

Birds of passage—immigrants who return to the homeland once a sizable income has been earned in America—are but an extreme variation on the same theme.

A further consequence of low socioeconomic status is the inability to produce ethnic candidates who might mobilize immigrants for political participation. Wolfinger notes the relationship in proposing what he calls the "mobilization theory of ethnic voting." Wolfinger's contention is that immigrant-stock voters receive a powerful stimulus to political activity when they see a co-ethnic heading a party ticket. For the ethnic group member to reach such a position, however, requires the achievement of middle-class status and concomitant resources and skills. Thus ethnically based voting is greatest among the second and third generations of immigrant families, groups more likely to have moved up the socioeconomic ladder. That the immigrant generation itself might produce a sufficiently middle-class candidate is a lesser probability, as is immigrant political participation on this basis.[107]

It might also be mentioned that all of these factors have a certain reinforcing effect. In other words, an individual's disposition to participate is often a function of the social group with whom that person most closely associates.[108] Given the likelihood that an individual immigrant will probably associate with compatriots of a similar socioeconomic station, he or she will receive little encouragement to participate. The consequences of group characteristics making for limited participation in politics will be magnified in the orientations of individual members of the group.

This general perspective on the nonparticipatory inclinations of the foreign-born may be refined by taking into account the degree of cultural exoticness among the various immigrant groups. Not all groups are equal, of course, when it comes to their cultural distance from the Anglo-American norm. The farther away immigrants are from that norm—i.e., the greater the degree of heterogeneity they introduce into the American system—the less likely they are to share the dominant liberal creed. Yet it is precisely by virtue of this exoticness that immigrants have little disposition to become politically active. Language and social customs are elementary cultural obstacles to participation, but lack of cultural orthodoxy also goes far in determining socioeconomic status—a further correlate of participation. Hence, as opposed to what conventional antiheterogeneity analyses imply, the most culturally exotic immigrants are also the least probable to create political instability. Contrariwise, it is those ethnic groups most nearly akin to the Anglo-American cultural standard that have the confidence to participate and thus are in fact most politically "suspect" because the impulse to participate meets with fewer cultural barriers.

An absence of cultural impediments helps to explain Irish political participation, the outstanding exception to the rule of immigrant passivity. Despite entering the American economy at or near the bottom, nineteenth-century Irish immigrants possessed qualities compensating for the political effects of low socioeconomic status. Language, of course, was not an issue for most of the Irish, English having been a familiar tongue in Ireland. Additionally, Irish immigrants were distinctive in their general political awareness, made acute in the struggle for autonomy from Great Britain. Not only were the Irish already conversant with Anglo-Saxon political institutions upon their arrival in America, but they also had a considerable amount of organizational experience in politics. Unable or unwilling to avail themselves of the official English political institutions, the Irish established institutional alternatives—underground legislatures, executives, and judiciaries—to govern their affairs. This and the experience gained in nationalist organizations gave them a political sophistication absent in other immigrant groups. Small wonder that the Irish should take so quickly to American politics.

Irish-Americans have been advantaged when it comes to participation in at least one other way: they have perceived themselves to be a relatively coherent and unified ethnic group, ready for political mobilization in the name of common objectives. For many immigrants this has not been the case, as intragroup diversity has inhibited the collective identity necessary to ethnic politics. In some instances, local loyalties may be stronger than national ones: in Italian immigrant communities, for example, sentiments of *campanillismo* have sometimes overwhelmed belief in a unified Italian identity,[109] whereas among Chinese-Americans, differences in origin among Hong Kong, Taiwan, and various provinces on the mainland have impeded ethnic solidarity.[110] In other situations it may be the diverse class backgrounds of various immigrant streams that create a lack of cohesiveness: in this respect the Mexican-American community is pertinent, divided among descendants of Spanish colonial elites, middle-class refugees of the revolution, and various peasants who have crossed the border at various times in search of prosperity.[111] The consequence of such lines of cleavage within the immigrant-stock community is frequently a reduced presence in American political life.

Patterns of geographic mobility may also affect the immigrant's inclination to participate. For birds of passage, individuals whose orientation is consistently toward the country of origin, any sense of identification with, and thus inclination to participate in, American politics is extremely limited. To this group should be added immigrants who intend to make America their home but who, in search of adequate employment—often in seasonal industries such as construction or agriculture—display considerable impermanence of place.[112] Clearly, migratory patterns of this sort inhibit those enduring attachments to local communities that enhance the desire to participate in politics.

Participatory inclinations are more likely to the extent that immigrants look outside of their own ethnic communities and begin to interact with a broader American social milieu. The inclination to adopt this perspective suggests the acculturation of the immigrant-stock group, that is to say, the adoption of certain valuational and behavioral norms typical of the host society's dominant cultural ethos.[113] An immigrant who is acculturated will understand the social customs common to the preeminent Anglo-American culture, will comprehend the social environment in which political activity takes place, and will begin to internalize the American political creed itself, including that portion encouraging participatory democracy. The more comfortable the immigrant feels in American society, the more likely he or she will be to participate in its political life.

But acculturation takes time, time to develop a positive orientation to life outside the immigrants' own ethnic community. Despite a natural affection for America stemming from the lifeboat perspective, rare is the immigrant who will readily leave the cocoon of cultural familiarity. The community of compatriots is a refuge in which immigrants can relax in an atmosphere of ethnic assurance and in which their identity is grounded. When it is found in a city, such an environment may resemble what Herbert Gans has called an "urban village," an attempt to transfer the well-worn traditions of the Old World to the new.[114] Such entities can be socially self-sufficient, replete with churches, schools, mutual aid societies, newspapers, beer gardens, saloons, and lodges all focused on the life of the immigrant community itself. Should the panoply of social institutions be comprehensive enough to maintain the interest of the immigrant, and should the Old World furnish a steady supply of ethnic reinforcements, immigrant attentions turn inward, away from the larger American society, and away from political interest in that society.[115] Prejudice and discrimination, perhaps best illustrated in the case of Chinese-Americans, lead to the walls of cultural and political isolation being built even higher.

Finally, the dynamics surrounding the immigrants' reception in America may well inhibit any willingness to participate in politics. The substance of government legislation, as well as the spirit of nativism periodically infusing American public opinion, suggests the limits of American hospitality. Simply by virtue of foreign provenance, immigrants tend to be viewed as politically suspect, possessing the potential to undermine the political consensus regulating American politics. Any political activity on their part may be cited by the native-born as evidence that this disruptive potential has come to fruition. In order to remain in the good graces of the host society, immigrants must be sensitive to the constraints which are placed on their political behavior. From the immigrants' point of view, it may be wise to call as little attention to themselves as possible.

In this respect, the threat of deportation has been a reminder to immigrants of their precarious political status. Although it is difficult to gauge the precise effect this has had on participatory inclinations, it would seem to be of some consequence. For one thing, the threat has not been idle: almost 600,000 immigrants were deported during the first seventy years of the present century—a proportionately small but not insignificant number.[116] The enthusiasm with which the government has periodically sought to repatriate the foreign-born— most famously during the "Red scares" of 1919–1920 and the 1950s—must be sobering to the immigrant contemplating political activity. Equally intimidating is the fact that the ambit of the deportation law has been quite broad; neither long-time resident aliens nor naturalized citizens have been able to escape its reach.[117] Moreover, the expressly ideological criteria under which deportation procedures have been initiated serve direct notice of America's concern with the political character of immigrants. The cumulative effect, it may be imagined, is that immigrants come to regard political participation as a very risky business.

Political Radicalism, Labor Militancy, and Civic Corruption

Before the argument of the present chapter can be concluded, a further matter requires attention. Scholars of the American political experience have often pointed to foreign-born support for unorthodox political movements, including the more aggressive varieties of trade unionism and involvement in the operation of the urban machine, as empirical evidence of immigration's political disruptiveness. Owing to the decline of the institutions in question, immigrants of the recent past are unlikely to be indicted on similar grounds. Yet this alleged propensity for radicalism and civic impropriety is of more than simply historical interest as it suggests the manner in which immigrants, lacking sufficient understanding of democracy American-style, may promote political instability. In the interest of defending the lifeboat thesis against a potential line of criticism, a response is warranted.

Certainly the connection between immigrants and radicalism is not completely unfounded. If by radicalism is meant any political movement out of the liberal American mainstream, then any number of immigrant groups might be called "radical." Taking commitment to unconventional principle to the logical end, some of these groups concluded that the survival of their ideals required institutional separation from the American political system. The distinguished historian of immigration, Carl Wittke, counted seventy-eight such immigrant utopias in America by 1868, all organizing themselves according to "communistic" social and economic principles. The bulk of these societies had explicitly religious persuasions—the Ephrata community of Pennsylvania or the Amana group in Iowa, for instance. But some were more directly devoted to political and economic theories, most famously Robert Owen's socialist experiment in New Harmony, Indiana. New Harmony was not unique, however: German Marxist societies were established in Minnesota and Missouri; Norwegian communists took up residence in Green Bay, Wisconsin; an English socialist colony was established in Tennessee; and Fourierite communities were founded in Kalamazoo, Michigan, and Brook Farm, Massachusetts.[118]

Yet because of their limited number and even more limited success, separationalist communities are generally not at issue among individuals concerned with immigrant radicalism; rather those immigrants who have sought to change the American political system by participating in it are the focus of concern. Evidence of this form of immigrant activism is readily available. But left unqualified, the association between immigrants and radical politics is highly misleading. Although well represented in the radical ranks, the majority of immigrants have been far from radical. In national as well as municipal elections the overwhelming tendency has been for immigrant-stock voters to support the mainstream Democratic or Republican parties.[119] Thus populism, feeding on the agrarian discontent of the late nineteenth century, found few members or sympathizers among immigrant farmers,[120] the nativist tinge of the movement (among other things, the Populist party wished to prohibit alien landownership) serving to dissuade.[121] At best, its appeal was to the children of the immigrant generation, a reaction against their fathers' political cautiousness, and even here the tangible consequence was the formation of moderate parties essentially confined to state politics—the farmer-labor coalitions of the upper Midwest, for instance. Nor were immigrants very keen on the more mildly reformist Progressive movement that overlapped and succeeded the Populist one. Perhaps most importantly, at the level of urban affairs there was an elementary divide between the ethos of the Progressive politician committed to honesty in government, nonpartisan elections, and civil service reform and the desire of immigrants to avail themselves of the patronage of the big city machine.[122] (That is not to say Progressive candidates never received immigrant-stock votes: in the presidential election of 1924, Robert LaFollette, Sr., received a good deal of support from various ethnic constituencies, especially Germans—understandable given his base in Wisconsin.) And if socialists fared better among certain ethnic contingents, typically they did so by advocating nothing more grandiose or abstract than enhanced social welfare measures—hardly the stuff of which revolutions are made.[123]

Even if such sentiments count as radicalism, the extent of immigrant support for radical parties can be exaggerated. At its high-water mark in 1912, of the 118,000 members of the American Socialist party, less than 16,000 were members by virtue of foreign-language affiliation; by the time foreign stock made up a majority of the party, its membership was in decline—this for America's premier radical party of the twentieth century.[124] The Communist party in America must be viewed in similar perspective. During the 1920s, when those of immigrant stock dominated the party, its membership never exceeded 20,000; by the time party membership peaked in the 1930s and 1940s, the proportion of its foreign-stock supporters was diminished, and in any case the party's staunchest advocates were found among the smallest of the immigrant communities—the Finns and Lithuanians in particular.[125] Moreover, even though ethnic-related socialist societies have often been quite visible in the United States, their relative importance can also be exaggerated. One of the best known of these, the Alliance of Polish Socialists—related to the Polish Socialist party of Poland, an organization in the forefront of the struggle for Polish independence whose leader, Joseph Pilsudski, eventually became president of Poland—never had more than a few thousand members, only a small fraction of those who were loyal to rival organizations, the Polish Roman Catholic Union and the Polish National Alliance.[126] Fascist organizations have received an even less favorable reception. Despite efforts to attract Italian immigrants, the Fascist League of North America could gain no more than 13,000 members by 1929, and this was before Mussolini's adventurism and the pact with Hitler made fascism even less appealing.[127] In short, radical movements and parties have never formed more than a tiny portion of the American political landscape, the immigrant-stock component of that portion, for reasons already advanced, tinier still.

That is not to gainsay immigrant participation in radical political movements. Even before the Civil War, German immigrants—William Weitling being perhaps the best known—were busy organizing workers' alliances and congresses in support of a program of state socialism. Indeed, German immigrants and their descendants were especially important in the early years of the American socialist movement. The first Socialist party in America (established in 1867) was an outgrowth of the German Communist Club and the German Workers' Society of New York, and most members of the succeeding Social Labor Party (established in 1877) were German.[128] Cities with a high concentration of German-stock citizens were also politically influenced by the German attraction for socialism. By the 1910s, Milwaukee possessed an especially powerful Social Democratic Party, which dominated municipal politics on the strength of its support in German wards and which sent Victor Berger to the House of Representatives in 1918.[129] Later immigrant contingents also established socialist associations—the Poles, Finns, and Czechs being of particular note.[130] But it is with the Eastern European Jews, particularly those from Russia, that the socialist connection is most famously drawn. It was Russian Jews who assumed leadership of the American socialist movement soon after the turn of the century and who guided the movement until well into the 1950s.[131] Daniel DeLeon, Morris Hillquit, and Meyer London, leading lights of American socialism from the 1890s through the 1920s, were produced by and had their strength in the Jewish immigrant communities of New York City, while Jewish-dominated trade unions such as the International Ladies Garment Workers Union, and Jewish newspapers, most notably the *Jewish Daily Forward,* added financial and moral support to the socialist cause.[132] Immigrant membership in the American Socialist party was sizable: by 1919 foreign-language federations accounted for more than half of all party members.[133]

Socialism, however, has not been the whole of immigrant radicalism; anarchism, communism, and fascism have all had adherents. The appearance of anarchism in America can be traced to German immigrants—eight of the ten individuals indicted for murder in the Haymarket incident, for instance, were of German extraction.[134] Jewish radicals provided much of the leadership and a significant portion of the membership of the American Communist party in the 1920s and

1930s; Lithuanians and Finns were also well represented.[135] In fact, only 15% of the membership of the Communist party during the 1920s was English speaking.[136] And at the opposite end of the political spectrum, Italian immigrants evinced a certain weak attraction for Mussolini's fascism, seeing in it the possibility of reconciliation between church and state in Italy, as well as resoluteness in attacking the social and economic problems plaguing the homeland.[137]

Following the logic of the Hartz thesis, it is not remarkable that radical ideologies should be of foreign import, it being improbable that they could develop independently in an American environment. What is surprising, however, is that more immigrants have not been attracted to radical politics, especially in view of the disadvantaged position from which many have confronted the American economy. Even though many immigrants have been sympathetic to radical political movements—in some cases furnishing the majority of support for these movements—on the whole, immigrants have not been so inclined. For one thing, the perspectives and objectives of most foreign-born workers have not been the same as those of socialist leaders who have wished to build parties based on working-class support. Given that the greater number of the foreign-born have come to the United States for economic reasons, the desires of the immigrant worker have tended to be short term, pragmatic, and geared to an improved material and social position. To the extent that radical politicians have addressed the mundane but crucial issues of the workplace—wages and working conditions—they have caught the ear of the immigrant. But flourishes of ideology might gloss over such bread-and-butter issues and in doing so become irrelevant to immigrant workers.[138]

Radical politicians have also competed with leaders of the immigrant community who usually are staunchly opposed to their agenda: the immigrant clergy. Although the affinity of the immigrant for the church in America has varied among national groups, in most it has been regarded as a focal point of the immigrant community and a conservative one at that. Historically, political liberalism in the old country indicated anticlericalism as well; the church transplanted in America had little reason to doubt that the relationship still held. Besides this, the teachings and functions of the church could run against the radical political grain. An insistence on the communion of all believers and a providential God made the prospect of class conflict remote for many of the faithful. Moreover, the church furnished emotional, and sometimes physical, sustenance for the immigrant and did so through the comforting auspices of timeworn traditions.

Compared to this, radical politics could offer only a secularized vision of a better future.[139]

Additionally, since the immigrant's relatively limited political interest has most often centered on the country of origin, it should not be surprising that much immigrant-stock radicalism has had the same focus. So, whereas certain Russian Jewish socialists, German communists, and Italian anarchists have debarked in the United States with their political orientations already in place, still other immigrants, already resident in America, have come to support radical politics because of subsequent developments in the homeland. In this manner the attraction of communism for various immigrant groups may be related to the Russian Revolution: between December of 1918 and April 1919, Russian and Slavic membership of the American Socialist party tripled; when the Communist party was established from a fragment of the Socialists, almost two-thirds of the new party's members were born in countries either part of the former Russian Empire or inhabited by Slavs.[140] Similarly, the support fascism received among the Italian-American community, albeit limited, was directly tied to the unfolding story in Italy:

> The Italian American population was not split at all regarding Mussolini. They upheld support for the Italian government, regardless of who was ruling. It could have been Attila the Hun, or it could have been the Pope. This was the first time that they had seen Italy as a nation achieve something which, in their view, was commensurate with what other governments were achieving. Almost all the Italians I knew supported the government. Most of them were probably monarchists. All the people I knew in the Italian radio seemed to be. My grandmother gave her gold ring and I think she no more had an idea about fascism than she did of any other political systems. The popular view of fascism was a naive one. Finally, someone had come along to make Italians do what they were supposed to do and the English world seemed to respect them.[141]

As the Italian case suggests, the countervailing attraction of nationalism among immigrant groups must not be underestimated, a perspective frequently in tension with cross-ethnic belief systems like socialism and communism (though not, of course, fascism). That is not to suggest that nationalism and radicalism are incommensurable. As Eric Foner has argued with respect to Irish working-class radicalism during the Gilded Age, nationalist sentiments for homeland independence can merge with critical reform movements in both the country of origin and of adoption.[142] Yet, the political center, and

122   Counterthesis

frequently the destiny, of such radicalism lies in foreign hands. And just as the attraction to radical politics might occur because of homeland considerations, so might the aversion, events in the home country causing immigrants to renounce, or significantly reorient, their radical political persuasions. Thus the strength of the Alliance of Polish Socialists moved in tandem with the struggle for an independent Poland; after Versailles accomplished that objective, the Alliance dissolved, those still interested in socialism joining the Polish section of the American Socialist party. So, too, the invasion of Ethiopia, support for Franco, and the alliance with Hitler all reduced Italian-American enthusiasm for the fascists, just as Stalinist pogroms and Khrushchev's denunciation of his predecessor tempered Jewish radicalism.

Finally, and perhaps most importantly, immigrants who desire permanent residence in America have been eager to demonstrate unreproachable patriotism. One of the surest ways to gain social acceptance in America is to wave the flag enthusiastically, and this is not lost on immigrant citizens. Given that they are frequently under suspicion for incomplete allegiance, immigrants make special efforts to present themselves as even more loyal Americans than the native-born. To that end, millions of German- and Scandinavian-stock citizens condemned the Haymarket anarchists as traitors, their churches adopting resolutions pledging absolute loyalty to America.[143] Other immigrants broke with the Socialist Party when it opposed American participation in World War I.[144] Likewise, Italian-Americans fully supported the United States in World War II, despite the propaganda efforts of the fascist government.[145] Radicalism has simply been no match for Americanism within the immigrant community.

Running parallel to political activism in the name of radical objectives is labor activism with radical consequences, and just as the foreign-born have been implicated in the first sort of undertaking, so have they in the second. Evidence of immigrant involvement in the trade union movement is not difficult to come by. From the beginning of the attempt to organize labor, the foreign-born have played a part. Early efforts to coordinate a labor movement, in the 1830s and 1840s, were made by English and Scottish immigrants; by mid-century, Germans had revitalized such attempts by organizing unions in trades—cabinetmaking, baking, watchmaking, upholstering—in which German artisans dominated.[146] Many of the best-known labor leaders have been immigrants: Samuel Gompers of the American Federation of Labor and David Dubinsky and Sidney Hillman of the Congress of Industrial Organizations are among the most prominent. Certain unions have been dominated by immigrant membership; the garment workers unions and, more recently, the United Farm Workers Union are prime examples. There have also been numerous industrial actions led by immigrant-dominated associations. The Fall River textile strikes as well as the Molly Maguire disturbances during the latter third of the nineteenth century; the Hart Shaffner and Marx strike of 1910–1911 in Chicago; the 1912 and 1919 mill walkouts in Lawrence, Massachusetts; and the 1930s job actions by eastern Pennsylvania's United Anthracite Miners Union were all spearheaded by immigrants.[147] Indeed, on those occasions when immigrants have been active in the interests of labor, a sense of ethnic group unity has often enhanced the cohesiveness and effectiveness of their efforts.

Yet the affinity of immigrant workers for unionism has not been automatic, varying among workplaces and ethnic groups. To the extent generalizations can be made, however, it would seem that during the formative years of the American labor movement, the foreign-born were as much an obstacle to labor activism—and to the development of labor as an independent political force—as its facilitator.[148] In part, this may be attributed to a natural conservativism among certain immigrant-stock workers, their precarious economic status making them reticent to participate in industrial actions interrupting the accumulation of income and even more ominously threatening permanent loss of employment.[149] More than this, immigrants arriving in the late nineteenth and early twentieth centuries were frequently used as strikebreakers, a fact that provoked the restrictionist urge among native-born workers and weakened the prospects for working-class solidarity.[150] Due to a desire for quick earnings, such immigrants were unlikely to have been sympathetic to a strike even if they had previous knowledge that one was taking place. That they did not always have such knowledge was sometimes due to contract labor (made illegal in 1885), which both insulated immigrants from the wider society and was recruited from the ranks of the less permanent individuals, those more willing to work despite the conditions.[151]

More debilitating to the prospects of a vital trade unionism, however, was the emergence of an ethnically segmented labor force. Describing the labor movement between 1870 and 1930, one social historian writes, "Both from necessity and intent the organization of work reflected the dominant ethnic character of workers. There is agreement on one critical point: that notwithstanding exceptions, the factory during the formative period of the American working class was subdivided into numerous ethnic boundaries that lacked a linguistic, psychological, and operational basis of common action and development."[152] Although absence of a lingua franca was the most elementary inhibitor of working-class unity, antagonisms among immigrant laborers of different nationalities (hostilities often escalated by employers) further reduced the prospects for worker organization and coordination. In other instances, ethnic concerns were linked to pledging to a union. In the late nineteenth century, for example, Irish support of union activities was often predicated on the union championing the cause of Irish independence—national loyalty competed with loyalty to the union movement.[153] Many immigrants have possessed an innate distrust of any agency without a distinctive ethnic stamp; immigrant moneys have followed their affections, contributions to churches, benevolent associations, and fraternal orders leaving little for union coffers.[154]

Additionally, during the same period an ample supply of unskilled immigrant labor advanced the development of industrial capitalism in the United States, once again to the detriment of working-class unity. As the production process was broken up and mechanized, skilled laborers—most often native-born or foreign-born of British, Irish, and German origin—began to lose their privileged position within the working class. Wage levels were depressed as a premium was placed on unskilled labor.[155] Unlike their native-born counterparts, immigrants had few institutional expectations of the American workplace and were not resistant to changes being introduced into the economy. To be sure, the immigrant was in some respects a ready-made capitalist, desirous of wage labor and a free labor market. That many were only temporary sojourners in America made the concern for maximum profits, at the expense of longer-term labor objectives, that much greater.[156] Consequently, over the course of the late nineteenth and early twentieth centuries, native-born workers increasingly viewed the immigrant, not as a fellow laborer, but as a competitor, a threat to cultural values and economic livelihood. Exclusionism, of course, was the natural outgrowth of such a perspective, Chinese laborers on the West Coast being the first to feel the full force of the restrictionist logic that would culminate in the quota laws of the 1920s—legislation, incidentally, welcomed by the A.F.L.[157]

Predictably, then, early attempts at nationwide labor organizations did not build on the foundation of immigrant workers. Although initially successful in attracting the urban laborer, the Knights of Labor by the late 1880s had little support in cities where large numbers of immigrants resided; the organization gradually became rural and middle class in perspective.[158] Nor did the American Federation of Labor fill the breach. Though moderate and reformist in objectives, characteristics that immigrant workers might have found appealing, and despite being led by the foreign-born Gompers, the A.F.L. seldom recruited actively among immigrants. It was the skilled craft unions that provided the bulk of A.F.L. membership until well into the twentieth century, few attempts being made to organize the unskilled workers among which the majority of immigrants were found.[159] Among immigrant-stock workers, the Irish showed the greatest affinity for the A.F.L., and this was because they dominated many of the skilled trades from which the A.F.L. drew its strength.[160] And if, by contrast, the Industrial Workers of the World were one of the few labor federations earnestly to seek immigrant members, immigrants were rarely comfortable with the Wobblies. Immigrant membership of the I.W.W. did realize a rapid increase in the years preceding the famous Paterson, New Jersey, and Lawrence, Massachusetts, strikes of 1912 and 1913, strikes conducted under I.W.W. auspices. But once the strikes ended, affection for the Wobblies waned and immigrant support was lost, a circumstance that may be attributed to unmediated immigrant inclinations as well as the anti-I.W.W. efforts of employers and the government.[161] In any event, the I.W.W. never had a secure base in the eastern United States where most immigrants resided and among whom its radical agenda was not well received; its real strength lay west of the Mississippi where its foundational unions, like the Western Federation of Miners (admittedly, a union led by Irish-Americans) were located. Not until the creation of the Congress of Industrial Organization in the 1930s were the lower ranks of the immigrant labor force actively and comprehensively organized.[162]

Hence, immigrants have tended to be only sporadically involved in radical politics and labor militancy. But a further and more subtle claim demands consideration: that immigrants have introduced an alien and self-seeking ethos into American municipal politics, thereby securing the development of the urban political machine. So, for instance, assessing immigration's impact on municipal reform, Edward Banfield and James Q. Wilson contrast more high-minded Anglo-Saxon middle-class beliefs with the political ethos of the typical immigrant, the former emphasizing public spiritedness, efficiency, honesty, impartiality, morality, and procedural integrity, the latter fixed on the acquisition of material benefits and personal improvement.[163] Although the authors assume a posture of evenhandedness, it is not difficult to discover where their preferences lie. The political machine, supported by immigrant constituents, is referred to as a "system of organized bribery," relying on citizens who are uninterested in issues or candidates and uncommitted to any particular political principle, while the swelling of the middle class is welcomed for the salutary effect it will have on the administration of civic institutions.[164] Of course civil service reform and (although this is more debatable)

federally directed social welfare programs have greatly reduced the
capacity of city machines to distribute the patronage perpetuating the
system Banfield and Wilson seem to find objectionable. Nevertheless,
the implication remains that immigrants, consciously or not, have been
inclined to support a form of government whose political principles
deviate in many respects from those held by right-thinking Americans.

That immigrants have been an essential constituency of city
machines is well established in much of the research concerning urban
politics.[165] Although not all immigrant groups have been courted with
equal diligence, machines have frequently made special efforts to
register the immigrant faithful.[166] Many of the best known "bosses"—
William Tweed, John Kelly, Charles Murphy in New York, Anton
Cermak, Edward Kelly, Richard Daly in Chicago, Michael James Curley
in Boston—were either themselves immigrants or had recent immigrant
roots. As one analyst suggests, "Any disciplined grass-roots organization rests upon a docile mass base which has in some manner been
rendered dependable, predictable, and manipulable."[167] Equipped with
only vague notions of civic responsibility and democratic virtue,
immigrants have appeared to fit the bill.

But if immigrants have been important to the well-being of city
machines, the relationship must not be misread. It is not a matter of
the foreign-born arriving in America with prefabricated value systems,
intending to establish organizational beachheads with which to corrupt
city politics. Strangers to the democratic process they may be, but that
does not mean that immigrants have actively espoused alternatives
to the American creed. Machine politics is politics without ideology,
politics revolving around needs—the need of constituents for social
and economic gain, and the need of the organization to perpetuate
itself. Of the Irish experience in New York, William Shannon writes:

> Irish machine politics was carried on in an intellectual void. It was the
> intuitive response to practical necessities and unrelated to any compre-
> hensive theory of politics and society. . . . The larger society outside
> the Irish community looked upon the party bosses as grotesque; politics
> seemed a morality play in which, despite frequent scandals and
> exposures, vice always triumphed; and the gloomier observers despaired
> of democracy. But for the Irish, politics was a functioning system of
> power and not an exercise in moral judgement.[168]

If a party leader was prepared to court an immigrant group with
material assistance, social respect, and ultimately political appointments, the loyalty of the group would likely be his. It was on this
pragmatic basis that machine politics proceeded.

What the machine offered was not a particular political philosophy, rather an attempt to meet the central interest of the immigrant—survival. Jane Addams, despite her opposition to the machine, well understood its appeal:

> Any one who has lived among poorer people cannot fail to be impressed with their constant kindness to each other; that unfailing response to the needs and distresses of their neighbors, even when in danger of bankruptcy themselves. This is their reward for living in the midst of poverty. They have constant opportunities for self-sacrifice and generosity, to which, as a rule, they respond. . . . It seems to such [men] entirely fitting that [their] Alderman should do the same thing on a larger scale—that he should help a constituent out of trouble just because he is in trouble irrespective of the justice involved. . . .
>
> What headway can the notion of civic purity, of honesty or administration, make against this big manifestation of human friendliness, this stalking survival of village kindness? The notions of the civic reformer are negative and impotent before it.[169]

If the immigrant tolerated what reformers called "corruption," it was because it served the interests of social welfare narrowly conceived; pledging a vote was a small price to pay for tangible, immediate, personal assistance. None of this meant that the immigrant consciously rejected the American political value system. The attraction of the machine for the immigrant represented the rejection of the political for the practical.

Furthermore, the predilection of the native-born for machine politics must not be forgotten. Immigrants have not been the only constituents for machines, which have operated in some places without much immigrant support at all. Nor has machine politics been the invention of the foreign-born.[170] Immigrants did not burst on to the municipal political scene unannounced; they were invited in by native-born American politicians, their votes solicited for the political benefits they could bring. Recognizing this, Bryce wrote, "New York was not an Eden before the Irish came; and would not become an Eden were they all to move on to San Francisco. . . . There is a disposition in the United States to use the immigrants, and especially the Irish, much as the cat is used in the kitchen to account for broken plates and food which disappears."[171] Even Tammany Hall began as a middle-class and nativist organization until the expansion of the suffrage and large-scale Irish immigration made such an approach politically unwise.[172] Bosses reached out to the immigrants; they were not the bosses' creation. In supporting the politics of the urban machine, immigrants may have behaved in a way as American as apple pie.

In sum, the standard pieces of evidence used to indicate the immigrant's uncertain commitment to the norms of the American democratic order are suspect. Radical politics has attracted some, but the great majority of immigrants have not been so disposed. Labor militancy, and for a long while the trade union movement itself, has been coolly received by the foreign-born, or, alternatively, the labor movement has been cool to the immigrant. In the case of machine politics, immigrant participation has been stimulated by economic necessity, not ideological conviction, and in any event has not been an exclusively immigrant-stock attribute. At a minimum, then, immigrants have seemed little inclined actively to oppose the American political creed.

Conclusion

The foregoing discussion has been consciously speculative. But if the case for immigration's contribution to American political stability can be sustained, and prima facie evidence suggests it can, that America is a settler society may go far toward explaining the success of its experiment in democracy. Ethnic heterogeneity, at least that produced by immigration, may not have the disruptive consequences that traditional democratic theory anticipates. Immigrants do not undermine the consensual foundations of the American democratic order and may in fact make that order more secure. In the first place, immigrants demand little from American government and beyond ritualistic displays of civic virtue do not have much of an active political presence at all. Such political passivity insulates the body politic from any immigrant-induced ideological conflict. But more positively, the process of immigration itself makes for political allegiance. Patriotism is a quality that immigrants readily exhibit, an expression of gratitude for the promise of America implicit in the act of immigration, as well as an attempt to demonstrate an unswerving loyalty. Granted, immigrants may not possess the full complement of liberal-democratic virtues—surely democracy requires more than uncritical support—but neither are they likely to question the procedures and policies of the liberal-democratic polity. And political stability, while not the only end of government, is not an end to be lightly dismissed.

If contribution to political stability alone is at issue, immigrants may well make better citizens than the native-born. It is not that the latter are insufficiently devoted to the American republic; in comparative terms, Americans—immigrant stock or not—are a highly patriotic people. Yet immigrant patriotism would seem to have a different, more reliable quality. Both immigrant and native-born may believe that America is to be esteemed because it encapsulates political goodness, but the source of that goodness is not the same in each case. To borrow from David Easton, the "diffuse" support of the native-born relies on the political system's ability to encompass the common values of the citizenry; "specific" support—centered on the government's capacity to deliver desired material goods and services—is too tenuous a basis for political allegiance.[173] This is why theoretical arguments about the creed are relevant. In a certain sense, native-born Americans are patriotic because ideally the United States enshrines their dearest beliefs about freedom, equality, autonomy, and so forth. Such individuals will not, of course, be as analytic about their convictions, but their behavior indicates the origin of their affections. This is most apparent in the realm of foreign affairs. When the United States confronts a country whose beliefs are supposedly opposed to its own, political leaders rally the faithful by appealing to shared political values rather than material welfare. Patriotic Americans are urged to "make the world safe for democracy"; pleas to "make the world safe for prosperity" are rarely heard.

The immigrant, at least initially, is unable to ground loyalty to America on shared values. Not having grown up in the United States, he or she has not necessarily been socialized to think of the liberal creed as normative. The immigrant's support for America is based, as is the native-born's, on the subjective perception that America offers the good life. But the immigrant forms his or her opinion on the basis of information native-born citizens may not have: what life is like elsewhere. The immigrant knows what is worthy about America because he or she has the comparative data. The immigrant recognizes that America is a good place to live because he or she has lived in a worse place, has experienced a harder life, has been victimized by the country of birth. America may not be perfect, the newcomer thinks, but it is better than the homeland. For this reason the immigrant may be more unreservedly patriotic than the native-born. Without having experienced life elsewhere, how can the latter be certain that the benefits of the American political system cannot be exceeded? And how can the native-born know what for many immigrants is the preciousness of American identity; for the native-born that identity is not earned but comes as a birthright. The comparative experience, gratitude for American sanctuary, the prospect of assuming American nationality, pressure to demonstrate civic rectitude in the eyes of the host society, in short all of the factors that entrench the commitment of the immigrant to America and that inhibit the development of a politically disruptive spirit, are absent in the instance of the native-born. The native-born assesses America according to an ideological ideal; as the standard of judgment is so exacting, America's shortcomings are more likely to be discovered.[174] But immigrant patriotism turns on the pragmatic determination of how the past measures up to the present, and relative to the histories of many immigrants, America is a distinct improvement. If anything, immigrants have an exaggerated view of the benefits of the host country; hence they are the most enthusiastic of flag-wavers and the most ardent champions of American rectitude.

The case can be made, therefore, that immigrants not only have not been bad for America, bad in the sense of politically troublesome, but also have been positively good and a force for political stability. Beyond the evidence already cited, the full argument for immigrant goodness would require an analysis of immigration's consequences for the American political economy. The totality of that discussion is beyond the scope of the present study, but the argument's essential features can be highlighted.

The starting point for such a disquisition would be the labor needs of settler societies. All newly established colonies must secure a labor supply commensurate to the economic tasks confronting them, a labor force that can most efficiently develop the material resources of the territory at hand. Subjugation of an indigenous population is one means of obtaining this labor, but in America that method of procurement was a nonstarter. The Indian population was not sufficient (not the least because their numbers had been diminished by European-borne diseases) to provide an adequate supply of cheap agricultural labor, nor did Indians adapt well to European agricultural methods. From the standpoint of white settlers, it was more expedient and profitable to dispossess the Indians of their land, eventually isolating them on reservations—the institutionalization of their economic marginality. And even though Mexicans living on land annexed by the United States in the 1830s and 1840s were incorporated into the regional economy of the Southwest, they constituted only a minor source of the total labor that the American economy demanded.[175] So, given the inviability of indigenous alternatives, America turned to an imported work force. Not all of this, of course, was free labor. During the early colonial period, indentured servants and redemptioners were a sizable proportion of the working population, especially in the South. But the expense involved in hire and maintenance, the limited duration of employment obligations, and, periodically, the scarcity of potential emigrants led to the gradual replacement of indentured servitude by chattel slavery as the forced labor supply of choice.[176] Slavery, too, was at best only a partial solution for America's labor needs as it was closely, though by no means exclusively, tied to a southern economy based on large-scale production of staple crops—rice, tobacco, and most importantly cotton. It was not suited to an economy centering on commerce and manufacturing, the sort of economy that first developed in the North and that required free, mobile, and cheap labor—precisely the opposite of what slavery had to offer.[177] Given the unsatisfactory nature of the alternatives, then, voluntary migration was the only scheme whereby America could meet the greater part of its laborpower requirements. Colonial authorities implemented an open immigration policy—one that did not discriminate on the basis of country of origin—as a simple matter of economic necessity.

Free immigrant labor has been crucial to the development of industrial capitalism in America. By the early twentieth century, the foreign-born constituted the majority of America's unskilled and semiskilled work force.[178] It was this work force that facilitated the mechanization of production necessary to industrial growth. Unlike skilled native-born workers, immigrant laborers were not threatened by, and thus did not resist, technological change. Nor were the material expectations of immigrant workers as high as their native-born counterparts. The perspective of most immigrants dovetailed nicely with conditions required by industrial capitalism—an emphasis on labor mobility and payment in wages.[179] As previously noted, a majority of immigrants arrived in America primarily motivated by the desire for economic gain, wealth that they estimated could not be acquired in the homeland. Despite the very real hardships immigrants encountered as they made their way in the American economy, the determination was made that the prospects for making money were yet better in the New World than in the country of birth. This comparative point of reference, when combined with the transitional mentality of many immigrants and their fear of antagonizing the host society, suggests why immigrants proved to be such a relatively docile and malleable work force, one reducing the severity of the birth pangs of economic modernization. In truth, the most vociferous opposition to unfettered industrial capitalism has come from native-born workers. It is the native-born who have made up the bulk of the trade union movement in general and who have been in the vanguard of labor militancy in particular. This is not to gloss over the exploitation that many immigrants suffered, nor is it to maintain that immigrants have been impervious to economic duress. Instead, it is to point out that American prosperity has been built on the backs of typically noncontentious immigrant laborers. The immigrant contribution to the dynamism of the American economy is undeniable; in that sense immigrants have been good for America.

Such economic benefits might well have carried political costs—certainly this would seem to be the expectation of those political theorists advancing the antiheterogeneity thesis. But in fact, the political disruptions latent in an ethnically heterogeneous society, a population generated by America's demand for labor, never transpired—quite the opposite. In immigrants, America acquired not only the industrial reserve army necessary to propel its economic expansion but also a citizenry that was withal patriotic. Gratitude for the advantages to be had in the New World, a lack of resources for political activity, and a concern not to offend the conventions of the host society all contributed to the immigrants' quiescent and allegiant demeanor. These, plus a political culture designed to absorb ethnic groups, indeed a culture that insisted on it, wedded the immigrant to the American political community. If fortuitous, the conditions for the development of a flourishing and stable political economy could hardly have been better.

Hence, the counterthesis in its totality. As noted at the chapter's outset, it claims only the status of a hypothesis; discrete sources of evidence suggest it may have a good deal of explanatory power, but more data must be collected. The subsequent chapter represents a step in this direction. In order to lend contemporary flavor and empirical support to the case being constructed, the essay will draw upon data taken from Laotian immigrants to America. The Laotian community will be approached as an extreme instance, extreme by reason of cultural exoticness and refugee status, against which to test the validity of the counterthesis. It is to the task of marshaling further evidence that the essay now turns.

Notes

1. See, for example, Kerby A. Miller, *Emigrants and Exiles: Ireland and the Irish Exodus to North America* (New York: Oxford University Press, 1985), pp. 345–63.

2. See, for example, Thomas Kessner and Betty Boyd Caroli, *Today's Immigrants, Their Stories: A New Look at the Newest Americans* (New York: Oxford University Press, 1981), pp. 30, 168.

3. For instance, see Miller, *Emigrants and Exiles,* p. 107.

4. James Stuart Olson, *The Ethnic Dimension in American History* (New York: St. Martin's, 1979), I., p. 182. On the theme of family obligation also see Richard D. Alba, *Italian-Americans: Into the Twilight of Ethnicity* (Englewood Cliffs: Prentice-Hall, 1985), pp. 28ff.

5. John Bodnar, *The Transplanted: A History of Immigrants in Urban America* (Bloomington: Indiana University Press, 1985), p. 168; Oscar Handlin, *Boston's Immigrants: A Study in Acculturation,* 2nd ed. (Cambridge: The Belknap Press of Harvard University Press, 1959), p. 131; Edward M. Levine, *The Irish and Irish Politicians* (Notre Dame: University of Notre Dame Press, 1966), p. 48; Miller, *Emigrants and Exiles,* p. 528; Peter Skerry, "The Ambiguity of Mexican-American Politics," in *Clamor at the Gates: The New American Immigration,* ed. Nathan Glazer (San Francisco: ICS, 1985), pp. 251–55; Carl Wittke, *We Who Built America: The Saga of the Immigrant* (New York: Prentice-Hall, 1940), pp. 222–26.

6. Quoted in Miller, *Emigrants and Exiles,* p. 330.

7. Alba, *Italian-Americans,* pp. 38–39; Maldwyn A. Jones, *American Immigration* (Chicago: University of Chicago Press, 1960), p. 107.

8. Hansen notes that the idea of obtaining status through consumerism as opposed to birth was already gaining acceptance in Europe before the middle of the nineteenth century. See Marcus Lee Hansen, *The Atlantic Migration 1607–1860* (Cambridge: Harvard University Press, 1940), pp. 215–16.

9. Handlin, *Boston's Immigrants,* p. 132.

10. As employed by most scholars, the term *immigrant stock* refers to the immigrant generation as well as its second- and third-generation American-born offspring.

11. Wittke, *We Who Built America,* p. 193.

12. Thomas N. Brown, *Irish-American Nationalism, 1870–1890* (Westport: Greenwood, 1966), p. 24.

13. Kessner and Caroli, *Today's Immigrants,* p. 181.

14. Marcus Lee Hansen, *The Immigrant in American History* (1940; rpt. New York: Harper and Row, 1964), p. 86.

15. Oscar Handlin, "The Immigrant and American Politics," in *Foreign Influences in American Life,* ed. David F. Bowers (New York: Peter Smith, 1952), p. 86.

16. Lawrence H. Fuchs, *The Political Behavior of American Jews* (Glencoe: The Free Press, 1956), pp. 100*ff.*, 175.

17. See, for instance, Lee Benson, *The Concept of Jacksonian Democracy: New York as a Test Case* (Princeton: Princeton University Press, 1961); Michael Holt, *Forging a Majority: The Formation of the Republican Party in Pittsburgh, 1848–1860* (New Haven: Yale University Press, 1969); Paul Kleppner, *The Cross of Culture: A Social Analysis of Midwestern Politics, 1850–1900* (New York: The Free Press, 1970); Joel H. Silbey and Samuel McSeveney, eds. *Voters, Parties, and Elections: Quantitative Essays in the History of American Popular Voting Behavior* (Lexington: Xerox College, 1972); Robert Kelley, *The Cultural Pattern in American Politics: The First Century* (New York: Knopf, 1979).

18. Humbert S. Nelli, *From Immigrants to Ethnics: The Italian Americans* (Oxford: Oxford University Press, 1983), p. 42.

19. Caroline Golab, *Immigrant Destinations* (Philadelphia: Temple University Press, 1977), pp. 99–100.

20. John Bodnar, *Immigration and Industrialization: Ethnicity in an American Mill Town, 1870–1940* (Pittsburgh: Pittsburgh University Press, 1977), p. 55.

21. Ewa Morawska, "The Sociology and Historiography of Immigration," in *Immigration Reconsidered: History, Sociology, and Politics* (New York: Oxford University Press, 1990), p. 195; Thomas Sowell, *Ethnic America: A History* (New York: Basic Books, 1981), pp. 136, 160, 250.

22. Morawska, "The Sociology," p. 195; also see Guillermina Jasso and Mark M. Rosenzweig, *The New Chosen People: Immigrants in the United States* (New York: Russell Sage, 1990), pp. 127–29.

23. Foreign governments recognized this function of America and attempted to accommodate it. For instance, the Italian government, in an effort to promote seasonal migration, regulated ship prices and conditions, provided facilities for the remittance of U.S. currency through Italian banks, and, when the Americans imposed a literacy test for admission to the United States, established night schools so that Italians might learn English. See Kessner and Caroli, *Today's Immigrants*, p. 210.

24. On the vagaries of the assimilative process, see Virginia Yans-McLaughlin, ed., *Immigration Reconsidered: History, Sociology, and Politics* (New York: Oxford University Press, 1990), especially the essays by Tilly and Morawska; Ewa Morawska, *For Bread with Butter: The Life-Worlds of East Central Europeans in Johnstown, Pennsylvania, 1890–1940* (Cambridge: Cambridge University Press, 1985); Robert C. Ostergren, *A Community Transplanted: The Trans-Atlantic Experience of a Swedish Immigrant Settlement in the Upper Middle West, 1835–1915* (Madison: University of Wisconsin Press, 1988).

25. The United Nations Convention Relating to the Status of Refugees defines a refugee as "an individual who, owing to a well-founded fear of being persecuted for reasons of race, religion, nationality, memberships of particular social groups or political oppositions, is outside the country of nationality and is unable, or owing to such fear, is unwilling to avail himself of the protection of that country; or who, not having a nationality and being outside the country of his former habitual residence as a result of such events is unable or, owing to such fear, unwilling to return to it." Cited in Gunther Beyer, "The Political Refugee: Thirty-Five Years Later," *International Migration Review*, XV, Nos. 1–2 (1981), 27.

26. Fernando Ainsa, "Utopia, Promised Lands, Immigration and Exile," *Diogenes*, No. 119 (1982), 51.

27. See, for example, William J. Thomas and Florian Znaniecki, *The Polish Peasant in Europe and America* (1918; rpt. New York: Dover, 1958), II, p. 1483.

28. Hansen, *The Atlantic Migration*, p. 119.

29. William V. Shannon, *The American Irish* (New York: MacMillan, 1963), pp. 25–26.

30. Maldwyn Jones, *American Immigration* (Chicago: University of Chicago Press), p. 102.

31. Hansen, *The Atlantic Migration*, p. 295.

32. Bodnar, *The Transplanted,* p. 50; Sowell, *Ethnic America,* pp. 160–64.

33. Gil Loescher and John A. Scanlon, *Calculated Kindness: Refugees and America's Half-Open Door—1945 to the Present* (New York: The Free Press, 1986), p. xiv.

34. The Displaced Persons Act of 1948 charged refugees against the future quota allotments of a given country; the Refugee Relief Act of 1953 permitted, temporarily, entry outside the quota allotments.

35. The Refugee Assistance Act also established a separate quota of fifty thousand for refugee admissions, a figure that can be increased should circumstances demand.

36. Quoted in David M. Brownstone, Irene M. Franck, and Douglass L. Brownstone, *Island of Hope, Island of Tears* (New York: Penguin, 1986), p. 23.

37. Philip Gleason, "American Identity and Americanization," *Harvard Encyclopedia of American Ethnic Groups* (1980), p. 32. Also see Hans Kohn, *American Nationalism: An Interpretative Essay* (New York: Macmillan, 1957), pp. 7–9, 135–37.

38. Morawska, *For Bread with Butter,* pp. 24ff. Miller, *Emigrants and Exiles,* p. 59; Bodnar, *The Transplanted,* p. 28.

39. Quoted in Brownstone et al., *Island of Hope,* p. 17.

40. Hector St. John de Crevecouer, *Letters from an American Farmer* (1782; rpt. London: J. M. Dent, 1912), p. 43.

41. Alejandro Portes and Ruben G. Rumbaut, *Immigrant America: A Portrait* (Berkeley: University of California Press, 1990), p. 10; Guillermina Jasso and Mark R. Rosenzweig, *The New Chosen People: Immigrants in the United States* (New York: Russell Sage, 1990), pp. 240–43.

42. See Richard A. Easterlin, "Immigration: Economic and Social Characteristics," *Harvard Encyclopedia of American Ethnic Groups* (1980); Sowell, *Ethnic America,* pp. 27–35, 138–40, 162–76, 249–61; Philip Taylor, *The Distant Magnet, European Emigration to the U.S.A.* (New York: Harper and Row, 1971), pp. 169–207.

43. In 1908, the Dillingham Commission on Immigration found that two-fifths of all immigrant families made less than $500 per year and two-thirds less than $750—this in an era when $800 per year was considered the minimum acceptable income for a family of five. For a discussion of the precarious social and economic position of many immigrants, see Taylor, *Distant Magnet,* pp. 175–205.

44. See, for example, Ted Robert Gurr, "The History of Violent Crime in America: An Overview," in *Violence in America: The History of Crime,* ed. Ted Robert Gurr (Newbury Park: Sage Publications, 1989), I, pp. 11–20; Roger Lane, "On the Social Meaning of Homicide Trends in America," in Gurr, *Violent Crime,* pp. 55–79; Eric H. Monkkonen, "Diverging Homicide Rates: England and the United States, 1850–1875," in Gurr, *Violent Crime,* pp. 80–101.

45. See Daniel Bell, *The End of Ideology: On the Exhaustion of Political Ideas in the Fifties* (Glencoe: The Free Press, 1960), pp. 129–35; Humbert S. Nelli, *The Business of Crime: Italians and Syndicate Crime in the United States* (Chicago: University of Chicago Press, 1976), esp. pp. 254–55; Jenna

Weissman Joselit, *Our Gang: Jewish Crime and the New York Jewish Community, 1900–1940* (Bloomington: Indiana University Press, 1983); Ivan Light, "The Ethnic Vice Industry, 1880–1944," *American Sociological Review,* 42 (1977), 464–79.

46. Quoted in Theodore C. Blegen, *Land of Their Choice: The Immigrants Write Home* (St. Paul: University of Minnesota Press, 1955), pp. 180–81.

47. Quoted in Salvatore J. La Gumina, *The Immigrants Speak: Italian Americans Tell Their Story* (New York: Center for Migration Studies, 1979), p. 188.

48. Quoted in Kessner and Caroli, *Today's Immigrants,* p. 131.

49. Stephan Thernstrom, *Poverty and Progress: Social Mobility in a Nineteenth Century City* (Cambridge: Harvard University Press, 1964), pp. 164–65. Also see Gordon W. Kirk, *The Promise of American Life: Social Mobility in a Nineteenth-Century Immigrant Community, Holland, Michigan, 1874–1894* (Philadelphia: American Philosophical Society, 1978), p. 133., and Morawska, *For Bread with Butter,* pp. 114, 135–37.

50. Liem T. Nguyen and Alan B. Henkin, "Vietnamese Refugees in the United States: Adaptation and Transitional Status," *Journal of Ethnic Studies,* 9 (1982), 108–15. Also see Daniel Montero, *Vietnamese Americans: Patterns of Resettlement and Socioeconomic Adaptation in the United States* (Boulder: Westview Press, 1979), pp. 22–40.

51. Eleanor M. Rogg, *The Assimilation of Cuban Exiles: The Role of Community and Class* (New York: Aberdeen Press, 1974), p. 129.

52. Sowell, *Ethnic America,* p. 28, p. 61; Roger Daniels, *Coming to America: A History of Immigration and Ethnicity in American Life* (New York: Harper Collins, 1990), p. 183; Morawska, *For Bread with Butter,* p. 69; Yuji Ichioka, *The Issei: The World of the First Generation Japanese Immigrants, 1885–1924* (New York: The Free Press, 1988), pp. 45–46.

53. Leonard Dinnerstein and David M. Riemers, *Ethnic Americans: A History of Immigration and Assimilation* (New York: Harper and Row, 1975), pp. 99–101.

54. Bodnar, *Immigration and Industrialization,* pp. 61–62. On immigrants' success in accumulating property, also see Thernstrom, *Poverty and Progress,* pp. 155–57.

55. Morawska, *For Bread with Butter,* pp. 146–48, 216.

56. See, for example, Bodnar, *The Transplanted,* pp. 169–175; Stephan Thernstrom, *The Other Bostonians: Poverty and Progress in the American Metropolis* (Cambridge: Harvard University Press, 1973), ch. 6. Morawska, *For Bread with Butter,* pp. 151ff., 213–15. Also see, Hartmut Kaelble, *Social Mobility in the 19th and 20th Centuries: Europe and America in Comparative Perspective* (New York: St. Martin's Press, 1986).

57. Thomas Kessner, *The Golden Door: Italian and Jewish Immigrant Mobility in New York City, 1880–1915* (New York: Oxford, 1977), pp. 113–18.

58. Ibid., p. 126.

59. Kirk, *Promise of American Life,* p. 133.

60. Josef J. Barton, *Peasants and Strangers: Italians, Rumanians, and Slovaks in an American City, 1890–1959* (Cambridge: Harvard University Press, 1975), pp. 100ff.

61. John Bodnar, Roger Simon, and Michael P. Weber, *Lives of Their Own: Blacks, Italians, and Poles in Pittsburgh, 1900–1960* (Urbana: University of Illinois Press, 1982), 138, 252.

62. Barry R. Chiswick, "The Economic Progress of Immigrants: Some Apparently Universal Patterns," in *Contemporary Economic Problems, 1979,* ed. William Fellner (Washington, D.C.: American Enterprise Institute for Public Policy Research, 1979), p. 197. Also see Francine D. Blau, "Immigration and Labor Earnings in Early Twentieth Century America," in *Research in Population Economics,* vol. II, ed. Julian Simon and Julie da Vanzo (Greenwich: JAI, 1979).

63. Jasso and Rosenzweig, *New Chosen People,* pp. 305–06. As the authors use the term, *recent entrants* indicates individuals arriving in the United States less than five years before a given census.

64. Melvin M. Tumin, "Some Unapplauded Consequences of Social Mobility in a Mass Society," *Social Forces,* 36 (1957), 32–37.

65. Brownstone et al., *Island of Hope,* p. 279.

66. See, for example, Richard Hofstadter, "The Pseudo-Conservative Revolt," in *The Radical Right: The New American Right,* ed. Daniel Bell (Garden City: Anchor Books, 1964), pp. 88–99.

67. Frederick C. Luebke, *The Bonds of Loyalty: German Americans and World War I* (DeKalb: Northern Illinois University Press, 1974), pp. 200–01. On the question of immigrants and the war effort see Luebke, *The Bonds of Loyalty,* ch. 7 and 8, and also H. Nelli, *Italians in Chicago: A Study in Ethnic Mobility* (New York: Oxford, 1978), pp. 201ff.

68. Maldwyn A. Jones, *The Old World Ties of American Ethnic Groups* (London: H. K. Lewis, 1976), pp. 4–9.

69. Shannon, *American Irish,* pp. 132–34.

70. Of the Irish draft riots, at least two further observations should be made. First, proportionately, immigrant enlistments in the Union—and for that matter the Confederate—army exceeded their numbers in the population at large. In that respect, immigrants cannot be accused of shirking military obligations. Conversely, immigrants might be forgiven for challenging the apparent ability of the better-heeled among the native-born to be released from their military commitments, this being one source of the dissatisfaction leading to the riots. Second, the riots merged discontent stemming from the Union's prosecution of the war with Irish antipathy to the black population. As northern blacks were frequently perceived to be in economic competition with the Irish, and as the causes of nativism and abolitionism were often viewed by the Irish as all of a piece, the draft riots may be seen as acts of interethnic violence for which there was precedence (the Philadelphia riots of 1844, for instance) as much as political defiance.

71. See, for example, Harold F. Gosnell, *Getting Out the Vote: An Experiment in the Stimulation of Voting* (Chicago: University of Chicago Press, 1927), pp. 81–100; Robert E. Lane, *Political Life: Why and How People Get Involved in Politics* (New York: The Free Press, 1959, pp. 235–37; Charles E. Merriam and Harold F. Gosnell, *Non-Voting: Causes and Methods of Control* (Chicago: University of Chicago Press, 1924), pp. 227–30.

72. See, for example, Thomas D. Boswell and James R. Curtis, *The Cuban-American Experience: Culture, Images and Perspectives* (Totowa: Rowman and Allanheld, 1984), p. 174. Also see Alejandro Portes and Rafael Mozo, "The Political Adaptation Process of Cubans and Other Ethnic Minorities in the United States: A Preliminary Analysis," in *Latinos and the Political System,* ed. F. Chris Garcia (Notre Dame: University of Notre Dame Press, 1988), pp. 152–70.

73. See, for instance, Fuchs, *Political Behavior,* p. 62; Frederick C. Luebke, *Immigrants and Politics: The Germans of Nebraska, 1880–1900* (Lincoln: University of Nebraska Press, 1969), p. 38; Merriam and Gosnell, *Non-Voting,* p. 28; Raymond Wolfinger and Steven J. Rosenstone, *Who Votes?* (New Haven: Yale University Press, 1979), pp. 91–93. Cross-national data, if sparse, also tend to confirm that immigrants vote at lower rates than native-born citizens. See Mark J. Miller, "Political Participation and Representation of Noncitizens," in *Immigration and the Politics of Citizenship in Europe and North America,* ed. Williams Rogers Brubaker (Lanham: University Press of America, 1989), p. 133.

74. Paul Kleppner, *Who Voted? The Dynamics of Electoral Turnout, 1870–1980* (New York: Praeger, 1982), p. 37.

75. Ibid., pp. 89, 183.

76. Reed Ueda, "Naturalization and Citizenship," *Harvard Encyclopedia of American Ethnic Groups* (1980), p. 745.

77. Humbert S. Nelli, *Italians in Chicago,* p. 116; also see Alba, *Italian-Americans,* p. 54., and Helen Z. Lopata, *Polish-Americans: Status Competition in an Ethnic Community* (Englewood Cliffs: Prentice-Hall, 1976), p. 84. It should also be recognized that for several immigrant groups, East Asians in particular, naturalization was once prohibited as a matter of American law.

78. U.S. Bureau of the Census, *Statistical Abstract of the United States: 1990* (Washington, D.C.: G.P.O., 1990), p. 41.

79. H. F. Gosnell, "Non-Naturalization: A Study in Political Assimilation," *American Journal of Sociology,* 33 (1928), 938.

80. Ibid., p. 939.

81. Merriam and Gosnell, *Non-Voting,* pp. 143–44, 176.

82. Andrew Greeley et al., "Political Participation Among Ethnic Groups in the United States," in *Ethnicity in the United States: A Preliminary Reconnaissance,* ed. Andrew Greeley and William C. McCready (New York: John Wiley and Sons, 1974), p. 147.

83. Wolfinger and Rosenstone, *Who Votes?* pp. 91–93.

84. See, for example, John A. Garcia and Carlos H. Arce, "Political Orientation Behaviors of Chicanos: Trying to Make Sense Out of Attitudes and Participation," in *Latinos and the Political System,* ed. F. Chris Garcia (Notre Dame: University of Notre Dame Press, 1988), p. 147.

85. Michael J. Parenti, *Ethnic and Political Attitudes: A Depth Study of Italian Americans* (New York: Arno, 1975), p. 300.

86. Raymond E. Wolfinger, *The Politics of Progress* (Englewood Cliffs: Prentice-Hall, 1974), p. 35; also see Robert Dahl, *Who Governs?* (New Haven: Yale University Press, 1961), pp. 53–54.

87. See, for example, Holt, *Forging a Majority*; also Kleppner, *The Cross of Culture*.

88. Shannon, *American Irish*, p. 69.

89. Steven P. Erie, *Rainbow's End: Irish-Americans and the Dilemmas of Urban Machine Politics, 1840–1985* (Berkeley: University of California Press, 1988).

90. See, for example, Skerry, *Clamor at the Gates*, p. 256.

91. Quoted in Edward R. Kantowicz, *Polish-American Politics in Chicago, 1888–1940* (Chicago: University of Chicago Press, 1975), p. 74.

92. Edward T. Kantowicz, "Voting and Parties," in *The Politics of Ethnicity*, ed. Stephen Thernstrom (Cambridge: Belknap, 1982), pp. 46–47.

93. Shannon, *American Irish*, pp. 327–32.

94. See Alba, *Italian-Americans*, p. 84; Dahl, *Who Governs?* pp. 40–4; Fuchs, *Political Behavior*, p. 65; Garcia, *Political Orientation Behaviors*, pp. 14–15, 276ff.; Kantowicz, *Polish-American Politics*, pp. 95, 174ff.; Stanley Lieberson, *A Piece of the Pie: Blacks and White Immigrants Since 1880* (Berkeley: University of California Press, 1980), pp. 77–95; Nelli, *Italians in Chicago*, pp. 113, 223; Nelli, *From Immigrants to Ethnics*, p. 108. Alejandro Portes and Ruben G. Rumbaut, *Immigrant America: A Portrait* (Berkeley: University of California Press, 1990), pp. 127ff. Dahl speaks of a "massive invasion" of ethnic politicians into New Haven in the 1950s—yet for the Irish, Italians, and Jews to whom he refers, the breakthrough occurred 50–90 years after sizable numbers of each group began to reside in New Haven.

95. It should be noted that the state itself—as realized, for example, in measures taken by the Immigration and Naturalization Service to control Mexican immigration, efforts that many Chicanos perceive as unjust—may be a further stimulus to immigrant political mobilization. See Cynthia Enloe, "The Growth of the State and Ethnic Mobilization," *Ethnic and Racial Studies*, 4, no. 2 (1981), 123–36.

96. For a good discussion of the German-American experience in this regard see John A. Hagwood, *The Tragedy of German-America* (London: G. P. Putnam, 1940).

97. Kessner and Caroli, *Today's Immigrants*, pp. 142–44; Illsoo Kim, *New Urban Immigrants: The Korean Community in New York* (Princeton: Princeton University Press, 1981), pp. 227–36; Stanford M. Lyman, *Chinese-Americans* (New York: Random House, 1974), pp. 182–83.

98. Kantowicz, *Polish-American Politics*, p. 38; Boswell and Curtis, *Cuban American Experience*, p. 171; Maria de los Angeles Torres, "From Exiles to Minorities: The Politics of Cuban-Americans," in *Latinos and the Political System*, ed. F. Chris Garcia (Notre Dame: University of Notre Dame Press, 1988), pp. 81–98.

99. Jones, *Old World Ties*, pp. 4–9; Thomas and Znaniecki, *Polish Peasant*, p. 1581; Lopata, *Polish-Americans*, p. 22.

100. See Brown, *Irish-American Nationalism*; Kantowicz, *Polish-American Politics*, p. 169; Rogg, *Assimilation*, p. 41.

101. Richard Hofstadter, *The Age of Reform: From Bryan to F.D.R.* (New York: Vintage, 1955), p. 181.

102. Even the most basic reading and writing skills may be scarce: the Dillingham Commission on Immigration reported that 26.7% of immigrants in their early-twentieth-century sample could neither read nor write in any language. Easterlin, in *Harvard Encyclopedia*, p. 478.

103. Ibid. This is not to suggest, of course, that immigrants without facility in English have been completely lacking for political information; among certain groups, the foreign-language media has been a partial remedy.

104. L. W. Milbrath, *Political Participation: How and Why Do People Get Involved in Politics?* (Chicago: Rand McNally, 1965), pp. 16, 54; Sidney Verba and Norman Nie, *Participation in America* (New York: Harper and Row), p. 19.

105. On efficacy see Bernard Berelson, Paul Lazarsfeld, and William N. McPhee, *Voting: A Study of Opinion Formation in a Presidential Campaign* (Chicago: University of Chicago Press, 1954), p. 27; Angus Campbell, Gerald Gurin, and Warren E. Miller, *The Voters Decide* (Evanston: Row, Peterson, 1954), p. 194; L. W. Milbrath, *Political Participation*, p. 54; Verba and Nie, *Participation in America*, pp. 125–26.

106. Kessner and Caroli, *Today's Immigrants*, p. 203.

107. Wolfinger, *The Politics of Progress*, p. 49. Also see Eric M. Leifer, "Competing Models of Political Mobilization: The Role of Ethnic Ties," *American Journal of Sociology*, 87 (1981), 23–47.

108. Berelson, *Voting*, p. 25.

109. Barton, *Peasants and Strangers*, p. 203; Bodnar, *Immigration and Industrialization*, p. 111; Joseph Lopreato, *Italian Americans* (New York: Random House, 1970), p. 106.

110. Shih-Shan Henry Tsai, *The Chinese Experience in America* (Bloomington: Indiana University Press, 1986), p. 191.

111. Skerry, *Clamor at the Gates*, pp. 242–43.

112. See Wolfinger and Rosenstone, *Who Votes?* pp. 50–55; Nelli, *From Immigrants to Ethnics*, p. 48; Bodnar, *Immigration and Industrialization*, p. 58.

113. Milton Gordon, *Assimilation in American Life: The Role of Race, Religion and National Origins* (New York: Oxford University Press, 1964), pp. 71–77; also see Raymond H.C. Teske and Bardin H. Nelson, "Acculturation and Assimilation: A Clarification," *American Ethnologist*, I (1974), 351–67.

114. Herbert Gans, *The Urban Villagers: Group and Class in the Life of Italian-Americans* (Glencoe: The Free Press, 1962), p. 4.

115. On this theme see Alba, *Italian Americans*, p. 70; Lopata, *Polish-Americans*, p. 4; Lopreato, *Italian Americans*, p. 119; Miller, *Emigrants and Exiles*, p. 330.

116. U.S. Bureau of the Census, *Historical Statistics of the United States: Colonial Times to 1970* (Washington D.C.: G.P.O., 1975), p. 114.

117. Rudolph J. Vecoli, "Immigration, Naturalization, and the Constitution," *News for Teachers of Political Science*, No. 50 (1986), 10–13.

118. Wittke, *We Who Built America*, pp. 339ff.

119. See John M. Allswang, "Immigrant Ethnicity in a Changing Politics: Chicago from Progressivism to FDR," in Silbey and McSeveney, *Voters, Parties,*

and *Elections*, pp. 278–80; also see Kantowicz, *Polish-American Politics*, pp. 87–95.

120. Hansen, *The Immigrant and American History*, pp. 90–95; Luebke, *Immigrants and Politics*, pp. 114–15, 164–65.

121. David H. Bennett, *The Party of Fear: From Nativist Movements to the New Right in American History* (Chapel Hill: University of North Carolina Press, 1988), p. 178.

122. See, for instance, Hofstadter, *Age of Reform*, pp. 177–84.

123. See Donald T. Critchlow, ed., *Socialism in the Heartland: The Midwestern Experience, 1900–1925* (Notre Dame: University of Notre Dame Press, 1986); Fuchs, *Political Behavior*, p. 124; also see Moses Rischin, *The Promised City, New York's Jews, 1870–1914* (Cambridge: Harvard University Press, 1962), p. 219.

124. Gerald Rosenblum, *Immigrant Workers: Their Impact on American Labor Radicalism* (New York: Basic, 1973), p. 153.

125. Wolfinger, *The Politics of Progress*, p. 59.

126. Kantowicz, *Polish-American Politics*, p. 38.

127. Nelli, *Italians in Chicago*, p. 242.

128. Wittke, *We Who Built America*, p. 241.

129. Sally M. Miller, "Casting a Wide Net: The Milwaukee Movement to 1920," in *Socialism in the Heartland: The Midwestern Experience, 1900–1925*, ed. Donald T. Critchlow (Notre Dame: University of Notre Dame Press, 1986), pp. 18–41; Luebke, *Bonds*, pp. 295–300.

130. Bodnar, *The Transplanted*, p. 107; Wittke, *We Who Built America*, p. 415.

131. Rischin, *Promised City*, p. 227; Stephen J. Whitfeld, *Voices of Jacob, Hands of Esau: Jews in American Life and Thought* (Hamden: Archon, 1984), pp. 79–82.

132. On the Jewish-Socialist connection see Fuchs, *Political Behavior;* Rischin, *Promised City*; and Whitfeld, *Voices.*

133. Rosenblum, *Immigrant Workers*, p. 153.

134. Hansen, *The Immigrant in American History*, pp. 88–89; Wittke, *We Who Built America*, p. 241.

135. Fuchs, *Political Behavior*, p. 129; Whitfeld, *Voices*, p. 81; Edgar Litt, *Ethnic Politics in America* (Glenview: Scott, Foresman, 1970), p. 96.

136. Seymour Martin Lipset and Earl Raab, *The Politics of Unreason: Right-Wing Extremism in America, 1790–1970* (New York: Harper and Row, 1970), p. 132.

137. Nelli, *Italians in Chicago*, pp. 239–41.

138. Bodnar, *The Transplanted*, p. 110; Litt, *Ethnic Politics*, p. 87.

139. Bodnar, *The Transplanted*, p. 109; Kantowicz, *Polish-American Politics*, p. 29; Litt, *Ethnic Politics*, p. 97. Also see David J. Goldberg, *A Tale of Three Cities: Labor Organization and Protest in Paterson, Passaic, and Lawrence, 1916–1921* (New Brunswick: Rutgers University Press, 1989), pp. 51–53; David Montgomery, *The Fall of the House of Labor: The Workplace, the State, and American Labor Activism, 1865–1925* (Cambridge: Cambridge University Press, 1987), pp. 304*ff.*

140. Rosenblum, *Immigrant Workers,* p. 154.

141. Quoted in LaGumina, *Immigrants Speak,* p. 134.

142. Eric Foner, *Politics and Ideology in the Age of the Civil War* (New York: Oxford University Press, 1980), ch. 8.

143. Hansen, *The Immigrant in American History,* p. 89.

144. Bodnar, *The Transplanted,* p. 112.

145. Nelli, *From Immigrants to Ethnics,* p. 171.

146. Bodnar, *The Transplanted,* pp. 85–86; Wittke, *We Who Built America,* p. 237.

147. Bodnar, *The Transplanted,* p. 90, 102–04; Nelli, *From Immigrants to Ethnics,* p. 82; Montgomery, *The Fall,* pp. 106–10.

148. See, for example, Gwendolyn Mink, *Old Labor and New Immigrants in American Political Development, 1875–1920* (Ithaca: Cornell University Press, 1986).

149. See, for example, David M. Emmons, *The Butte Irish: Class and Ethnicity in an American Mill Town, 1875–1925* (Urbana: University of Illinois Press, 1989), pp. 190*ff.*

150. To cite an extreme example, Chinese railroad laborers were alleged to be so adverse to strike activity that they were disparagingly referred to as "Crooker's Pets" after the chief executive officer of the Union Pacific Railroad, Charles Crooker.

151. On the controversy surrounding contract labor see A. T. Lane, *Solidarity or Survival? American Labor and European Immigrants, 1830–1924* (Westport: Greenwood Press, 1987), pp. 62*ff.*

152. Gabriel Kolko, *Main Currents in American History* (New York: Harper and Row, 1976), p. 75. For the classic statement of this position, see Selig Perlman, *Theory of the Labor Movement* (1928; rpt. New York: Augustus M. Kelley, 1949).

153. Bodnar, *The Transplanted,* p. 90.

154. Lopata, *Polish-Americans,* p. 85; Rischin, *Promised City,* pp. 181–82.

155. Bodnar, *The Transplanted,* pp. 92–94.

156. Lopata, *Polish-Americans,* p. 86; Rosenblum, *Immigrant Workers,* pp. 121–33; Kolko, *Main Currents,* pp. 69*ff.*

157. On labor's role in the drive to restrict Chinese immigration, see Alexander Saxton, *The Indispensable Enemy: Labor and the Anti-Chinese Movement in California* (Berkeley: University of California Press, 1971), also Ichioka, *The Issei:* pp. 91*ff.* For a general discussion of the transformation of labor's attitude toward immigrant workers, see Lane, *Solidarity or Survival?*

158. Rosenblum, *Immigrant Workers,* p. 135.

159. Bodnar, *Immigration and Industrialization,* p. 49; Rosenblum, *Immigrant Workers,* pp. 156–58; Montgomery, *The Fall,* p. 461.

160. Shannon, *American Irish,* pp. 140–41.

161. Gary Gerstle, *Working-Class Americanism: The Politics of Labor in a Textile City, 1914–1960* (Cambridge: Cambridge University Press, 1989), pp. 74–76; Bodnar, *The Transplanted,* pp. 102–04; Rosenblum, *Immigrant Workers,* p. 165.

162. Bodnar, *Immigration and Industrialization,* p. 145.

163. Edward C. Banfield and James Q. Wilson, *City Politics* (Cambridge: Harvard University Press, 1965), pp. 117, 128.

164. Ibid., pp. 339*ff.*

165. See for example John M. Allswang, *Bosses, Machines, and Urban Voters* (Baltimore: Johns Hopkins University Press, 1986); Elmer E. Cornwell, "Bosses, Machines, and Ethnic Groups," *The Annals of the American Academy of Political and Social Science,* 353, (1964), 27–39.

166. Allswang, *Bosses,* pp. 45, 51, 54, 89.

167. Cornwell, in *Annals,* p. 28.

168. Shannon, *American Irish,* p. 67.

169. Jane Addams, "Why The Ward Boss Rules," *The Outlook,* 58 (1898), rpt. in *The Irish: America's Political Class,* ed. James B. Walsh (New York: Arno, 1976), pp. 879–82.

170. See Amy Bridges, *A City in the Republic: Antebellum New York and the Origins of Machine Politics* (Cambridge: Cambridge University Press, 1984); Raymond E. Wolfinger, "Why Political Machines Have Not Withered Away and Other Revisionist Thoughts," *The Journal of Politics,* 34 (1972), 364–98; and Raymond E. Wolfinger and John Osgood Field, "Political Ethos and the Structure of City Government," in *Perspectives on Urban Politics,* ed. Jay S. Goodman (Boston: Allyn and Bacon, 1970), pp. 454–95.

171. Quoted in Wittke, *We Who Built America,* p. 146.

172. Allswang, *Bosses,* p. 40; Shannon, *American Irish,* p. 49.

173. David Easton, *A Systems Analysis of Political Life* (New York: John Wiley and Sons, 1965), pp. 273–87.

174. Cf. Samuel Huntington, *American Politics: The Promise of Disharmony* (Cambridge: Harvard University Press, 1984).

175. Stephen Steinberg, *The Ethnic Myth: Race, Ethnicity, and Class in America* (New York: Atheneum, 1981), pp. 14–24.

176. Wittke, *We Who Built America,* pp. 9–13.

177. Steinberg, *Ethnic Myth,* pp. 25*ff.*

178. Kolko, *Main Currents,* p. 74; Taylor, *Distant Magnets,* pp. 182–87, 195–97.

179. See Kolko, *Main Currents,* pp. 73*ff.*; Rosenblum, *Immigrant Workers,* pp. 121*ff.*; Steinberg, *Ethnic Myth,* pp. 35*ff.*

5

The Politics of Laotian Immigrants

According to the true thesis of this study, immigrants have contributed to the vitality of the American political system. On this view, ethnic heterogeneity has not threatened America's democratic order, and since in the United States heterogeneity is largely the consequence of immigration, neither has immigration. By making for individuals who demand little from government yet are highly patriotic, immigration has in fact advanced the cause of American political stability.

The present chapter furnishes further evidence in support of that claim. The verbal testimony of Laotian refugees, solicited in interviews specifically designed to probe the insights of the thesis, constitutes the empirical data with which the immigrant experience is assessed. Mindful of the exploratory nature of the investigation, conclusions based on the interview testimony must be tentatively offered. In truth, the perspectives of those interviewed are not always uniform; hence one can only speak of tendencies and trends in the responses given. Still, a distinct image, hazy but perceptible, emerges from the interview data, indicating that the bare bones of the thesis are correct. All Laotians considered in the current investigation pledge a staunch allegiance and scrupulous obedience to the government of the United States, and if not completely agreed on the virtues of the American creed, their disinclination to become active in American political life suggests that any points of disagreement are not decisive.

The decision to study Laotian immigrants requires a word of explanation. Although the author was interested in and had had contact with the Laotian community before the research project commenced, the choice of Laotians was also deliberate. To begin with, by reason of their cultural exoticness, Laotians provide a particularly good test case of the standard immigrant political analysis. Implicit in that analysis is the presumption that the greater the degree to which an immigrant group departs from American ideological norms—that is to say, the greater the cultural gap between the immigrant group and the host society—the more likely the group is to disturb the consensus on which American democratic stability rests. Conversely, the contention of the present study is that culturally exotic immigrants should be the least likely to unsettle the political system, their exoticness serving as a barrier to political participation and disruptive behavior.

But Laotians illuminate the present thesis for an additional reason—the overwhelming majority have entered the United States as refugees. Individuals whose migration is not the product of their own volition, the urgency of flight not permitting much premeditation, might be expected to have only a limited enthusiasm for the host society, a society thrust upon them rather than entered into freely. Admittedly, in the instance of the Laotians this characterization must be slightly qualified, since their sojourn in Southeast Asian relocation camps may have given them some time to choose where they wish to be resettled. Still, for most Laotians a desire for family reunification, or the fear of refusing a resettlement opportunity, has lent an immediacy to the decision to come to America typifying refugee movements in general. The theoretically significant point is that although refugees experience more intensely the fear and uncertainty confronting all immigrants, and thus may exhibit a heightened gratitude for the sanctuary of the host society, this may be outweighed by the involuntary character of the act of migration from the homeland. If so, the interview testimony should suggest ambivalence regarding the Laotians' commitment to America. As it happens, when it comes to the subject of allegiance, the responses that follow are anything but tepid. Despite good reasons to expect otherwise, the Laotians' status as refugees does not appear to diminish the high esteem in which the host society is held.

The ensuing discussion consists of two major sections. First, in order to establish the political context from which Laotians have emerged, a modicum of historical background is presented. Second, the integrity of the thesis is examined in light of the testimony of Laotian refugees. In order that the reader might associate particular respondents with their basic social characteristics, a biographical schedule has been included in Appendix A. A number appears in parentheses after each quotation in part two of this chapter. By referring to the same number in the biographical schedule, the reader can formulate a demographic sketch of the author of the quotation without betraying the promise of anonymity. Appendix B describes the construction of the research project and includes a consideration of the representativeness of the population group under study.

The Historical Background

Laos's experience with democracy, indeed with self-government at all, has been both brief and incomplete. The characteristic principles of the democratic ethos have not defined the essence of the Laotian political tradition, nor, for the most part, have they been regarded as normative by the Laotian citizenry. In the context of the present study's concerns, this general unfamiliarity with the precepts and practice of democracy is an important point to note. Laotians would seem to be just the type of immigrants to challenge the American political consensus, thus undermine the democratic order; certainly they could not have learned many of the democratic virtues in the homeland.

If a single theme may be said to run through Laotian history, it must be that of foreign intervention. Since the fourteenth-century establishment of the Laotian kingdom of Lan Xang, rarely has Laos been free to develop in an independent manner. Strictly speaking, the entity that is presently called Laos did not exist until the first decade of the twentieth century, pieced together by way of French imperialism. Before then, Laos was little more than a geographical expression, divided into a complex array of small principalities serving as vassal states to more powerful Southeast Asian neighbors, Vietnam and Thailand in particular. Given its traditionally prone political position, Laos afforded little resistance to European colonialists. Concerned with the British presence in Burma, and ostensibly having been invited by the king of Luang Prabang (one of the Laotian principalities) to protect his country from Thai expansionism, France readily asserted official control of Laos in 1893, thereby adding to Indochinese acquisitions in Vietnam and Cambodia.[1]

Save for a brief Japanese interregnum, French imperial authority was maintained in Laos until 1954. By this time the Vietnamese factor in Laotian politics had once again become salient. With the support and tutelage of the Communist Party of Vietnam, a Laotian communist movement centering on an armed resistance organization, the Pathet Lao, began operations in Laos. With the assistance of the Viet Minh, by the early 1950s the Pathet Lao had assumed control of northeastern Laos, establishing itself as a force to be accommodated in plans for an independent Lao state.

The Geneva Conference of 1954, through which the French formally withdrew from Indochina, permitted the Pathet Lao a certain autonomy in the provinces under its control pending full participation in an independent Royal Lao Government (RLG). Yet over the next twenty years all three attempts to create an integrated state met with failure.

Each coalition arrangement broke down amidst mutual recriminations and mistrust, leading to an escalation of the civil war between the RLG and its communist adversaries.

As the French withdrew from Indochina, the United States moved to fill the vacuum. Motivated by cold war considerations, America threw its weight behind the anticommunist forces in the Vietnamese conflict; Laos quickly became an integral part of this Second Indochinese War. In an attempt to cripple North Vietnamese military operations as well as undermine the communist insurgency in Laos itself, the United States began to conduct a secret Laotian campaign. To that end, the Central Intelligence Agency created a guerrilla force among Hmong and Yeo tribesmen living in the mountainous regions of Laos, an effort extended by American bombing raids on Laotian territory, particularly the Ho Chi Minh Trail. More conspicuous were the transfer payments meant to complement these operations, the United States channelling millions of dollars of military aid to the Royal Lao Army, while providing further humanitarian assistance to the hundreds of thousands of Laotian victims of the war. Having in this manner become a central prop of the Laotian government, America's withdrawal from Southeast Asia under the terms of the 1973 Geneva agreement promised the demise of the RLG. By December of 1975, the forces of the Pathet Lao had claimed the victory, inaugurating the Lao People's Democratic Republic (LPDR).

Foreign interests continue to determine the political disposition of Laos. Since 1975 the Vietnamese and Laotian governments have professed to have a "special relationship," and on both the level of party and government a commonality of purpose and action is displayed. In part, this unity of approach is a product of the historical indebtedness of the Laotian communists to their counterparts in Vietnam. Until recently, the connection was made manifest by the scale of the Vietnamese presence in Laos. By one account, in the early 1980s fifty thousand troops, six thousand civilian advisers with key posts in Laotian government ministries, and eight hundred secret police seconded by Hanoi were stationed in Laos.[2] And although this contingent has since been significantly reduced (estimates of the number of Vietnamese in Laos, circa 1990, vary between ten thousand and zero),[3] the explanation has as much to do with Vietnam's economic difficulties and its desire to normalize relations with China and Thailand as with advancing Laotian political autonomy.

In the precolonial era, Laotian governments were monarchical in form, absolutist in theory, but typically decentralized in practice. Advised by a council of ministers drawn exclusively from those of noble birth, the king was recognized as the source of preponderant political power. The government's presence at the regional level was maintained by district chiefs, officials of aristocratic descent who were sometimes autocratic in their own right. A mandarinate based on merit, staffed by commoners with the requisite qualifications, filled out the remainder of the political structure. In principle, the monarch wielded absolute authority; all land belonged to the king, and all public officials were accountable to him and served at his pleasure. The king's legitimacy derived both from his royal lineage and from his position as protector and interpreter of the Buddhist faith. Yet all in all, the hand of the central government rested quite lightly on the Laotian people. Most kings ruled in a benign and paternalistic manner and in any case were prevented by inadequate communication links with the periphery from becoming absolutist in fact. For this reason, one historian has described the traditional Laotian political system as "quasi-feudal."[4]

By grafting colonial institutions on to preexisting governmental forms, French authorities contributed to the political consolidation of Laos. Ultimate political responsibility in the colonial period rested in the hands of French ministers at the pinnacle of the bureaucratic hierarchy. These were relatively few in number—by 1940 less than six hundred French colonial officials were administering a country of more than one million inhabitants.[5] At the subaltern grades of the civil service, French-speaking and French-educated Vietnamese officials were most often employed, French-educated Laotians gradually coming to occupy only the lowest rungs on the bureaucratic ladder. It is true that under the French several of the Lao princely houses lost their official standing—only the royal family of Luang Prabang retained its status. Still, France preserved many of the customary channels of Laotian government, generally placing value on the political savvy of indigenous elites, particularly those at the local levels of administration.[6] With respect to Laotian society at large, the French did institute a few changes, most notably abolishing slavery and introducing the direct ownership of land by commoners. But save the imposition of taxes that could fall quite heavily on the Lao peasantry, especially on ethnic minorities, under colonial rule the lives of most Laotians proceeded much as before.[7] If the French left a lasting imprint on Laotian society, it was more in the gallicization of a segment of the Lao elite than in the legacy of specific policies.

Prior to their departure, French administrators helped articulate the structure of government for an independent Laos. The Royal Lao Government had its genesis in the constitution of 1947, a joint French-Laotian creation that determined that Laos was to be a constitutional and democratic monarchy within the French Union.

Under the constitutional dispensation, the king of Luang Prabang was made head of state, the government was to be led by a prime minister and cabinet accountable to a popularly elected bicameral legislature, an independent judiciary was established, and the system of French administrative decentralization was maintained. Buddhism was recognized as the religion of state, the king retaining his position as keeper of the faith.

Yet the practice of politics in an independent Laos was far from the democratic ideal. Constitutional aspirations to the contrary, elections had little impact on the conduct of public affairs, political parties behaved more as special interest groups than as representatives of a broadly based public opinion, and the autonomy of provincial and local officials was highly restricted. Political decisionmaking was dominated by a handful of French-trained Lao politicians, frequently members of one of the traditional Lao princely clans, to whom the legislature readily deferred. Nor was experience in democratic methods assisted by the numerous coups and countercoups afflicting the RLG or by the persistent civil war that eventually concluded in the assumption of power by the Pathet Lao.

Although the government of the Lao People's Democratic Republic constitutes a sharp departure from Laotian political tradition, most expressly in the abolition of the monarchy, continuities can be found. For instance, under the LPDR the Buddhist clergy and Buddhist ceremonial life have been preserved, although transformed in a manner consonant with Marxist ideology.[8] Until lately, however, the LPDR has been by its own description a Marxist-Leninist state, whose political institutions suggest old-order Soviet inspiration, and where political decisions are taken according to the principle of democratic centralism.

As one observer remarks, "Three basic elements permeate the administrative and institutional structures of Laos: the Party which directs; the government which manages; and the mass organizations which execute."[9] The Lao People's Revolutionary Party (LPRP) constitutes the core of the LPDR's political system, the party determining government policy and leading party officials making up the governing elite. The provincial and local tiers of government, while possessing a measure of independence, are likewise subject to central party control through revolutionary committees associated with the LPRP. Similarly, popular elections for district, provincial, and national councils—first held in 1988 and 1989—have been subject to party guidance, the LPRP selecting the majority of nominees from party membership rolls even while generally observing the norms of multiple candidacies and secret balloting. The government is headed by a president who serves as presiding officer of the seventy-nine-member Supreme People's Council.

The council is charged with producing a constitution for the LPDR, and though a draft document was made public in 1990, as yet no new constitution has come into effect. In the interim, the council functions as the LPDR's legislature, currently called the Supreme People's Assembly. The judiciary is also incomplete, presently a combination of local "people's courts" to which the Supreme Court has been added. The Lao Front for National Construction rounds out the formal political structure, operating as an umbrella group for the various social and political organizations promoting national solidarity under communist auspices, and whose approval has been necessary for all candidates for election.[10]

It is the establishment and operation of the LPDR that have triggered the outflow of refugees from Laos. Between 1975 and 1991 approximately 346,000 Laotians left for Thai refugee camps, an exodus of approximately ten percent of Laos' entire population.[11] For many of these, the trauma of displacement was already known. As the Indochinese conflict produced an estimated 600,000 to 700,000 refugees within Laos during the 1960s and early 1970s, the post-1975 migration may be understood as the culmination of a longer and all the more tragic sequence of population movements.[12]

The refugees' reasons for leaving fall into three general categories. First, a number of individuals have abandoned Laos because of their association with the Royal Lao Government and its struggle against the Pathet Lao. Many of the earliest refugees were RLG ministers and leading civil servants as well as high-ranking officers in the RLG military. These groups were joined by tribal minorities, most notably the Hmong, who had been mobilized as anti–Pathet Lao guerrillas by American advisers.[13]

The perceived oppressiveness of the LPDR has been a further motive for flight. In part, such sentiments are related to the severity with which the LPDR initially sought to deal with opposition. Wishing to assert its authority as quickly as possible, the new regime moved to purge the army and government of any rightist remnants, sending such individuals for undetermined periods to "seminars" or reeducation camps in remote areas of the countryside, places where hard labor was the order of the day. One analyst claims that of 120,000 RLG soldiers and civil servants, 70,000 were either in reeducation camps or prison by the late 1970s.[14] But beyond this, refugees have expressed more general fears: the indeterminate nature of a government operating without constitutional restraint, the LPDR's inability to tolerate dissent, the political stigma attached to anyone even remotely associated with the RLG, and an often arbitrary and harsh dispensation of justice. All of these elements have given the LPDR a capricious quality prompting numerous Laotians to quit their homeland.

Finally, Laotian refugees have migrated in response to economic circumstances. Soon after coming to power, the government of the LPDR effected economic transformations that many Laotians found disagreeable in the extreme, including the imposition of price controls, new taxes, restrictions on the sale of farm produce, the nationalization of manufacturing concerns, and a system of labor conscription. Perhaps the most far-reaching of these innovations was an ambitious program of agricultural collectivization, a policy whose success, given the resistance of the Laotian peasantry, has been halting at best.[15] And although the LPDR has forsaken much of its early economic agenda, having increasingly turned to the market and privatization as the most fruitful means to socialist ends, prosperity has not been forthcoming. Laos remains one of the poorest countries in the world, with a per capita gross national product, according to 1988 World Bank estimates, of U.S. $180.[16] Industrial development is in its infancy, manufacturing accounting for less than six percent of the gross domestic product in the mid-1980s and employing less than one percent of the work force.[17] Even though the government has recently claimed self-sufficiency in food production, economic modernization has been inhibited by woefully inadequate transportation and communication networks. Moreover, basic commodities such as medicine are in extremely short supply, as are qualified physicians and other health personnel, factors contributing to Laos's high infant mortality rate (151 deaths per 1,000 deliveries) and low average life expectancy (fifty years old).[18] Confronted with such a precarious economic existence, many refugees have left the country in search of simple material sustenance.

Virtually all Laotian refugees first enter Thailand in search of asylum. Considered illegal immigrants by the Thai government, most make their way as soon as possible to one of the United Nations assisted refugee camps. There they can regain legal status as displaced persons in the eyes of Thai authorities and as refugees according to the United Nations High Commission for Refugees (UNHCR). Yet reaching the camps does not automatically bring relief from anxiety. In the first instance, life there is not uniformly amiable, conditions varying with respect to size, construction, and amenities of the compounds. And on average, at least through the mid-1980s, refugees might expect to remain in one of these holding centers for at least two to five years before gaining permission to be relocated overseas.[19] Furthermore, the Thai government has been a grudging host. Worried by a drop in resettlement, over the last few years Thai officials have become more strict concerning the disposition of Indochinese refugees on Thai soil.[20] Consequently, as of 1 July 1985, all asylum seekers have been subject to formal eligibility tests carried out by Thai authorities as monitored by UNHCR observers, a procedure reaffirmed under provision of the Comprehensive Plan of Action—the convention on refugee policy signed by seventy-six countries in 1989; individuals failing to qualify are either repatriated under UNHCR protection or housed indefinitely in specially designated camps with no possibility of third country emigration.[21]

More than half of all Laotian refugees have been resettled in the United States: an estimated 202,602 by the end of fiscal year 1989 (see Table 5.1). Laotian entry to the United States is characterized by three demographic waves, the first peaking in 1976; a second, much larger wave reaching its apex in 1980; with a third wave, intermediate in size, cresting in 1987.[22] Until 1980, Lao refugees were the beneficiaries of the U.S. Attorney General's parole authority. This granted special permission to enter the country apart from the normal quota system of immigrant selection. Since 1980, however, Laotians have been covered by the terms of the Refugee Act, legislation establishing a more generous and uniform admission procedure for refugees of all countries. Most Laotians have come to America by virtue of this special dispensation; by contrast, between July 1974 and June 1989, barely 1,900 Laotians were admitted under the quota system, and before 1975 only a handful of Lao immigrants had established permanent residence in the United States.[23]

The U.S. State Department acknowledges ethnic distinctions among refugees from Laos, though it collapses them into just two categories. Of the Laotian influx, approximately forty percent are "highland" Lao, the largest component being Hmong. The remaining sixty percent are classified as "lowland" or ethnic Lao.[24] It is the characteristics of this latter contingent, historically the politically and culturally dominant group in Laos, that the present chapter will explore.

Laotian Refugees and the American Creed

Laotian refugees are not fully agreed on the merits of the American creed. While possessing a certain esteem for the values of freedom and capitalism, perhaps a natural reaction of individuals whose flight is motivated by a desire to escape authoritarian government and economic hardship, the refugees' appreciation of the remaining elements of the creed—individualism, equality, participatory democracy—is incomplete. Even in the case of freedom and capitalism, Laotians understand these concepts in a fashion that distinguishes

TABLE 5.1 Laotian Refugee Migration to the United States, Fiscal Years 1975-1989

Year	Total Number of Laotian Refugees
1975	800
1976	10,200
1977	400
1978	8,000
1979	30,200
1980	55,500
1981	19,300
1982	9,400
1983	2,900
1984	7,200
1985	4,724
1986	11,130
1987	15,508
1988	14,561
1989	12,779

Sources: FY1975 through FY1984, Linda Gordon, "Southeast Asian Refugee Migration to the United States," Paper prepared for the Conference on Asia-Pacific Immigration to the United States, September 20-25, 1984, East-West Population Institute, Honolulu, Hawaii, p. 29; FY1985 through FY1989, U.S. Immigration and Naturalization Service, 1989 Statistical Yearbook of the Immigration and Naturalization Service (Washington, D.C.: G.P.O., 1990), p. 52.

them from the host society. Such a lack of consensus is not remarkable. If Americans are "born Lockean," Laotians are not. Fidelity to the creed requires conversance; most of the Laotian participants in the study simply have not lived in America long enough to have had sufficient exposure. So, although all of those interviewed share a desire to affirm the value system necessary to become fully American, the political virtues they applaud often deviate from the American norm.

For Laotian refugees, freedom is the sine qua non of the American creed. In a generic sense, of course, freedom's absence is what compels all journeys from the homeland. Emigrants calculate that they can no longer lead a life of their own choosing, that the essential freedoms necessary to the pursuit of a life plan have been denied, indeed that a future of their own making has been denied. In comparison, the emigrant's destination is pregnant with possibilities. In the first instance, simply because it represents a new beginning, the country of resettlement may appear as a repository of lost freedoms. But as America is a society in which liberal principles are regarded as normative, the effect is magnified. Several Laotians explicitly identified freedom with the United States. One respondent testified that the very word *freedom* caused him to think of "the American government who has given us the privilege of doing what we want" (18). Other immigrants conveyed similar sentiments:

> I think I am just like everybody else in that the thing I like most about America is freedom. Here we have complete freedom, to say what we want to say, to think what we want to think, and to live the lifestyle we want to live without restriction.
> Everyone knew that in Laos you could not do what you wanted to; you could not say what you wanted to say. In Laos you worked like a machine or like a slave. If the communists said you had to do it, you had to do it; you had no choice. (15)

> In America, if you want to do something, or you need something, and you have the ability, you can go ahead and do it with no questions asked. Back in Laos if you wanted to do something, even if you had the ability to do it, you might not be allowed. Before you could do anything, the communists would examine your family history and your former connections. If you had connections with the former government, or if you had not been to a seminar and taught by them, you might not be allowed to do what you wished. (11)

Yet many refugees confessed that the freedom to be had in the United States was something of a mixed blessing, American society being too indulgent. Freedom of children from parental authority was considered symptomatic of this. Several Laotians agreed with the following analysis:

There may be too much freedom in America, especially among young people. I don't think it affects older people as much as it does young men and women. For instance, children growing up in school in America hear so much about freedom that they feel they can do what they want to when they are fifteen, sixteen, or seventeen years old. Even Lao children do this; they don't want to obey their parents, and they talk about getting apartments and living alone. This is very different from Lao culture. (24)

More politically pertinent, however, is the connection that refugees drew between freedom and licence. On this view, too much freedom allowed for criminal activity. One of the respondents attested, "One of the things I don't like about America is that this society has so much freedom that people abuse it. Many people drink too much and break the law. Or they fight or steal and carouse and do things that are breaking the law. It is easy to do in this country" (29). And echoing such perceptions, a fellow immigrant noted that "sometimes the rules are too loose. In Chicago there are all kinds of people who just live on food stamps and public aid; they don't do any work. And they steal and they rob and they do all kinds of bad things. They have too much freedom" (15). This concern for freedom and law-abidingness may well suggest the lifeboat perspective. While grateful for the enhanced freedom to be found in America, Laotian immigrants simultaneously vow to exercise that freedom in a responsible manner and only within the bounds of the law, condemning those who do not do so.

The great majority of Laotians declared the freedom they sought in America was not without limit. When they addressed the issue of freedom of expression, such boundaries were clearly demarcated. For instance, several refugees were reluctant to agree that in the United States citizens should have the freedom to demonstrate against the government. One respondent felt the government should be able to stop demonstrations, commenting, "After all, the American government gives people enough to eat and to live on. Why should people complain about the government when it has been good to them?" (30). Another believed that "if people go beyond the confines of government policy, and say too many bad things about the government, they should be punished" (7). And still another thought that at least Laotians "should not do anything like that" since "the country has been good to us and let us resettle here" (25).

Other refugees were less restrictive than this, recognizing the freedom to oppose the government as a liberty central among

American political convictions. Nevertheless, with only one exception, the Laotians found it impossible to be equally charitable to all political perspectives.[25] Fear of communist mischief was still acute:

> Sometimes there is too much freedom even in [American] politics. For example, people can say what they want to about the government; this creates a lack of stability. . . . If there are too many people saying bad things about the government, a group like the communists can come in and influence those people and overthrow the government. (15)

> In America, people have the authority to demonstrate against the government. If someone did not like Reagan they could carry a sign over their head, or go out in the street and scream their disapproval. You could not do that in another country. America gives you that freedom.

> But communists should not be allowed to speak against the government because they are so terrible. I think the government should stop anyone who is trying to promote communism in this country. In fact, if communists were on the street making speeches and trying to convince Americans to become communist, I myself would be willing to try and stop them. (4)

> Ordinarily the American government should not punish someone who is making a speech because that is the freedom we have in America. . . . [Yet] I know this country does not like communism. I don't think someone should be allowed to promote communism in this country. They should be judged and not allowed to live here. Exile them. (16)

Of course, when expressing viewpoints such as these, Laotian immigrants may reflect American convictions more than they know, the threat of communism being a familiar shibboleth of American politics. Indeed, far from their different cultural background undermining the American political consensus, on this score one may speak of a natural resonance between the refugees and their hosts.

Unlike orthodox adherents to the American creed, however, those individuals interviewed seemed unconcerned with the possibility that the government might wrongfully intervene in their lives. This does not mean they were willing to give public officials carte blanche, their experience in Laos ruling it out. Still, the exercise of the American government's authority was usually viewed in a benign manner, in some cases not merely a necessary evil but a positive good. Without the intervention of the American government in its citizens' lives, one respondent feared that "the country would be in trouble" and "the communists might even take over" (10). Another individual cited moral instruction among the tasks of public officials, believing that citizens must be "taught to do good" by the government and should "constantly do what they are told to do" (11). And a further interviewee claimed that "the more involved the government is in the citizens' lives, the better," it being for the "benefit of the people" that the government "know about the people and their needs" (5). Such responses betray the suspicion of political authority that is a hallmark of the American political culture, yet they may be expected considering the circumstances of the refugee. For the individual who has achieved solace via the auspices of an accommodating host government, it may be difficult to imagine that the activities of that government could be anything but obliging.

Laotians paid special homage to the economic freedom implicit in capitalism, the freedom to accumulate without fear of unwarranted expropriation. "In America," one respondent maintained, "you are not breaking the law if you make money. You can buy a car, you can buy a boat, you can buy anything you want to and there are no restrictions" (26). Refugees often appeared to subscribe to the "boot-straps" theory of economic development. Many exuded confidence in the ability of an individual to become prosperous, provided he or she was willing to be diligent. There seemed to be two dimensions to this faith in the capitalist road to success. First, according to most of those interviewed it was possible for the average person to "get ahead" in America. One respondent explained that "every person who is now in an important position had to start somewhere. He had to start at the bottom and work his way up. He then becomes a good example. People look at that and say, 'Well, if he could start at the bottom and work his way up, so can I'" (12). And a fellow countryman expressed his belief that "anybody who is industrious, works hard, and studies hard can always succeed in America" (26).

But the corollary to the notion that America provides an environment in which it is "easy to make money" (6) is that poverty is largely the fault of the poor. According to a number of Laotians, the poor frequently do not take advantage of the plentiful opportunities available in America. One refugee claimed that "as concerns the poor people in this country, I assume that they want to be poor. This country is full of opportunity to do whatever one wants. . . . If [the poor] wanted to, they could go ask for training and improve themselves" (8). A countryman observed that the poor are poor "because they do not work. They do not do anything. In America . . . there are all kinds of factories and businesses that will hire people. If you really look for a job you can find one and take care of yourself. You don't have to be poor in America" (25). Another respondent made a similar point, using an illustration from his workplace:

I think poor people are poor because they don't work. Where I work, in a furniture upholstery factory, a young man came to work. He was given a staple gun, just like me, but he worked much more slowly than I did. I could do four or five chairs while in the same time he could do only one. Well, he was so lazy and worked so slowly that soon the boss fired him. He went on to get a job somewhere else where he only gets $3.00 or $4.00 an hour—a lower paying job. And as soon as he is out of work, he goes around to the bars and spends his paycheck. So, he has not had enough money to pay his rent, and he just sleeps in his car in a parking lot somewhere. So here is a poor man without enough money to pay his rent, but he is poor because he is lazy. (29)

Granted, several refugees were not as sanguine concerning their ability to achieve material success. These individuals noted that other factors beyond hard work can enter in to the prosperity equation—natural intelligence, family history, and educational background. And others claimed that life was by no means easy in America, that the demands of the workplace could be onerous. Yet such observations should not be taken as evidence of deep-seated discontent with the American economic system. Even among these refugees, opportunities for advancement in America were readily acknowledged.

Comparative criteria of judgment were apparent when refugees were asked about the propriety of government redistributing wealth. Again, immigrants professed fidelity to capitalist principles—that government should not seek to intervene in the operation of the free market. Predictably, the experience of the homeland, specifically the communist government, influenced responses. "In America," one refugee remarked, "hard work pays; you get what you work for, not like a communist country. There, everything goes to the government. If I work hard, it won't go to my family but to someone else. So why should I work hard at all?" (14). Another contended that it was absolutely wrong for the government to compel the rich to share some of their money with the poor, explaining that "it would not be right to make the rich give money to the poor in a country which boasts it is a democracy. If you start forcing people to do things like this, then you have communism, not democracy" (16).

Admittedly, not all those interviewed thought the free enterprise system virtuous in every respect, noting that some individuals might be "more interested in having things for themselves than using the money to help the country's economy" (3). Yet many deflected the reproach of avarice by pointing out that material success benefits more than just the individual earning the money.

In the first instance, the accumulation of wealth might be used to become self-sufficient, thereby relieving others of the burden for one's care. One interviewee was convinced that it was necessary to "make a lot of money and put it away for your old age in this country" (16), while a compatriot encouraged people to make as much money as possible so that they "can take care of themselves . . . and don't have to ask for any aid from the government" (25). Relatedly, interviewees often praised private charitable efforts to help the less fortunate. On at least two occasions, credence was even given to "trickle down" economic theories, the observation being made that affluent individuals could open factories and employ those who were impoverished. But perhaps most remarkably, the obligations of wealth were also said to extend to the civic arena. Clearly wishing to be thought worthy residents of their newly adopted country, in language uncharacteristic of most capitalists, several Laotians declared themselves willing taxpayers:

> People should be allowed to make as much money as they want. For example, I pay federal taxes, so when I work the government gets money, money which it uses to look after its people. Also, in this country people put their money in a bank and the bank can gain interest on the money, and that too is good. It is not like in Laos where people put their money under their pillow or buried it somewhere. Here they put it in the bank which uses it to help create a better country and helps America to make progress. (29)
>
> Making as much money as we want to is one of the privileges we have as Americans. As long as we earn all the money that we earn honestly, it is okay to earn it. The more money that you make, the more taxes you can give to the government, and the more taxes you give to the government, the more the government is able to progress economically and protect us from invasion. (15)

If such perspectives are to be squared with those concerning the impropriety of government-initiated redistribution, the government's care for its citizens must be conceived of in a minimal fashion, perhaps in terms of the maintenance of internal order and external security. In fact, refugees frequently suggested the role of the government as police officer and protector, notions complementary to America's Lockean creed.

Only intermittently, however, did refugee attitudes pertaining to individualism reflect the American ideological perspective. Laotians were generally agreed on the merits of economic individualism, even though most had at one time been the beneficiaries of public assistance. But the consensus among the refugees who addressed this issue was that welfare should be extended only to those in dire straits and in any case should be abandoned as soon as possible:

> In the case of refugees I think that it could be wrong if the government gives too much money to refugees or if refugees receive too much for free. When they are given too much they become lazy and they don't want to work. . . . There should be some kind of policy or some kind of plan where people would be encouraged to work and to make more money. . . .
>
> I know cases, for instance, where refugees get public aid and that public aid is more than they would get if they went and did a job for $3.35 an hour. So they can sit at home and not do any work and become very lazy and get their public aid. There should be some kind of program or a plan where they are forced to go out and get the job for $3.35 an hour whether they want it or not. (15)

> I think the government should help [the poor] at the times when they really have need, but I don't think they should give it to them all their lives. One person sees another person getting food stamps and the thinks, "Oh, I don't have to work either. I can get food stamps if I don't work." And soon there are a lot of people not working and they all want to get food stamps. (12)

Personal reputation may well be a consideration in this antipathy to public aid, welfare a badge of economic failure:

> I want all Lao people to get off public aid. Public aid should be looked at as a temporary thing, for when you really need it. Like when the first Lao people came, they don't know any English, they don't know any way to find a job, they don't have any car; the only way to survive is on public aid. . . .
>
> But public aid is a degrading thing. It is a shame to go in there with paper money [food stamps] to hand it to a checker and they look at you like you are a dummy. We have a lot of pride. It is understandable; we can excuse welfare when you are here for the first two or three months or so. After that, if you are still in the welfare office, then you look lazy. (5)

If government is responsible in more than a minimal sense for the immigrant's economic situation, according to the Laotians it is in the provision of opportunities for prosperity. In general, refugees expressed optimism concerning their ability for economic self-sustenance and prosperity in America, as long as they could avail themselves of sufficient opportunities to succeed. If the appropriate prospects presented themselves, especially educational ones, their own efforts might accomplish the rest:

I believe the government needs to give people the opportunities for them to develop. For me, what I would like to see more of is the education program geared toward the disadvantaged group of people to give them self-esteem and hope, and tell them they themselves can get out of the ghettos or the situation they are in. (5)

In this respect, Laotians are indeed devotees of Lockean individualism, acknowledging the importance of not becoming an economic encumbrance to government.

Nevertheless, expressions of self-interest to the exclusion of broader corporate responsibilities, arguably the tendency of the American national culture, are generally absent in the testimony of those interviewed. On a few occasions Laotians attested to having the intensity of their commitment reduced by the ingratitude of those they had tried to assist. At other times, sentiments of compassion were qualified by an inability to assist others materially; such refugees indicated that if they had the means they would be happy to help, but their own poverty diminished their capacity to do so. Nevertheless, most responses revealed an acute sense of social obligation, a feeling that was particularly earnest when other Laotians were in question:

I certainly do feel a sense of responsibility for Lao people. When they can't go places and they don't know how to get around and do things on their own, I feel responsible to help them. When they are not doing well or are not doing the right thing in this country I feel I should advise or help them. And when they lack money or lack the things they need, I should be willing to share with them whatever money I can share with them. I should advise them in how to live so that they can be a good person, and so that they in turn can help someone else. (11)

We should do everything we can to help people around us, and should take responsibility for those people. If we don't take responsibility for the people around us, soon they will hate us . . . as individuals who have more than they do. That leads to bad government and is how communists come in and take over a country.

I feel a special responsibility for Lao people, especially for those who need me to interpret for them. Maybe they have to go to the hospital and they can't explain things to a doctor . . . and they have to have someone help them. And I also feel responsible if I see refugees who have just come to this country and really don't have enough food. I feel responsible to share with them whatever I have so that they will have enough to eat. (9)

All the same, a minority of respondents doubted that selflessness was uniformly a Lao cultural trait. For them, America's powers of acculturation, in particular the premium placed on personal autonomy, may already have taken hold:

> I would like to help other Lao people. But since Laotian refugees have come [to the United States] a lot of things have changed. They have all gone their own way. And if you say too much to Lao people, or try to change them in any way, or are in contact with them too much, sometimes they say, "This is a free country and there is nobody over us here; we are all free to do what we want." So people tend to go and do their own thing, and are not concerned too much with other Lao people. They are just interested in living separate lives. (23)

There is less evidence, however, that Laotian immigrants speak the language of political individualism. That the individual stands at the center of the political system, or that the common citizen is ultimately the arbiter of political right and wrong, is a principle contrary to the substance of Laotian political tutelage. As previously noted, the traditional Lao political structure was quasi-feudal in form, if not always function, the bailiwick of princes and mandarins little subject to popular pressure. French colonial authorities reinforced such conventions, in part by superimposing imperial institutions on preexistent Laotian hierarchies. When independence was granted in 1954, despite a democratic constitution Laotian political practice remained far from democratic. A small elite was the locus of decisionmaking authority, elections and partisan politics doing little to empower the general population. And while the communist government of Laos has attempted to politicize the citizenry, a commitment to democratic centralism does not easily permit recognition of a citizen's independent political power. Doubtless the cumulative effect of Lao socialization experiences has been to dissuade refugees from thinking in individualistic terms regarding the American political system. It should not be surprising, then, that ready submission to political authority is a featured text of the Laotians' testimony, a theme that will be more fully developed below. At this stage suffice it to note that the Laotians perceived the ambit of the ordinary citizen to be highly restricted, rarely including the role of political initiator. Duties pertaining to citizenship were emphasized, not assertions of individual rights.

As to the egalitarian aspects of the American creed—legal, social, and political—Laotian support is similarly uneven. Affirming part of that creed, most refugees did evince unqualified optimism in the United States as a country of equal opportunity:

I think that if a person really puts their heart into a project or into work, and they really have a goal and work toward that goal, they can reach it. For instance, many refugees who have come to the States have determined that they were going to be somebody like a doctor or lawyer, or something like that, and have reached their goal because they are just determined that is what they are going to do. (19)

The privilege is given for all of us to work in America. The government never says to us, "Oh, you are a child of a very poor man so you can't have a good job or a high-paying job." You could be a child of a poor man and still get a high-paying job. . . . [In America] a poor person is not told that he can't have a position in the government just because he was born into a poor class of people. And a farmer isn't told that he can't have an education. . . . [When] I look back to my own country, in the past it was only the family of the government officials that ever got the good job or got the opportunities and education. (18)

[In America] everybody has an opportunity to accomplish their goals; no one tries to stop them. If my goal is to become rich, I can achieve that goal. Even an ordinary person in America can have the opportunity to buy a brand new car. In Laos there wasn't that kind of equality. If you were a trishaw driver in Laos, you would probably be that forever; there was certainly no continuing education over there! If you stopped school, you could never go back again. You started working and that was it. But over here after you graduate from high school, you can work part time and go to college in the evening. There is more opportunity here. (14)

Furthermore, Laotians expressed a good deal of confidence in the impartial administration of American law, a majority claiming the police would treat them no differently than native-born Americans. Admittedly there was a certain ambiguity in some of the testimony on this point. Thus one respondent contended, "If I was a citizen I am sure the police would treat me the same as anybody else. But as long as I don't know the laws and rules of this country, then perhaps he might not treat me the same." (21) Others served notice of what they believed to be ethnic prejudice:

There are times that a policeman may not treat you fairly. My wife recently had an accident where a truck hit her. Because she was Asian the policeman went to the truck driver and wrote the report saying that my wife was at fault. But it was not her fault. When the boss of the place where she works found out about it, she contested my wife's ticket. My wife's name was cleared in court, and it was definitely proven that it was not her fault. But the policeman had not talked to her at all; he had just talked to the driver because it was easier for him. (3)

Yet to put an optimistic gloss on this particular instance, the injustice may derive as much from the officer pursuing a path of least resistance as from more fundamental cultural antagonisms. If so, the Laotians' overall faith in the American system of justice may be—and given the general tenor of the testimony on this point, is in fact—preserved. From the immigrant's perspective, a more thorough application of the principle of legal equality may accompany greater knowledge of American law and of the English language.

As concerns social equality, the evidence seems less open to interpretation. Laotian refugees appeared reluctant to abandon completely the deferential relationships embedded in their cultural tradition:

> I see that Americans do not show any special respect for a person of higher status, not like Lao people. The Lao respect those who are "over them" more than Americans do. This has to do with good manners; children should have good manners toward older people, just as adults should have good manners to those who are over them. (22)

This attitude was particularly apparent in answers given to questions concerning the propriety of social status distinctions. Superior knowledge seemed the key criterion of social differentiation:

> I think that as concerns a lawyer or a doctor, or someone who is in that social rank, we should respect that person more than just an ordinary person. They have studied much more than we have. From the very beginning in our Lao culture we are taught to respect the person who is over us and who is more capable than we are. (19)

> When you talk about equality you have to recognize that people may be created equal but [that] their knowledge and ability is not always the same. There are some people who have more knowledge and ability. For instance, you. You may have more knowledge and ability than I do. Maybe our standard of living is the same, and we are equal as far as what we do and how we act. But when it comes to knowledge and ability, if you have more than I do, I have to look up to you and respect you. (11)

On the other hand, the interviews did reveal that some of the status distinctions maintained in Laos have been eroded in America. One individual drew attention to this as concerns the Hmong tribespeople in America:

> In Laos, the Hmong people were regarded as barbarians or slaves living in the mountains. The Lao were the ruling class, the people who lived

in the lowlands and the cities, who had education and governed the country. The Lao did not respect the Hmong nor show them any consideration. But even in Laos the Hmong were very industrious and intelligent; they simply had no opportunity for education. But in America the Hmong have prospered and have surpassed the Lao in what they have been able to do. (4)

Equality's political dimension points to the essence of democracy— the equality of decisionmaking influence. Most of the refugees were at least conversant with the meaning of democracy as the American creed would have it. In a few cases Laotian respondents claimed not to know the meaning of democracy, but usually they made some reference to the idea of a popular component in the corporate decisionmaking process. Indeed, democracy often seemed to be a cluster concept for all that was laudable; "freedom of choice," "opportunity," "honesty," and "goodness" were several of the terms used to describe its content. Still, many Laotians argued that such notions were only appropriate when discussing the American version of democracy, not the political arrangement called democracy in Laos, whether in the precommunist or postcommunist period:

> In Laos they said it was democracy, but it was not. The country was ruled by a few people who had a lot of money and a lot of power. . . . Here in America a governor or mayor is an ordinary person who listens to the people. If he walks down the street everybody does not bow to him; they treat him as an ordinary person. This was not true in Laos. If someone was in a government position in Laos, they did not pay attention to what anyone else thought. They would just rule the country the way they wanted to; they were not willing to make changes. And if anybody spoke against that person, they would be arrested and maybe never seen again. You would not dare speak against a ruler in Laos. (23)

> Democracy means that the majority of people rule. They said they had a democracy in Laos, but what that meant was that if the communists saw there was someone who did something wrong they might put his picture on a school wall or someplace. Then they would ask the people, "Do you think this man is an enemy of the government? Do you want him killed?" And if the people said yes, then they killed him. They said that was a democracy, but that is not American democracy. That is a false kind of democracy. (29)

Such professions of democratic conviction notwithstanding, Laotians seemed to conceive of a version of democracy that Americans would hardly recognize. Among those immigrants interviewed, commitment to an abstract concept of democracy was authentic, but many were reluctant to respond too readily to the clarion call of political equality, acknowledging limits on the political power of the average citizen. It was, for example, quite possible to make improper demands on governing officials:

> The government should listen to the majority of the people, but their request should come within the confines of government policy. When the people ask the government to do something, they should not ask it to do something which is impossible or wrong, or would in any way destroy the government. The request must be made within the framework of government. Even a majority should not be allowed to ask something that is absolutely wrong according to the policy and law of the government. (4)

> There may be times that the people support some policy for selfish reasons. Maybe they don't understand what the government is trying to do. At that time the government should explain its policy to the common people so that they will understand it. . . . The government knows what it is doing even if the people don't. (27)

> Democracy means that people have a choice, that the government will not do what the people do not like. . . . [The only problem with this] is if the people of the country ask the government to do something that is not right. It would be disadvantageous if the government was trying to do what the people wanted, and the people were asking for the wrong thing. (3)

The idea that the people could be wrong does not suggest the American belief in popular sovereignty, nor does the idea that government possesses superior knowledge and insight over and above the wishes of the citizenry. Yet these beliefs are common to the refugee testimony. One respondent insisted, "We need to do what the [government] says, because after all they are the ones who rule over us. They are better than we are. They are more intelligent than we are. They know more than we do. So when they say something, we should do it" (3). Another expressed the conviction that an attitude of supplication was appropriate when making political demands, claiming that "we should ask the government permission" to do what it is that we desire, and "do what they say" (6).

Relatedly, many of those interviewed couched the relationship between government and governed in paternalistic terms—the government as a father tending to the needs of politically immature citizens:

It is absolutely necessary that the government rules in a firm manner. In the same way that a father tends to the upbringing of his children, laying down rules to guide their behavior, and seeing to their nourishment, so must government give citizens rules to guide their conduct and give them what they need. People would be lost without government. (13)

If the government lays down rules, I think we are obligated to obey them just as children are obligated to obey their parents. . . . Government gives rules and ideas to the people, and if we don't follow them, we get in trouble. Just like a child. If his parents tell him that if he plays with fire he will get burned, and he plays with fire anyway and doesn't obey the rules, he will get burned. And the same is true with the government. (11)

We must have a government that rules over the people. You can't just let the people rule over themselves; that would never work. It would be like a family. If you had children without any parents to control them, it would not be good at all. (21)

Here, then, is the most fundamental of all inegalitarian relationships used as a metaphor for the relationship between ruler and ruled.

In sum, Laotian immigrants appear to possess an uncertain commitment to the idea of equality between rulers and ruled. Again, there is little in their experience of politics in Laos to suggest that things could be otherwise.[26] One individual described the traditional Lao political ethos in these terms:

If a leader in our country wished to sit down and discuss something with common citizens, they would not all sit around a table at the same level; the leader would sit in a chair and the people would sit on the floor. And even if a person disagreed with the leader, he dare not voice that disagreement because he was afraid of the leader. . . . The governor told [the common citizen] what to do, and he had to do what he was told. People had to bow and scrape in front of the leaders; they really did not have the power to express themselves. (23)

And although the LPDR has made certain gestures in the direction of egalitarianism, Lao refugees have either left the country too quickly to be affected by these or believe that the supremacy of the Communist Party elite makes such gestures hollow:

In the Communist Party the government says the rich and poor people have the same rights and are equal, but they do not give the people, any of the people, the power to choose the government or make decisions. . . . They are afraid they would lose their power if they gave the people authority to speak up. So they control the people; they don't let the people control the government. (9)

Without much practice in its methods, the full logic of liberal democracy as yet escapes many Laotian immigrants. Consequently, their disposition to participate in American politics also remains inchoate. The very idea that participation could make a difference is too often absent.

Participatory Orientations Among Laotian Refugees

Immigrants, it has been assayed, will tend to be quiescent citizens, a passivity insulating the political system against the potentially disruptive consequences of an incomplete acceptance of the dominant American political ideology. This hypothesis is confirmed as regards Laotian refugees. The Laotians in the present study confessed to having only moderate political interest, even less inclination to participate actively in political affairs. To begin with, they lack the knowledge of American politics that might foster their participation. In large measure because of the cultural distance between themselves and the host society, resources that might be employed to gain political understanding are scarce. So, while cultural exoticness may indicate unfamiliarity with America's integrative political creed, a failing that on the conventional theoretical wisdom would seem to place stability at risk, it also means that for many Laotians the world of American politics is impenetrable because it is mystifying. For that reason, among others, Laotians are unlikely to be politically demanding or disruptive residents of the United States.

Lack of facility with the English language is an elementary cultural deterrent affecting Laotian refugees. More than any other factor, those interviewed cited an inability to speak and read English as an impediment to political education. "American politics is difficult for me because I don't understand all the things they say," said one respondent. "I don't know the language well enough to follow politics; somebody would have to explain to me what is going on," (23) declared another. "If I knew English better I would probably be more interested," explained still another. "I try to follow a little political news in the *Chicago Sun-Times,* but there are so many idioms it is very hard to understand" (1). Perhaps the most telling statement was made by the oldest participant in the study: "American politics is only difficult to understand because I don't know the English language," he maintained. "If it was all interpreted into Lao I probably would be able to debate them in politics, but I can't do it in English" (21). Without a sufficient knowledge of English, the world of American politics remains remote.

Disparity between the homeland's political conventions and those of the host country serves as a further cultural barrier to participation. In this case, even the political information immigrants do receive is frequently difficult to comprehend. It is not unusual, for instance, to hear accounts of immigrants who have not appeared in court, their political experience in Laos leading them to believe that bail money is a bribe to the judge for their freedom. Several Laotians explained their lack of civic sophistication in terms of the disparate political practices between America and Laos. "Most Laotians don't really understand American politics," explained one interviewee, "because there is such a tremendous difference between the actual operation of the government here as compared to Laos. They find the way American government runs very confusing" (4).

Low socioeconomic status, itself often a function of cultural exoticness, is a further hindrance to Laotian political activity. For refugees no less than native-born Americans, time is a precious commodity that must be expended if one is to take an enduring interest in political life. A majority choose to direct their energies toward more immediately gratifying activities, specifically the pursuit of economic well-being. Given that Laotians enter America with little capital, and that public agencies offer limited assistance, the drive for economic sustenance is often a full-time enterprise. Politics is in many respects the sport of a leisured class; few Laotians feel economically secure enough to participate. One refugee noted, "Our family lives day by day. We only are concerned about our children, and school, and work; we don't pay attention to anything more than that. We go to work, we get tired, and we come home. We don't worry about the government" (14). "I am not interested in politics," concurred a countryman, "because I don't have any problems that would involve politics. My own problems concern working, making a living, and taking care of my family" (20). Even if income sufficient to maintain the immigrant and his or her family is achieved (as Appendix A suggests, several Laotian families in the interview sample seem to be fairly well off), there is no guarantee that attentions will be turned toward political matters. Immigrants come to America, not to participate in politics, but to make better lives for themselves, i.e., to pursue the American dream of affluence. Once unleashed, the acquisitive impulse may leave little time for involvement in political matters.

But high socioeconomic status is no certain indicator of greater participatory inclinations for an additional reason. Unlike the native-born, among immigrants formal education in America is not necessarily correlated with income. It is entirely possible for members of a Laotian family to achieve considerable earnings without being much exposed to the American school system, an exposure that might instruct them in the basic elements of American political practice. Though this may seem a minor point, it should not be discounted. A number of Laotians echoed the sentiments of a compatriot who explained, "I don't understand American government because I have never studied anything about it. I have never studied the laws of America. All I can do is just be an ordinary person in my house who eats and sleeps. I can't be involved in politics here" (28). And while naturalized citizenship (five individuals in the interview sample had their citizenship papers) requires conversance with basic American political institutions, it is unlikely that this is an adequate substitute for the healthy doses of civic education administered in secondary schools, nor is naturalization a requirement for refugees to maintain residence in the United States. Moreover, not possessing one of the resources used to acquire political knowledge magnifies the effect of not possessing another. Without adequate language skills, for example, immigrants are unlikely to expend the limited spare time they may have to obtain political knowledge, it being simply too much of a chore. Thus Laotians are doubly impoverished, the cumulative effect being an enhanced aversion for the political world. Again, the circumstances of immigration itself suggest barriers to the procurement of political knowledge promoting participation.

To the degree that Laotians are wanting for the resources used to gain political knowledge, their sense of political efficacy will be greatly diminished. When efficacy is in doubt, immigrants are disposed to direct their attentions elsewhere; they think that if they cannot make an impact politically, why bother being concerned with politics at all? As one of the Laotians expressed it, "I am not too interested in politics right now because I don't have the power to do anything about it" (15). For reasons just indicated, information permitting successful redress of grievance as well as the appropriate skills—language in particular—used to lobby for that redress are in short supply. "I don't think I could do much [to change a harmful law]," said one, "because I am not able to express myself in English. Even when they put up a sign about voting, I really don't know what it says" (11). A compatriot agreed that "Lao people could not have much impact on the government because they don't have as much knowledge as the people who live in this country." "Besides," he observed, "the Lao are a minority race here" (30). Newness to the country was certainly a factor in all this. Many claimed they could not influence the direction of American politics, because "we are still foreigners and not powerful enough to make the government pay attention," (8) or because "we are outsiders and don't know how to influence the government yet" (20). But furthermore, little in their experience of politics in Laos suggests to the refugees that an ordinary person might make a political difference. When asked why he would be unlikely to try and change a harmful law, one refugee explained:

> I don't think I would have enough strength to do anything about it. When the communist government did things that were wrong, we would just shut our eyes and let them do it. We didn't say anything. We didn't act like we heard about it or knew anything about it. That was the best way to get along. (21)

Nevertheless, the Laotians' doubts concerning the impact of individual political action pertained to themselves, not to the wider American citizenry. In the main, the refugees expressed confidence in the ability of average Americans to effect political change and in the parallel desire of the government to listen to the demands of common citizens. This perspective seems congruent with their general attitude toward American government. As previously remarked, refugees tend to understand American democracy in idealized and idiosyncratic terms. As the guardian of "true democracy," that the United States government might completely ignore the wishes of its citizens is not a possibility the Laotians are likely to contemplate, even if citizens do not always make appropriate requests.

Participatory orientations can be affected by a variable even more fundamental. For many immigrants, and especially political refugees, the word *politics* itself carries a negative connotation. According to numerous Laotians, the concept implied corruption and falsehood, a perception informed by the homeland:

> When I think of politics I think of someone who is doing something underhanded. Most politicians try to sell themselves to you by telling you all the good things about themselves, whether or not they are true. They also make a lot of promises to the people which they don't keep. . . . In Laos the government lied to the people to try to get them to have faith in it. (9)

> Lao people say they don't want anything to do with politics because it is all a bunch of lies. The people got this idea because their leaders came to them and made all kinds of promises. But of course the leaders only were trying to promote themselves and get elected to office; once they left the village they never actually kept their promises. (13)

It should be mentioned, however, that such testimony was frequently accompanied by a disclaimer: politics Laotian-style is not necessarily reproduced in America. Organized political activism by Laotians in America may display the bad old habits of the homeland, but on the Laotian view, American politics does not suffer from the same stigma. "The difference between politics in America and politics in Laos," contended one respondent, is that "here it seems that the government tells the people what it is going to do, and is more apt to carry out what it is going to do" (1). "American government officials do not lie," agreed another. "They are too smart for that" (13). Nevertheless, the association of the political realm with the vices of the Laotian system must do little to whet the refugees' appetite for American politics:

> Many people think politics is not a good thing. When they talk about it, they say it causes trouble in the country and affects their living situations. They just don't want to have anything to do with it.
> When I think about politics, I think about when I was a student. We used to have political demonstrations and rallies, but that ended up causing us to have a lot of fear and uncertainty about the future. So even though I used to be interested in politics, I am not interested in it now. (19)

More than this, for many Laotians "politics" evokes feelings of anxiety and danger, again a reflection of the homeland experience. As the flight from the homeland was compelled by fear of the political authorities, fear of death and imprisonment, the notion of politics is understandably imbued with ominous overtones. "I was not involved in politics even in my country," said one respondent, "because I was afraid that I might get my head cut off" (29). Another confessed reluctance to talk about politics in Laos because "nobody trusts anybody there. There were people who turned in their relatives to the communist government, and fathers who had their own sons imprisoned because of their anticommunist feelings" (1). The testimony of compatriots indicates that such anxieties are not peculiar. "Playing with politics" is a dangerous game:

> I wasn't too interested in politics in Laos—most young people weren't. There was a saying in Laos: if you play around too much with politics, pretty soon politics will play around with you. What this means is that if you don't know too much about a subject and you try to get involved in it, you better be careful. You might be punished for doing something that you didn't even know was wrong. (7)

> You have to be careful when it comes to politics. I really don't know too much about it, so I have to be careful what I say. If you don't

understand it, you might be talking about some issue or some person and saying the wrong thing. In politics it can be dangerous if you don't know the whole story. After all, politics is not something to play around with or talk about without knowing what you are saying. (11)

Indeed, according to several interviewees, aversion to things political has been the value inculcated by Laotian families:

In Laos I would never say anything about politics because I would be afraid that I would say something wrong. My parents taught me that I should never say anything wrong about politics because there was danger in that.

For instance, in our country, if we knew that there was someone who was very rich, and we knew that he got that money in a dishonest way, like taking it from the poor, even if we knew the story, we wouldn't say anything about it. We were always afraid that we would be punished for speaking up, and our parents always told us that even if we know about it, we still shouldn't say anything. (19)

When the lessons of childhood are of this nature, it is not difficult to imagine that, in an immigrant's estimation, a life devoid of politics is no great loss.

It would not be accurate to say, however, that the Laotians who were interviewed expressed no concern with politics whatsoever. Certain refugees professed considerable interest in American government. Curiosity seemed to be sparked by their analysis of history, that in some sense the fall of Laos to the communists was attributable to political ignorance. "I feel that we lost our country because we did not know anything that was going on in our government," explained one refugee, "so I am more interested in finding out what is going on here" (27). "In our country people did not know about politics," allowed another. "Therefore our country did not progress. In America people do know what the government is doing—that is why the country is so prosperous—so I want to know more about it too" (13). Nonetheless, the few instances when refugees did indicate interest in American political life must be taken in tandem with the factors impeding the pursuit of that interest—a language barrier, attention to more pressing economic concerns, and a consequent lack of political knowledge. Thus, even if Laotians might like to expand their political horizons, circumstances often narrow their scope for doing so.

But language and political knowledge are not restrictive as regards interest in the politics of Laos itself. Unquestionably, many Laotians expressed an abiding interest in the disposition of their country of birth. In the opinion of one respondent, "For the most part when Lao people begin to talk about politics, they talk about what is going on in their own country—that is what they are interested in" (16). In some cases, the major topic of conversation concerns "how we can oppose the government and what we can do to get it back the way it was" (18). For Laotians wishing to take action to that end, a distinct minority among those interviewed, various Lao political organizations exist to forward the objective. These "parties" serve both as conduits of information about Laos and vehicles by which to raise money for the anticommunist resistance. As one refugee disclosed:

> I do meet with my friends to talk about politics. There are four political groups in Illinois which meet when there is something to take care of—maybe once a week, or every two weeks. We collect money so that we can help the rebels who are fighting. We do this because we have a heart for the people back in Laos, the people who were not able to get out like we were. Sometimes we ask for five- or ten-dollar contributions to buy medicine, or [we] use the money is some way to help those who are fighting to take back Laos.
> We collected three thousand dollars to send a former army colonel to Thailand so that he could fight with the rebels. (23)

By no means do all Laotians view such political groupings in favorable terms. Several refugees contended that the political organization of Laotians in America would simply reproduce the corrupt and self-serving political climate that existed in Laos. Further testimony questioned the motivations of those Laotians leading the organizations:

> The reason I don't go to these political meetings is that I know the people who are running the parties; I know their background. They were politicians in Laos, most of them, who made money from poor and uneducated people. They were people who used their power over the people to control them. Here, in this country, they are doing the same thing. They say they want to take Laos back from the communists, but they don't have a plan that can accomplish anything. I really don't care about having anything to do with them. (15)

> When they came to America, the people who used to be in the government in my country tried to keep some of their former power. They act like they still have that power; they want to be government officials, colonels, and generals as they used to be. But they find that when they come here, what they used to be counts for nothing. The American government won't allow them to keep the authority they had in Laos. Now, if they are American citizens, all they can do is vote. They are not so important any longer. (2)

Testimony of this nature notwithstanding, Laotians who are actively disposed to homeland politics, participating in such organizations, or giving them financial and moral support, do have a bearing on the arguments of the present thesis. First, it should be noted that many of those interviewed spoke of the activities of these political associations in hushed tones. A distinct impression was imparted that any homeland-directed activities should be secretive for want of offending the wider American society. Perhaps fear of the accusation of divided loyalty, historically directed at so many different immigrant groups, or a generalized sense of impropriety stemming from uncertainty concerning the norms of American political practice, makes Laotians reticent to speak too freely about their political efforts. In any event, they implicitly seem to realize that as newcomers they must be on their best behavior and that political organizations promoting homeland causes may appear to the host society as evidence of an uncertain commitment to America. No doubt this once more suggests the politics of the lifeboat; having gained sanctuary in an accommodating country, refugees must be certain that their conduct is not perceived as untoward.

The few refugees expressing an enduring interest in the goals and activities of Laotian political organizations are what might be termed *political birds of passage.* In the past, birds of passage have come to America solely for economic betterment, returning to the homeland when that was achieved. Their commitment to America being based on an economic nexus, the political orientation of these individuals was restricted. A related phenomenon can be observed among Laotian refugees. While it is true that the flight of refugees may be prompted by economic factors in the homeland, most Laotians have come to America to escape political persecution pure and simple. For some of these, the United States is a place to regroup for the continuing struggle for their country of origin. It is this prospect that sustains their attention to the politics of Laos:

> I think there is hope because things in the world are never settled; nothing is for certain. There is a Lao proverb that says when the water goes up, the fish eat the ants, but when the water comes down, the ants eat the fish. The communists may have a lot of power right now, but later they may lose it. (21)

> We have to remember that our country is a very old country. Our country has a long and glorious history, and we don't want to lose it. We have to think about the people who are still there. We have to believe that we can take it back; if we didn't have that belief, we wouldn't be able to do anything. (23)

> I think there will come a day in the future when the communists will be forced to leave the country. They have caused too much poverty and suffering; nobody likes it or wants it that way. At some point the people will drive the communists out of Laos, and if so, I would go back. (26)

Refugees harboring like aspirations are not apt to have much concern for American government per se. For them, any interest in the politics of the United States is largely the by-product of a preoccupation with Laos:

> Certainly we are interested in American politics, especially in having the support of the American government for what we are trying to do. It is hard for us as a small group of refugees to raise three thousand dollars to send somebody back to fight. If we had more help from the government we could do this. . . . In the beginning the communists were only a small group, but they maintained their relationship with the Soviet government. (23)

If and when Laotians feel comfortable enough to petition the American government for assistance on a regular basis, in the manner of immigrant-stock lobbyists who promote foreign policy objectives of ethnic concern, their political presence may become more conspicuous. For reasons already advanced, however, presently Laotians are hesitant to publicize their cause.

If political information is scarce and political interest is limited, one would expect levels of actual participation in political life to be low. Data solicited from the refugees confirm this expectation. Table 5.2 lists the Laotians' responses to questions concerning their political activity in Laos and the United States. Although the small sample size makes it impossible to extrapolate the results to the wider Laotian community, the data do provide insights into the political behavior of the interviewees. The outstanding conclusion is that, in the aggregate, the Laotians have become less politically participatory in America than they were in Laos, and this despite the fact that three of those canvassed were teenagers when they left Laos and hence unlikely to have participated much in Laotian politics for reasons of youth alone. The one exception to the general pattern concerns the discussion of political affairs; in the United States, Laotians showed a greater inclination to talk about politics. This is probably the product of two factors: (1) many refugees feel freer to speak of political matters in America, the political atmosphere in Laos being less relaxed; and (2) discussing politics with friends and family is not as subject to

TABLE 5.2 Political Activities of Laotian Refugees in Laos and the United States (N = 30)

Activity	Laos		United States	
	Yes	No	Yes	No
1) Discussing politics with friend or family	13	17	19	11
2) Voting	20	10	1[a]	29
3) Personal contact with government officials (face-to-face or by letter)	14	16	5	25
4) Attending political meetings or rallies, or participating in election campaigns	15	15	2	28
5) Holding office in a political party or having a government job	16	14	1[b]	29
6) Circulating petitions to influence public policy	2	28	1	29
7) Participation in demonstrations, boycotts, or strikes	12	18	3	27

[a]It should be noted that only five immigrants had their citizenship papers.
[b]The one individual in this category was a public school teacher.

resource barriers—particularly, limited command of English—as are other varieties of participation.

One further word of explanation regarding Table 5.2 seems in order. According to the data, Laotians are ready participants in unorthodox political behavior—demonstrations, strikes, and boycotts. This appears to be especially the case in Laos and, relative to their involvement in other sorts of participation, in America, too. But on this account the data are misleading. By their own admission, most of the demonstrations in which Laotians participated in the homeland were ritualistic marches of support orchestrated by the government or their opponents, not independent expressions of activism. "I was involved in the demonstrations as the communists were coming in," recalled one individual, "but I did it more because my friends were all doing it, and I was afraid they would be angry with me and might hit me if I didn't go along" (19). Similarly, although more Laotians participated in demonstrations in America than voted, this must not be taken to indicate their willingness to go to the streets with their political demands. All three individuals in this category explained that they participated in demonstrations surrounding "captive-nation's" week, a broadly based effort to heighten public awareness of countries under communist rule, not to pressure directly the American government.

Not only do the Laotians show themselves to have low levels of participation in American politics; they also attest to having serious reservations about the importance of participation. One respondent voiced his belief that "the only thing we need to do is to know the important things, like who the president is, but as far as getting involved in politics more than that, I don't think it's necessary" (28). Another doubted the very propriety of participation, declaring, "I don't think Lao people should be allowed to influence the American government. This country is running well; if we come in here and cause a lot of confusion and trouble, I think that is absolutely wrong" (30). Many refugees simply suggested they had no difficulties requiring political attention.

Any political act more aggressive than voting was viewed with the greatest caution. Respondents shared the belief that although a high political profile may be appropriate for long-established American citizens, Laotians must simply obey. To oppose the American government is the cardinal sin. "I don't think I really have the power or the right to oppose the government," declared one respondent, "because I am just a simple resident of this country. Even before we came here we were told that we were to obey the laws of the country and do what was right" (9). Relatedly, in the view of one individual there was a proper and an improper manner to petition the government. "If people agree to sign their names to a petition, asking the government to do something, that is all right. But if they are trying to fight something the government is already doing, that is not right." (30). Others were reluctant to petition the government at all, particularly if they were not fully citizens. The lessons of Laotian politics played a part in their timidity. "I don't think I could ever present a petition to government officials," confessed one individual. "I don't think I would be brave enough. I was afraid to do something like that in Laos, and I guess I am still afraid" (29). Making a parallel observation, a countryman remarked that "you wouldn't do that sort of thing in Laos because they wouldn't pay attention to you—common men didn't have any rights in Laos" (10).

If circulating petitions is regarded as a defiant action, anything more unconventional should be thoroughly proscribed. Thus, while the Laotians generally affirmed the right of Americans to take part in demonstrations, strikes, and boycotts, they did not readily see themselves as participants in such activities. "I don't think that Lao people would ever do anything like that because their characteristic is not to cause friction but to live in peace and harmony," averred one individual, adding that "I don't think they should have the privilege to do that yet because most of them aren't citizens" (23). Another respondent related a story whose moral seemed to be that Laotians might reap advantages by not being "rabble-rousers":

> There was an American who owned a factory where Laotians worked. The Mexicans in the factory decided to strike, but they didn't tell the Laotians—there were only two Laotians working there at the time. The owner of the factory had a big party at his house and invited all the employees. The Mexicans told the Laotians not to go, but the Lao went anyway, and they discovered they were the only two employees there! After that, the owner of the factory fired all his Mexican workers and hired only Laotians to take their place. So in this instance not striking helped the Lao people. (29)

Additional testimony made it clear that a major vehicle of political socialization—the Laotian school system—did not do much to develop the politically evaluative skills making activism probable. For older respondents, French imperialism was the culprit. One individual remembered that "we never said anything about politics in school because we were a colony of France. If we had said anything about the government, we could have been arrested and taken away. . . . The French controlled everything; we were like slaves in our own country" (21). Nor was postcolonial Laos fertile ground for formal political education. A former student recalled that neither "teachers, nor the heads of the schools, nor the head of the government, would have been too happy if students did a lot of talking about politics. They would be afraid that the students might establish a communist party" (9). One of the few interviewees with direct experience of the LPDR's educational system attested that the curriculum has retained its nonquestioning character:

> When we talked about politics, we talked only about the good things, never the bad. . . . We talked about what a good leader Soupanouvong [the president of the LPDR] was, and how we didn't need a king, and how unlike a king we had a leader who the common people could see, and how he cares for us, and how the people had to be united and should think together. (17)

There is at least one notable exception to the reluctance of Laotians to participate in politics, however. When it comes to political acts having symbolic significance, the symbolism being an expression of support for the American government, Laotians profess to be eager participants. For many Laotians, voting is an act of this nature, a means of legitimating the regime by giving it popular approval, as well as a sign of identification with American society. An interviewee declared, "I live in America. When I become a citizen I have a *responsibility* to take part in choosing the leaders who will bring peace and prosperity to the country" (emphasis added) (15). When asked about the 1984 presidential election, another of the refugees responded:

> I was very interested in the last presidential election. At the time I wished that I could be a citizen and vote. I kept thinking about when I would be able to do that. I wanted to give one more vote for president. I wanted my vote to count. I didn't know who I would vote for. . . . I really didn't know which one was good and which one was bad. All I could think of is that I would like to have the privilege of voting. (7)

Such sentiments imply that it is not the ebb and flow of American politics that captivate the immigrants, but rather the opportunity to fulfill the duties imposed by the host society and thus become part of the American community.

To conclude, Laotian refugees lack the participatory inclinations that might disturb the smooth functioning of the American political system. Their tendency toward quiescence stems both from cultural barriers to their participation and a desire to show themselves as citizens beyond reproach—willing to demonstrate avid support for the American government, but unwilling to do anything calling that support into question. Of course, few immigrant groups have been self-starters politically. Instead, it has been the mobilizing efforts of native-born Americans, in the name of partisan politics, especially patronage-dispensing urban machine politics, that have brought them into the political mainstream. In that respect, Laotians are at something of a political disadvantage when compared to earlier immigrant groups. Given the decline of the machine, they have been generally unable to avail themselves of an organization that, if corrupt in the eyes of municipal reformers, at least introduced many of the foreign-born to a variety of participatory politics. Contemporary political parties, by contrast, as yet have shown slight interest in the Laotians, their comparatively small number and residential diffusion serving as disincentives. Thus it would seem they will have to find their own way in the American political system, relying on the forces of assimilation to provide the impetus. Until then, Laotians are likely to become politically involved only as an acknowledgment of what they take to be their civic obligations, voting prime among them.

Laotian Refugees and the Politics of the Lifeboat

As the thesis under consideration has maintained, patriotism is the immigrant alternative to consensus on the American creed. While immigrants may not own the precise configuration of values deemed important for the operation of American democracy, they are nonetheless among the most tenacious defenders of the republic's political rectitude. Their advocacy, on this view, is a natural concomitant of the very act of migration; America is sanctuary, the "Utopia that already exists in another place," the lifeboat bringing release from the adversity of the homeland. If for reason of gratitude alone, immigrants are inclined to be highly allegiant to their adopted country.

Tellingly, those interviewed often used the words *refugee* and *Lao* interchangeably, at least one indication that the former is a concept central to Laotian identity in America. The motive compelling the majority of the respondents to flee the homeland, either for their own or their family's sake, was fear of political persecution. One individual described the pervasive atmosphere of unease: "I left because the communists took over our country, and I no longer had any freedom. We could not even trust ourselves to talk to our own wife or our own family because the communists had their people everywhere, listening and checking up on us" (26). Others worried that they were the specific targets of the new authorities because of their connection—as civil servants, soldiers, or party members—with the former government or its allies:

> The reason I fled was because I was a government official. From the time the French left until the time the communists took over, I served as a policeman. But when the communists took over, they immediately began to take people from the old government and send them off to seminars to indoctrinate them. I was sent off for two years and six days in an area of Sarawan, and while I was there I saw people persecuted and even killed. So I was afraid for my own life, and when I got a chance, I left. (16)

> It absolutely would have been dangerous for me to stay in Laos. People like me, who used to work at the American Embassy, they were usually called C.I.A. They didn't care who you were; they would put you in jail. If I had stayed there, I would have been killed for sure because I complained a lot about the communists. (2)

> I left Laos because I was a government official of the old government. In the new government I continued my job. I was a tax collector and had to deal with issuing deeds of property when the new government took over. I had to leave because I felt that the new government, which had a lot of power, did not have any trust in the people from the old government who were working for them—that they were always under suspicion. From the time they took over, I was always afraid that eventually they would grab me and send me off to a seminar, or that I would disappear like many of the officials over me disappeared. One by one they went off to seminars or just disappeared from their families. And every time I laid down to sleep at night, I did not know if they were going to knock on my door and take me away from my family, too. (4)

As this last passage suggests, the decision to emigrate was not always made immediately upon the establishment of the LPDR. For many refugees, a great deal of soul-searching prefaced that conclusion:

> When the communists first took over I was determined that I would not leave my own country. After all, that was the place I was born, the place where I grew up. And even though it was a small country and not very progressive, it was still the place that I belonged.
> I thought at first that I could be part of the new government [having been a policeman in the old one], and that I would change my thinking and do what they said. But I soon found out that this was not possible because they didn't treat the people who worked in the old government the same as those who had worked only for the new government. Even though there were policemen who knew how to serve the people, or generals who knew how to lead an army, or doctors who knew how

to take care of the sick, they still replaced them with their own people. They wanted to get rid of all the old employees. . . .

When the communists took over, all the police, and soldiers, and people who had worked for the former government were taken off to seminars. I was taken to one of the seminars too, only two to three months after the communists came into power. Yet these were not really places where people were taught, but were more like prisons where they tried to do brainwashing. I was in the seminar for five years, and during that time I decided that I had to leave. . . . If I had ever tried to flee from the camp, I certainly would have been killed. So I waited until I was released, in 1980, to leave Laos. . . .

The thing that was so disappointing was the fact that we, Lao people, could not live in our own country. We did not understand why we were not treated right by the new government; after all, it was our country as well as theirs. . . . But they simply didn't allow us to stay there. (23)

Needless to say, civil servants are not the only individuals threatened by political persecution. Although religion in Laos has not been a principal target of the authorities, the LPDR preferring to coopt the Buddhist *sangha* rather than dismember it, one respondent did indicate religious reasons for flight:

I was a priest and served in the temple. One of the things I was able to do was to cure people of diseases through spiritual means. This was contrary to the teachings of the communists, and when they began to curse me for doing this kind of thing, I decided to leave.

[The communists] didn't necessarily persecute people who followed a religion, but they persecuted anyone in whom the people had faith. If people had faith in some person other than a communist, that took away from their faith in communism. (12)

More frequent, however, was testimony relating the problem of family fragmentation to the government authorities. Several Laotians stated that they abandoned the LPDR to be reunited with family members who had already escaped. The following account is representative:

I left because when the communists took over in 1975, our whole family was affected. First, my husband's younger brother fled to Thailand because he was a pilot. I myself could not leave at that time because I was about three months' pregnant.

At first I did not want to go because Laos was my own country, where I had always lived. And I did not think I would have to leave because I was working in the hospital, something that didn't particularly have to do with the new government. But eventually I found that the communists had a plan for everybody that worked—even in the hospital.

After they took over we continued to work, but we also had to attend classes which indoctrinated us with communists ideas. . . . It meant that we had to get to the hospital and do all of our work, then immediately go to the classes and continue to study. I felt that . . . there was no hope for the future.

I was very afraid that something was going to happen because my husband was in the military. In the old government he had been a soldier who repaired airplanes. And the communists kept replacing people like that with their own people, and sending the former government's soldiers off to seminars. . . . You never knew what part of the country you might be sent to, or whether you would be separated from your family. . . . Finally my husband was sent off to a seminar. . . . After that, in 1978, my husband's brother, who was already in Thailand, sent word for me to get across as soon as I could. (24)

Once more, the reluctance with which Laotians left their country of nativity, as well as their fear of not doing so, is made manifest.

Economic motivations for seeking asylum are less significant in the instance of Laotians, but not negligible. Undoubtedly, political and economic factors are intertwined in the Laotian case. In this manner, the source of the economic misfortune compelling flight is traced to the policies of the new regime:

I left because of the poor economic conditions in the country. . . . When the communists took over they all made us work together in groups; nobody could just do their own work as before. Previously we had our own rice field, which we worked, and we had enough to eat. But when they took over the rice fields, and sent people in to work them, they only gave you just a percentage of what you reaped. There was never enough to eat. And sometimes, the people they sent to work the rice fields had never done it before and didn't know anything about it. How could people who had never done that kind of work before get any crops from the fields? There was never enough food, never enough medicine or anything else needed for a good life. The people were very poor. (30)

Even if the ills of life under the LPDR might be exaggerated, the refugees' declarations are nonetheless relevant. Indeed it might be expected that émigrés will magnify the deficiencies of the homeland. The decision to leave is so momentous that the reasons for leaving must be extraordinarily convincing. This is simply the obverse of the lavish praise many refugees bestow on America. What must be remembered in all of this is that the testimony of refugees cannot be utilized as objective descriptions of political virtue or vice. The importance of the testimony lies, not in the accuracy of what it depicts, but rather in the fact of depiction. Of interest is what immigrants say about the political world, no more than that. And what Laotian immigrants say about Laos is that their future in the country was so bleak, they had no choice but to leave.

If Laos was the embodiment of despair, in the Laotians' view, America is the incarnation of hope. The United States represents asylum from the apprehended terrors of the homeland as well as the purgatory of the refugee camps. Refugees have the comparative data, they know what life is like in a different place, and this perspective influences their evaluations of life in America. Naturally, their experience of the homeland is unfavorable, so much so that the painful decision to leave is made. All assessments of America are products of this historical matrix:

> When the communists took over Laos, everything was changed; our thinking, our whole lives were changed. We became like machines or slaves, just doing what we were told. And then we came to another country, America, and another change took place. We understood that now we could have freedom and rights. It changed my whole life. I realized I had been living in a communist country that did not allow me to develop, and I had come to a country where I could. (15)

It needs to be recognized, of course, that in the Laotian case a special dynamic promotes the allegiance of the immigrant to the country of adoption: Laotian immigrants have been ideologically self-selected, an anti-Communist contingent admitted into a host society equally anti-Communist. As America presents itself as the very antithesis of the sort of government that, according to the refugees, is responsible for their predicament, small wonder that Laotians are disposed to view the United States favorably.

Ideological considerations aside, to speak of America in less than glowing terms would be to contemplate that the decision to leave was ill-advised. Yet among the Laotian participants in the interview sessions, there was no evidence to suggest second thoughts. That is not to say that the disadvantages of life in America were not recognized: lack of job security, crime, loss of social status, and general cultural unfamiliarity were the most frequently mentioned liabilities. But many respondents claimed there was nothing about America that distressed them, several placing their remarks in comparative context:

> America is the best country in the world. If any refugees visit this country after having been sponsored in some other country, they tell us how much better it is here, and they don't want to leave. I am very

content that I came to this country and that I am going to live here.
(28)

> This country is the best in the world. Refugees who have gone to
> all the other different countries—none of them are treated as well or
> taken care of as much as they are in America. (10)

Even among those Laotians not quite so optimistic about their country
of adoption, present difficulties were said to pale in comparison to
the hardships left behind:

> One thing that is difficult for us is that young people often have to
> work two jobs in order to get ahead at all. Many Lao people work so
> much they have no time to eat and no time to sleep, and they still
> must give a lot to the government in taxes. But even having said all
> of that, *I still say that living in this country is a lot better than living
> in a Communist country.* (emphasis added) (16)

From the perspective of this individual, then, it would appear that
work without adequate rest and nourishment is yet an improvement
over the situation in the homeland, a revealing insight into one
immigrant's psychology.

Beyond general statements of approval, Laotians mentioned specific
features of American life they found especially praiseworthy. For
individuals seeking refuge from political persecution, relief from sheer
threat of physical violence is no mean achievement: "In Laos I lived in
. . . Luang Prabang, where there was the sound of gunfire all the time,
and I feared for myself and my family. The thing that I like [about
America] is the peace that I have in my heart being here" (3). But apart
from the menace of civil war, in Laos the arbitrary application of justice
was further cause for alarm. In America, by contrast, refugees claim
to have confidence in the impartial administration of the law:

> I particularly like the government and laws of this country, which are
> proper and honest—for instance, as regards soldiers or policemen. In
> Laos, if a policeman received an order to do something, he might come
> and take you whether you had done anything wrong or not. But in
> this country a policeman would have to have a reason to arrest you.
> In Laos . . . they might say that you had done something even if you
> hadn't, and the policeman would use his authority to put you in jail
> whether or not you were guilty. (11)

Testimony pertaining to security was not far removed from that
relating to freedom—on the Laotian view the greatest benefit of life
in the United States:

When I arrived in America, the first thing I felt was an ease of heart. I was impressed by the convenience of things in America. It was easy to live here. I had freedom to talk, freedom to do what I wanted to do, freedom to get a job, freedom to do anything. Back in my own country . . . we couldn't even say what we wanted to say. There was no freedom to go from place to place. Everything in our country was just the opposite from America; life was difficult, not easy. (16)

To many refugees, freedom suggested the chance to pursue one's personal ambitions without government interference. Certainly those interviewed possessed no shortage of aspirations, many pertaining to their children, the great hope of all first-generation immigrants. And crucial to the realization of those hopes was formal education, a commodity that, in the view of the Laotians, America liberally distributes:

My chief reason for coming to America is to find freedom, especially freedom in the way of education so that my children would have an opportunity to study and to prosper in this country. In Laos my children probably would not be able to go on to higher education unless they were part of a special clique; only certain people were chosen for education.

I think my children will be able to [become prosperous] because here they are free to learn. Jobs are plentiful, and when parents can work and earn money, they can help their children get an education. . . . If the parents and the government work together to teach the children, then the children have to be able to succeed. (15)

For myself I would say that I don't have any particular goal in mind, but I do have for my child. I dream about his future, and I would like to see him study and go to college, and even be a doctor someday. I don't know whether that will ever be possible. . . . But I think that if my husband and I plan for this, and save money, and if my son would cooperate with us and work toward the goal, I think it could be achieved. (19)

Interview testimony regularly included the conviction that the American promise of prosperity was not hollow. For several of the respondents, such optimism was buoyed by personal knowledge of others who had succeeded, in their opinion tangible proof of the proposition that the United States is a land of opportunity if only one applies the proper effort:

For refugees, who have come from a country of communist dictatorship, now, finally, they can breathe free air. They realize they can do something with themselves, now that everybody is equal. And they work hard. Our people have achieved tremendously. Anywhere we work, we are praised. We are hard workers and honest people and have developed self-esteem and respect. And in this area, we have so many people who are buying homes, who have become homeowners in less than ten years. . . . When we first came here, we didn't have anything. Sometimes our American friends wonder where we get all our money. . . . The reason we can [prosper] is that we usually live together in a big family and we share. . . . We divide our responsibilities and make things happen with a bigger number of people. (5)

That the United States' reputation for abundance can be established long before an immigrant sets foot on American soil was noted in an anecdote by one of the older interviewees. "When I was in school in Laos," he related, "I learned that Americans ate with dishes and silverware; then after they ate they threw it all away. I was taught that they drove a car for a while, then pushed it into the river and bought a new one" (16). Although this suggests that expectations of American munificence are high, additional testimony indicates they are not disappointed. Upon their arrival, the affluence of the United States is one of the first things that strikes Laotians. Subject to the economic deprivations of war, or the austerity measures of communist reconstruction, refugees believe that their new home brings relief:

This is an excellent country to live in because there is an abundance of everything. Here, there is no lack of food and water and things that make for a good living. This is extremely different from a communist country where you had to line up for food. And more than that you had to get a paper from the government that entitled you to food even before you could get in line. (29)

Moreover, according to several of those interviewed, poverty was not a major problem in the United States:

I have not seen very many people in America who are poor. It seems that almost everybody here is equal and has an opportunity to work. The only people that might be really poor in America would be old people, or refugees who don't know how to speak the language at all, or some kind of handicapped person. But I really haven't seen many poor people here. (24)

This supposed absence of privation was related to the foresight and benevolence of the American government. "There are not a lot of beggars here like their are in other countries," noted one individual, "because this country has a plan for welfare and public assistance"

(23). "The United States government cooperates with the people, and the people here have jobs and enough to eat," maintained another. "This country takes care of its people. You don't hear of anybody dying of poverty in America, but you do hear about people dying of poverty in Laos" (30). A countryman agreed, commenting, "Aid has been given to us. We have been given clothes to wear, and enough food to eat. Before, we never had a car, but now we have a car to drive. We can live comfortably here" (30). Of course this does not mean that levels of public assistance are in fact adequate, but that many refugees think them so. Laotians seem pleased simply to have left the poverty of Laos and to have found another country willing to take them in: any further effort to ease their way only enhances their positive impressions of the host society.

If, in the Laotians' perspective, the United States delivers refugees from the political and economic calamities of their past, it also offers them a less tangible, though equally significant, prospect: the chance to become American. Certainly, it must be acknowledged that the United States has been Janus-faced with respect to those not of Anglo-Saxon descent. Historically, non-Europeans have been socially stigmatized, their sense of identification with America thereby reduced. For that reason, the following testimony serves as a reminder of the difference between America's better inclinations and its worst ones:

> I still feel like a foreigner in this country because some people here don't like Asians. Every time I look in the mirror I remember that. Because some people don't like Asians in this country, and look down on them, I feel that I am still an Asian and not really a true American. (20)

Nevertheless, the opportunity for incorporation into the national society is not without substance; at least racism has no constitutional sanction. The operative principle of American government, apparent in public pronouncements, though unfortunately not always observed, is the equality of all persons. And a majority of Laotian interviewees appeared quite prepared to accept this all-inclusive vision of American democracy, recognizing that they might become thoroughgoing members of the host society, not merely its wards.

Naturally, not all respondents in the study readily considered themselves Americans. But for most of these, cultural barriers were the sticking point, not unwillingness on the part of the native-born. As one individual confessed, "When I first came [to America] I tried to become more like an American, to adopt more American customs and culture, but after all, a bird never changes" (23). Yet other

Laotians expressed a conviction that "Americans are a people of many races," and that it is "possible to be a Lao and an American at the same time" (13). "I will probably throw away some of the things of my old life," an interviewee imagined, "even my old religion. And I will accept the good things in American culture while retaining some of my own culture" (11). "I consider myself a Lao," noted another, "but I have the desire to learn and to know everything I need to know to be a good American" (7). For certain of the respondents, the process of acculturation already seemed to be proceeding quite rapidly:

> I feel that I am about eighty percent American now. I don't make my children do everything that I say. I let them go out with their friends even when I am not around. Also, I have been working alongside my husband. In Laos, women didn't work like this, but I am independent and go to and come from work just as my husband does. We work more like Americans in that way. (25)

By the same token, many of the first generation regarded their children as well on the way to becoming completely American. Several Laotians expressed the conviction that their offspring, suffering less from the cultural impediments confronting themselves, would be fully part of the American community. "They will become much more American than I am," one of the interviewees stated. "I want all my children and grandchildren to become full-fledged American citizens so that their lives can be easy in the future" (4). Nevertheless, a number of refugees regarded the prospects of their children becoming Americanized with a certain ambivalence. A concerned parent admitted, "That's one problem we worry about. They don't even want to speak Lao at home. We speak Lao to them and they answer in English. They speak very good English." (14). The theoretical importance of such declarations, however, lies in the fact that Laotian parents can imagine their children becoming members in good standing of the American commonwealth, a prospect, it may be ventured, less available elsewhere.

To be sure, a few of those interviewed understood American identity in strictly legal terms. One respondent voiced a certain amount of confusion on this point, saying, "I don't know what to say about myself being an American. I am not a citizen yet. I have a green card, but I don't know whether that makes me an American yet. I really don't know what race I belong to right now" (16). And there was some recognition of the instrumental benefits of acquiring citizenship, one interviewee claiming, "I think it is very important to be a citizen.

For instance, when you fill out a job application form there are little squares that ask if you are a citizen or not. I just feel if you could write down that you were a citizen, it might be helpful" (23).

Yet beyond such pragmatic considerations, the rite of becoming a citizen is rich with symbolic meaning, connoting formal admission to the national society, and thus one of the most important steps taken on the road to becoming fully American. "I think I want to be a citizen," one Laotian declared, "because I want to be a real resident of America for the rest of my life. If I am a citizen I will feel more like a part of the population here . . . and a part of whatever is going on in America" (4). So, too, does citizenship represent the abandonment of the past, a declaration of intent to make a new life in the place of refuge. For those Laotians indicating their desire to become American, it was clear that the break with Laos had been made. An air of resignation characterized their responses:

> I will have to become an American; I will become one. I will have to learn how to live and act, what to do here, how to support my family. In the future, I hope even to become a citizen. I probably never will be allowed to go back to my country. . . . It is important [to become an American] because I live and work in this country, I need to be a part of it. I will probably die right here, so I have to learn to become part of this society. I don't have any plans to go back to Laos. I left it, and there is no reason to return. (11)

> I am an American because this is the country that I live in, and I don't have anyplace else to go. This is the place I am going to be for the rest of my life. (9)

> I think I am an American. This is a good country to live in. We are just poor people and they have accepted us here. And, after all, there is no chance for us to go back [to Laos]. So we have to stay on and consider ourselves Americans. (30)

As the lifeboat analogy would have it, commitment to the country of adoption begins with the "tragic rejection" of the homeland. Refugees understand the import of naturalization; they are people without a country, persona non grata in the place of their birth. Into such a situation comes the tender of citizenship from the country of sanctuary, a chance to become established for individuals cut adrift. And more than just citizenship is proffered; there is the possibility to become American in all the senses—legal and extralegal—of the term. If refugees are enthusiastic about America, in part it is because in its more generous moments America indicates that it wants them.

Yet there are limits to the magnanimity of America, as immigrants are well aware. In some measure because they are from another place and have not been socialized to American political norms, a veil of suspicion hangs over all immigrants. In America, the political stability of the republic presumably relies on acceptance of a precisely arranged configuration of attitudinal values, a cultural matrix that few immigrants share. Thus the native-born have certain misgivings about the new arrivals. Immigrant groups seem subject to a probationary period of sorts, a time when they must prove worthy of the assistance that has been extended to them. To show that their allegiance to America is beyond question, appropriate displays of patriotism must be made. But more than this, immigrants must keep low political profiles. They cannot seek to be too active in the political process and furthermore must project an image of law-abidingness.

By this standard, Laotians exhibit the attributes of ideal immigrants. Their propensity to be enthusiastic, yet undemanding residents of their adopted home has already been cited. Barely visible on the American political scene, Laotians show little interest in becoming more influential. In truth, a segment of Laotian opinion believes that to become too strident in making demands on the host society is a sign of ingratitude. Hence, the one issue that does mobilize the efforts of the refugees—that concerning the destiny of Laos—is entered into with a certain trepidation; the activities of political organizations attempting to recapture the homeland are partially concealed for fear that Americans will regard them as untoward.

Additionally, Laotians testify to being an upright and obedient people. Expressions of commitment to law and order, and to the importance of obeying the government, permeate the refugees' remarks. For people lately emerging from the throes of civil war, and from what is regarded as the caprice of the LPDR, the security that comes from the uniform application of the law is comforting. Indeed, according to the Laotians, the major function of American government is the preservation of political order. On this account, life without government promises to be particularly grim:

If people were completely free to do what they wanted, there would be turmoil. People would be killing one another every day. In places like New York and Chicago you always hear about people being murdered. If there was no government, it would be worse than that. There would be war and killing all the time. (22)

Given such a pessimistic reading of human nature, it is understandable that government should be regarded as protector and sustainer. In fact, one interviewee wondered why the American authorities could not take more stringent measures against lawbreakers:

> One thing I do not understand is why, if a policeman is trying to catch a robber, he does not have the authority to shoot him? Many times in America, the policeman, the one who is doing what is good, is not allowed to shoot the robber, and instead gets shot himself. I think the policeman should have the power to punish or kill someone if he is doing wrong, and not get caught in a situation like that. . . . I do not understand why, if a policeman shoots a robber, that it is a criminal offense on his part. What kind of law would free the robber and put the blame on the policeman? (4)

Expressing related concerns, several individuals thought forced confessions were entirely appropriate. "If somebody has done something wrong they should confess it," insisted one respondent, "and if they are guilty they should be made to confess it. If they won't confess it, then [the police] should do whatever they have to do to make them confess. After all, they did something wrong" (30). A compatriot agreed, observing that criminals "have to be forced just like children. If children don't obey, you punish them to make them obey" (20).

In the present study, obedience to authority was the behavioral maxim of Laotian refugees. Time and again their testimony affirms the importance of doing as the government instructs. Reiterating the insights of many others, one respondent commented, "I don't think that ordinary people need to have anything to do with the government. If the government makes a law telling you what to do, you should do it. Your responsibility is just to obey the law" (30). Others amplified the notion that a citizen's prime obligation is "to obey the laws of the government and not do anything that would cause trouble in any way" (26). Furthermore, many refugees believed it was not only important that they themselves obey the law, but that they made certain others did so as well. "In Laos, many people did not obey the government," explained one individual, "and I need to show them that in their new life in America they should obey and listen to those in authority over them" (15). Indeed, of all people, refugees must be exceptionally concerned to observe the law:

> When we come here we must live within the confines of the law of this government. We must not do what is contrary to what the government requests us to do. . . . As refugees we are residents because of the graciousness of this country, which let us in. The expression we

use is that we have "fallen into this country." And as refugees we must not think that we are free to do whatever we want, but we must follow the rules of this government. (28)

Thus, Laotians are keen to swear allegiance to the American system of law, resolving to be paragons of political virtue. Their emphasis on law-abidingness suggests a recognition of the legitimacy of American government, a legitimacy established in the circumstances of flight.

Conclusion

Evidence gleaned from the testimony of Laotian refugees corroborates the expectations of the thesis: immigrants are supportive and quiescent members of the American republic. The present chapter has intended to demonstrate only that this assertion has some basis in empirical fact, and at least that much has been done. Because the research method employed cannot establish causal relationships, the verity of the thesis remains more promised than proved. But in no way does the evidence contradict the insights of the thesis, and in many respects it confirms them.

As expected, Laotians have no uniform affinity for all components of the American creed. With regard to their understanding and acceptance of the American ideals of individualism, equality, and participatory democracy, they are especially wide of the mark. Not much in the background of the refugees suggests things could be otherwise. Traditionally, the Laotian political system did not encompass such beliefs, and more recently, neither the constitutional monarchy nor its communist successor has regarded these values as normative. Socialization messages communicated in the homeland have centered on submissiveness, deference, and public obligation; systematic instruction in the rights-based liberal-democratic ethos has been absent. Testimony reveals that the lessons of the past as yet inform the perspectives of the present. Even in the case of freedom and capitalism, the two features of the creed that Laotians are most likely to embrace, the refugees frequently depart from the orthodox interpretation given these concepts in America. If consensus on a common core of political beliefs is a prerequisite of political stability in America, the Laotian presence cannot be welcome.

Yet if value dissensus is to threaten the smooth operation of American government, such values must become the basis of political action. Here lies the reason Laotians are not a negative influence on their host's political system: beyond formal displays of support,

Laotians do not participate in American politics. In the first instance, most Laotians lack the resources that must be mobilized if participation is to occur. Cultural unfamiliarity, the language barrier in particular, is a major source of this deficiency. So are the socioeconomic constraints restricting political participation. For some refugees, the struggle to keep self and family above subsistence levels of well-being may leave little time for political activity. For better-heeled others, pursuit of ever higher levels of prosperity may simply be more inviting than the esoteric attractions of the political world. And this suggests that besides being objectively ill-equipped for political action, subjectively, too, Laotians are improbable participants. Once more, socialization experiences have a certain amount of explanatory power. The political ethos of Laos rarely included the notion that common citizens might affect the direction of public policy, nor does the Laotians' situation in America lead them to draw different conclusions. Their testimony declares that they are too new, or do not know the language, or do not have the time, or have not studied American government sufficiently to become effective players in the political process. Doubting the efficacy of their action, the refugees' enthusiasm for participation is proportionately diminished.

Moreover, for many Laotians the very realm of the political is tainted. The word *politics* conjures up images of corruption, deceit, danger, and fear—understandably so, given that the reason Laotians fled the homeland ultimately can be attributed to political factors. Fear of political persecution motivated many to leave, while the economic hardship associated with the policies of the LPDR induced others. Even if the recollections of refugees magnify the severity of existence in their country of nativity, a distinct possibility when considering the testimony of any émigré, the oppression is nonetheless real to the refugees themselves. In the minds of many, the world of politics is a world of grief and sorrow best left alone. One must be careful when "playing around with politics."

As might be predicted, an inventory of the refugees' activities reveals that, save for discussing politics with family and friends and indicating an intention to vote, Laotians do not participate in American politics. But more than this, many are convinced they should not participate. Political demands, it is reasoned, not only show lack of appreciation for American haven; they also imply that the present policies of the American government are in some sense inadequate, and if there is one act that no Laotian seems inclined to commit, it is to voice opposition to the government of the United States.

Expressions of support are a different matter. The desire to vote, a political gesture that virtually all those interviewed wished to make, is relevant in this respect. Among Laotians, voting is not promoted for its instrumental effects but for its symbolic ones. From the refugee's perspective, voting is not so much a right as an obligation of citizenship, a chance to identify with the national community as well as to affirm the American system of government. In that respect, as the refugees testify, the result of an election is not as important as the fact of electing.

In only one other instance do Laotians indicate they are politically active: for a minority of respondents, the politics of the homeland retains its appeal. On those few occasions when refugees discuss political matters, usually Laos itself is the topic of conversation. Furthermore, the most zealous expatriates have established political organizations intent on recovering Laos from the communists, a subject of considerable controversy within the ethnic community. Yet in the foreseeable future, the impact of all this on the American political system should be meager. To begin with, Laotians devoted to liberating the homeland are unlikely to identify sufficiently with America to play an active part in its political life, their attentions being fixed on Southeast Asia instead. Neither are such individuals typically confident enough to be politically conspicuous. Wary of being called to account for their loyalty, immigrants indulge the politics of Laos with care. Almost intuitively, Laotians understand that the host society expects newcomers to adopt a politically compliant posture.

Because they are disinclined to become players on the American political scene, Laotians do not unsettle the democratic order. Hence, the thesis in its negative formulation is confirmed—immigrants do not harm the operation of American democracy. In its more aggressive formulation, however, the thesis maintains not just that immigrants are a negligible political force but that they have a salutary effect on the functioning of the democratic order. Immigrants are not only quiescent citizens but also loyal ones, an elementary patriotism compensating for any absence of commitment to the national creed. It is not the specifics of that creed that convince immigrants to transfer their allegiance to America; rather loyalty is a consequence of the process of immigration itself.

For Laotian refugees, America has served as a lifeboat offering sanctuary when it was most needed. The source of all immigrant allegiance lies in the rejection of the homeland, but in the instance of Laotians, indeed of most refugees, this rejection is two-sided. Laotians repudiate the homeland because they believe the circumstances of life there unacceptable. Yet simultaneously the homeland rejects them, making some individuals the specific targets of government persecution, while sealing off the possibility of return to all who would emigrate.

Deliverance from the uncertain status of the resettlement camps goes far toward assuring the refugees' positive impression of America. To restore hope to the hopeless is no small accomplishment. But America offers the Laotians relief in other ways as well: security from the violence of civil war and the violence that is done when the rule of law is disregarded; the freedoms necessary to aspire for those whose destiny has not been in their own hands; the promise of wealth, if not always its realization, for those suffering from economic destitution; a new focus of nationhood for political outcasts. In this manner, the very reasons motivating the flight from Laos—political persecution and economic distress—are at least partially resolved in the United States. Of course, America does not always deliver on its promises; it can be a very violent society, it can encourage people to exercise their freedom without giving them the means to make that freedom real, it is a country of abundance in which millions are impoverished. Yet immigrant assessments of the host society are filtered through remembrance of things past—the comparative vantage point is crucial to understanding the United States on Laotian terms. As many refugees maintain, despite the difficulties of life in America, it is, nonetheless, better than life in Laos. As long as the first generation and their progeny continue to make that evaluation, the politics of the lifeboat will endure.

Thankfulness for sanctuary alone might be reason enough for Laotians to be patriotic and obedient. But Laotians are prompted to display politically supportive behavior for a further cause: they are under pressure to demonstrate they are not a disruptive social force. Immigrants are welcome in America, but they can wear out their welcome. In the struggle between America's benevolent inclinations and its less laudable ones, any evidence that immigrants are less than quiescent, hard-working, and law-abiding citizens is grist for the nativist mill. Laotians understand the parameters of behavior within which they must operate, law-abidingness being a major theme of their testimony. The citizen's main responsibility, in the Laotian view, is to do what the government instructs. Even capitalism is justified not merely for the wealth accruing to individual entrepreneurs, but for the revenues that will go to the government in the form of taxes. Refugees are well aware of the image they must seek to project to the wider American community. Privately beneficial acts may need to be vindicated by an acknowledgment of public responsibilities. Like all invited guests, Laotians are on their best behavior.

In every respect, then, the wisdom of the thesis is confirmed in the observations of thirty Laotian refugees. The findings are tentative. But if these Laotians are in any sense representative of other immigrants, America's status as a settler society may go far toward explaining the success of its experiment in democracy.

Notes

1. Milton Osborne, *Southeast Asia: An Introductory History* (Sydney: George Allen and Unwin, 1979), pp. 64–65; Martin Stuart-Fox, *Laos: Politics, Economics, Society* (London: Frances Pinter, 1986), pp. 8–12.

2. Arthur J. Dommen, *Laos: Keystone of Indochina* (Boulder: Westview Press, 1985), pp. 123–25.

3. Joseph J. Zasloff, "Political Constraints on Development in Laos," in *Laos: Beyond the Revolution*, eds. Joseph J. Zasloff and Leonard Unger (New York: St. Martin's Press, 1991), p. 36; "Laos," *The Europa Yearbook* (1990 ed.), p. 1585.

4. Geoffrey C. Gunn, "Theravadins and Commissars: The State and National Identity in Laos," in *Contemporary Laos: Studies in the Politics and Society of the Lao People's Democratic Republic,* ed. Martin Stuart-Fox (New York: St. Martin's Press, 1982), p. 79. Also see Grant Evans, *Lao Peasants Under Socialism* (New Haven: Yale University Press, 1990), pp. 30–32.

5. Dommen, *Laos,* p. 28.

6. Donald P. Whitaker et al., *Area Handbook for Laos* (Washington, D.C.: Foreign Area Studies of the American University, 1972), p. 32; Evans, *Laos Peasants,* pp. 32–33. It should be noted that the relatively indirect form of colonial rule adopted in Laos represented a departure from the centralized pattern of administration instituted in the rest of French Indochina.

7. On ethnic restiveness in the colonial period see Geoffrey C. Gunn, *Rebellion in Laos: Peasant and Politics in a Colonial Backwater* (Boulder: Westview Press, 1990), pp. 55ff.

8. Gunn, "Theravadins and Commissars," in *Rebellion,* pp. 91–95.

9. Ibid., p. 86.

10. For a good overview of the institutional structure of the LPDR see Stuart-Fox, *Laos,* pp. 58–96.

11. "Laotians Consider Their Future," *Refugees,* No. 84 (April 1991), 28. At the beginning of 1991, more than 62,000 Laotian refugees remained in Thailand.

12. Paul J. Strand and Woodrow Jones, Jr., *Indochinese Refugees in America: Problems of Adaptation and Assimilation* (Durham: Duke University Press, 1985), p. 16.

13. Bernard J. Van-es-Beeck, "Refugees from Laos, 1975–1979," in *Contemporary Laos: Studies in the Politics and Society of the Lao People's Democratic Republic,* ed. Martin Stuart-Fox (New York: St. Martin's Press, 1982), pp. 324–27. Among the very first refugees were Tai Dam and Nung minorities, groups originally from North Vietnam that had settled in Laos after 1954. These groups included former soldiers in the French army, anti–Viet Minh guerrillas, and civil servants under the French colonial administration.

14. Amphay Dore as cited in Van-es-Beeck, *Contemporary Laos,* p. 327. By 1985, roughly five thousand Laotians were said to be held in reeducation centers; by 1989, perhaps one thousand. See The Economist, *World Human Rights Guide* (New York: Facts on File, 1986), p. 166; U.S. State Department, *1989 Human Rights Report,* as cited in Stan Sesser, "Forgotten Country," *The New Yorker,* 20 August 1990, p. 61.

15. See Stuart-Fox, *Laos,* pp. 98–104; Gary Y. Lee, "Minority Policies and the Hmong," in *Contemporary Laos: Studies in the Politics and Society of the Lao People's Democratic Republic,* ed. Martin Stuart-Fox (New York: St. Martin's 1982), pp. 210–12; Evans, *Lao Peasants,* pp. 44–64; Zasloff, *Political Constraints,* p. 34.

16. "Laos," *The Europa Yearbook* (1990 ed.), p. 1586.

17. Ibid.

18. United Nations Development Program, "The Economy of Laos: An Overview," in *Laos: Beyond the Revolution,* eds. Joseph J. Zasloff and Leonard Unger (New York: St. Martin's Press, 1991), pp. 68–71.

19. John L. Van Esterik, "Lao," in *Refugees in the United States,* ed. David W. Haines (Westport: Greenwood Press, 1985), p. 155.

20. "No Refuge," *The Economist,* 21 February 1987, p. 41, cols. 2–3; p. 42, col. 1.

21. It should be mentioned that the UNHCR has had a voluntary repatriation program in place for Laotian refugees since 1980. As of January 1991, slightly more than 6,500 Laotians had returned to Laos through UNHCR auspices, the majority in the previous two years, with a further 15,000 to 20,000 having returned independently. "Laotians Consider Their Future," *Refugees,* No. 84 (April 1991), 28. The gradual liberalization of the Vientiane government, as well as the considerable length of time that many residents have spent inside the camps albeit with limited prospects for third country resettlement, may help to explain this reorientation.

22. Linda Gordon, "Southeast Asian Refugee Migration to the United States" (Paper prepared for the Conference on Asian-Pacific Immigration to the United States, September 20–25, 1984, East-West Population Institute, Honolulu, Hawaii), p. 29.

23. Ibid., pp. 2, 8; unpublished data supplied by the United States Immigration and Naturalization Service.

24. Calculations based on U.S. Department of Health and Human Services, *Profiles of the Highland Lao Communities in the United States* (Washington, D.C.: G.P.O., 1988), pp. 6–7.

25. The single respondent who was willing to let a communist viewpoint be heard expressed his rationale in these terms: "Let them speak because the communists will claim that the communist way of life is better than the democratic way of life. Why, then, are so many people running away from the communist regimes? And if communism is so good, why do people have to steal secrets from [Western] technology. . . ? The communists can fool the people for awhile, but the truth will always come out" (5).

26. That is not to deny a rudimentary egalitarianism in traditional Laotian village life. See Gunn, *Rebellion in Laos,* pp. 63ff.

6

Conclusion

Immigrants have contributed to the stability of the American political system. This assertion, the major conclusion of the present investigation, stands in direct and fundamental opposition to the dominant theoretical interpretation of the immigrant experience. According to much of the literature of empirical democratic theory, immigrants are likely to disrupt the democratic equilibrium by reason of their alien political convictions; students of American politics have tended to follow this general line of analysis, believing that immigrants may well threaten the liberal political consensus on which the health of the American republic depends. But in fact immigrants have been pillars of the American political system, their character shaped by the process of immigration itself combined with an American culture specifically designed to integrate discrete immigrant groups.

Immigrants vote with their feet. If a government's right to rule is founded on the express consent of the governed, immigrants are one of the few unambiguous examples of individuals who have indicated such consent. Unlike many, perhaps most, of the native-born, immigrants consciously assent to the political rule of the country of adoption, choosing to place themselves under its jurisdiction. In a certain sense, the government of the host society does not need to justify its authority to the immigrant, such authority being confirmed in the very act of immigration. By contrast, those born to political rule cannot be said to have willingly acknowledged the authority of government. Mere residence cannot establish the moral basis for political dominion; hence Locke and others have invoked the notion of tacit consent as opposed to the express consent of the governed. But for immigrants, the question of legitimacy is settled once they set foot on the host country's soil. Whereas the native-born's allegiance must be won, the immigrant's allegiance is implicit in the act of migration.

Of course abstract notions of political commitment are far from most immigrants' thoughts. More significant are the prosaic calculations made with respect to life in the New World. Prime among these is the recognition that the New World brings respite from hardship, real or imagined. The comparative vantage point—what life was like in the homeland—provides the all-important filter through which life in the country of resettlement is evaluated. As long as the promise of the future outweighs the adversity of the past, immigrants readily promote the virtues of their adopted home. Indeed, in such a weighing-up, the scales are tipped in favor of the New World; the momentous decision to abandon the homeland virtually assures that this is so. To question the wisdom of that decision is to suggest the futility of immigration itself, a prospect few of the foreign-born are willing to contemplate. Hope is a precious commodity that the New World offers simply because it is new, and hope alone may buoy the immigrant's loyalty to the country of adoption. Should its potential be in any manner fulfilled, the devotion of the immigrant will be to that degree enhanced.

But more than gratitude affects the political disposition of the foreign-born; social pressure exerted by the host society also plays a part. The first generation's reception in the United States, at once accommodating and apprehensive (and at the limit, hostile), suggests to the newcomers that they are the guests of a host society, not temporary residents perhaps, but neither regarded as fully members of the American national community. In the measure that immigrants desire to move past this probationary status and gain complete social acceptance, with all the political and economic benefits thereby implied, they are extraordinarily concerned to demonstrate politically conscientious and supportive behavior. Consequently, for cause of the host society's expectations, as well as a genuine thankfulness for life in the New World, the foreign-born are inclined to ask little of government and are keen to demonstrate allegiance and obedience to political authority.

On this account, the insights of traditional democratic theory are not completely without substance, only misdirected. Those who advise of the immigrants' lack of conformity with the central tenets of the American political creed are correct; rarely do immigrants immediately partake in the American ideological consensus. If stability in America is in fact the product of a uniform system of political belief, the foreign-born do not further the cause of stability. Yet, as immigrants are not eager to participate in the American political system, their lack of ideological conformity is not of critical importance. Even if they do not share the same value system as the native-born, they are unlikely to operationalize those values by mobilizing for political action. Having neither the resources nor the inclination, immigrants are generally content to be politically passive residents of their adopted home. On this basis alone they do not threaten the democratic order.

But immigrants have a more positive effect on America's political stability: they are among the most ardent publicists of American virtue, quick to swear fidelity to their country of adoption. In part, immigrant allegiance is the product of what this study has called "the politics of the lifeboat." Enthusiasm for America and a strong desire to be viewed as politically dutiful and faithful are motivations emerging from the immigrants' historical context. Remembrance of things past determines their evaluation of the American polity. The United States is the terminus of a journey whose origin is discontent, a haven from the calamities of the homeland: to those fleeing political persecution, America offers security; to those fleeing economic impoverishment, America promises prosperity; to those fleeing cultural prejudice, America professes equality. Hence immigrants are firm believers in the civic faith and are more than willing to express their patriotic convictions. No doubt under the critical eye of the native-born, immigrants are especially eager to establish their loyalty. Genuine sentiments of patriotism are augmented by the immigrants' need to show themselves patriotic.

Immigrants are also wedded to the American political system because of the opportunity they have to become American. The United States possesses a political ethos able to integrate immigrants, both the cause and effect of an ethnically diverse population. As American national identity is defined in ideological terms, Americanism follows once the national creed is affirmed. In principle, this enables all immigrants, regardless of cultural background, to aspire to membership in the political community. Not that the status of American can be gained automatically; belief in the importance of ideological consensus is too strong for that. Nor has the United States been free of ethnic prejudice, a social barrier to entering the national community but at least one without constitutional justification. Nevertheless, it is true that immigrants have been solicited to stimulate economic growth or, more cynically, to function as empirical evidence of the superiority of the American political system. Moreover, once on American soil, the immigrant is expected to become American, to internalize the political creed at the heart of American identity. The significant point from the immigrant's perspective is that he or she need not remain an outsider looking in. As prospective Americans, immigrants come to have a direct interest in the success of the democratic order, a circumstance magnifying their support of the political system.

Whether the insights of this thesis are applicable to countries other than the United States remains an open question. A comparative study of the immigrant experience, necessary to establish the argument's general theoretical significance, has yet to be made. But it is doubtful that the American case is in all respects unusual. It is unlikely, for example, that immigrants will readily seek to participate in the politics of any host country and for the same reasons that they are reluctant or unable to do so in America. Prima facie evidence indicates that immigrants living elsewhere are similarly inclined to be politically quiescent. In Great Britain, for instance, studies of voter registration and turnout reveal that black Britons (New Commonwealth immigrants and their descendants) generally have lower rates of electoral participation than do their white counterparts.[1] Furthermore, although New Commonwealth immigration began on a sizable scale in the early 1950s, no member of this wave of migration was elected to the House of Commons until 1987, and candidacies have been rare (although this may be as much the result of party recruitment procedures as immigrant-stock preferences). In and of itself such data are inconclusive; nevertheless they suggest that the United States is not the only country in which immigrants have a low political profile.

As concerns the thesis' more positive claim—that immigrants actively support the host country's political system—the American experience may well be distinctive. It is not that the politics of the lifeboat ceases to obtain in other than an American context. Yet the United States does relate to its immigrants in a fashion uncharacteristic of other countries. In America, the immigrant can become American, a prospect enhancing the allegiance of the foreign-born to the political system. Conversely, in other democracies the possibilities for immigrants to be fully received into the national political community appear to be slim, and this is for at least three reasons. First, in most countries the concept of national identity is defined by certain cultural and behavioral attributes, not ideological ones. In the United States, the political creed delimits national identity; an immigrant can become American because becoming American is simply a matter of will, i.e., acceptance of the political ethos. But elsewhere, national identity is more strictly a matter of birth. Extrinsic characteristics of an individual, such as skin color, religion, and general way of life—in short, the characteristics subsumed under the concept of ethnicity—determine inclusion in or exclusion from the national community. To the degree that a country's political identity coincides with an exclusive cultural personality, those immigrants not sharing that culture can never feel completely allegiant to the host country's political system. This is what prompts immigrants and their children to understand themselves as West Indian before British, Jamaican before French, and Turkish before German; in a real sense it is impossible for them to feel otherwise.

Second, in certain cases there may be no well-defined national community into which immigrants can become integrated. The Canadian political system, for example, is often said to suffer from a "crisis of identity," a recurrent theme of Canadian political analysis being the attempt to determine just what constitutes a Canadian. As in the United States, but not the majority of Western European democracies, Canadian identity is not drawn in ethnically exclusive terms. Officially, it would appear, Canada understands itself as either a bicultural society—in which case neither of the "founding peoples," English or French, may claim to be the substance of what is Canadian—or a multicultural society—an acknowledgment of the division of the social structure into an ethnic mosaic and the denial of a single national-cultural identity. Unlike the United States, however, Canada has found it difficult to compensate for this absence of cultural unity by substituting a set of integrative values the acceptance of which would define one as a Canadian and to which immigrants might become assimilated. When a country's core political self-concept is in doubt, subject to a tug of war played out by major cultural (and given the concentration of French-Canadians in Quebec, political) groupings, immigrants are forced to choose sides. Precisely for this reason, it may be ventured, in Canada control over immigration policy has been an intensely debated issue. In such an environment immigrants may add fuel to the fire of national division rather than lend support to a central political authority; there is nothing with which the newcomers can identify and no certain focus for their political loyalty.

Finally, the political integration of immigrants may be closed off because of the host society's unwillingness to permit it. This attitude is frequently found in tandem with a national identity understood in culturally exclusivist terms. On this view, because it is crucial to preserve the cultural distinctives so closely identified with a country's political identity, integration is discouraged. Perhaps the *Gastarbeiter*, immigrants recruited to meet the labor shortages of postwar Europe, furnish the best illustration of this situation. While acknowledging the economic importance of these immigrants, the native-born have sought to keep them socially and politically isolated.[2] The very name *guestworker* suggests the predicament; the expectation of the immigrants' hosts, an unrealistic one, is that they are only temporary sojourners who will one day return to their countries of nativity. They may become acclimated to the host society, but integration is considered inappropriate. Such individuals are unlikely to develop a firm sense of allegiance to their host's political system, indeed they are actively deterred from doing so.

Should the arguments of the present thesis be sound, they would carry with them several implications for the theory and practice of democracy. In the first instance, democratic theory would need to look more closely at the relationship between stable democracy and ethnic diversity derived from immigration. Heterogeneity need not have the disruptive consequences that traditional political theory anticipates. Immigrants do not threaten the fragile foundations of the democratic order; they demand little from public officials, and beyond formal displays of civic virtue they do not have much of an active political presence at all. Thus the two major indictments brought against immigrants by conventional democratic theory—that they complicate the search for social equality informing a democratic idea of political community and that they challenge the valuational consensus on which the democratic order depends—must be reassessed. Immigrants would seem too politically quiescent to be guilty of the charges.

A reinterpretation of assimilation's significance for the stability of American democracy would also seem in order. The conventional explanation of the United States' ability to maintain its democratic political system, the one that American scholarship has tended to favor, focuses on pervasive social pressures to assimilate. On this view, in the interest of stable democracy an effort must be made to inculcate culturally diverse immigrants with the dominant political value system, stamping them into a common political mold. Furthermore, it would seem, this transformation must be swiftly accomplished, achieved before the immigrant generation has a chance to disturb the political order.

From the perspective of the current thesis, however, assimilation is not the whole of the immigrant story. To be sure, several social historians—Nathan Glazer, Daniel Moynihan, Michael Novak, and Andrew Greeley, among the best known—have challenged assimilation's explanatory power, revealing the persistence of ethnic idiosyncrasies, including political ones.[3] It should not be surprising that the political orientations of immigrants are distinctive and durable. Undoubtedly, the foreign-born most often enter the United States with political values dissimilar to those of the majority of Americans. Such perspectives will be communicated to successive generations. And though the depth of commitment with which they are held may diminish over time, they may not immediately give way to the American creed. American history provides ample documentation: big city machines *did* rely on the particular affinities of immigrant-stock voters, and in comparison to their following among native-born Americans, political radicals *have* been overrepresented within the immigrant community. In light of such evidence, an unqualified assimilationist explanation of American political stability is problematic.

Immigration is the crucial and complementary variable that must be introduced into the argument. Immigrants, though usually willing converts to the American political creed, are not always capable of fully comprehending it. The socialization experiences of the homeland, as well as the immigrant's cultural exoticness, prevent easy adoption of the host polity's value system. But rapid assimilation to the American creed may not be required to assure the stability of the political system; the immigrant by his or her very nature promotes stability. The allegiant and nonparticipatory disposition of the first generation insulates the United States from the ideological dissonance that immigration portends. Certainly, assimilation will be important for immigrant children and grandchildren, but only in proportion to the waning political legacy of their forbears.

If the theory of democracy might take note of what has been argued, so the practice. Undeniably the 1980s was a decade of restrictionism. In the United States the debate revolved around the issue of illegal immigrants, culminating in the passage in 1986 of the Immigration Reform and Control Act. At the core of that discussion, however, was the desire to "regain control of our borders," a phrase with ramifications far beyond the matter of illegal immigration. Recent attempts to ensure that America is unilingual emerge from a similar perspective. In the first instance, these initiatives seem motivated by the belief that high levels of immigration will adversely affect the economic well-being of the United States. Yet it is important to note that economic anxieties are often accompanied by fears that the essence of America's national identity is in jeopardy, allegedly by immigrant-stock individuals of Hispanic descent. From this perspective, restricting the entry of such individuals would not only assure America's economic health but would also simplify the task of assimilation necessary to political stability.[4]

America is not unique in its turn toward restrictionism. Northern European governments have shared the concern to secure themselves against unwanted immigrants. Apart from offering incentives to already established immigrants to return to their countries of origin, European states have adopted more prohibitive measures to dissuade immigrants from entering in the first place. Various policies are in place: placing limitations on the movement and employability of immigrant residents; heightening border security to screen unqualified applicants for asylum; financially penalizing airlines that transport individuals without legitimate claims to sanctuary; imposing stricter definitions of "refugee" to disqualify many who desire admission; or, as in the case of the British Nationality Act (1981), introducing a more exacting notion of what citizenship requires. The activities of anti-immigrant political parties have only served to fan the flames of restrictionist sentiment.

Restrictionism is most often justified on economic grounds. Retrenched population policies are a natural outgrowth of the uncertain economic climate of the last decade. Consequently, the few voices that speak against such policies have tended to argue on an economic basis as well, though occasionally the benefits of cultural diversity are noted, and the moral case for immigration is made. When the political dimension of the immigration question is raised in public debate, however, it typically weighs in on the side of restrictionism. Rarely is immigration praised for its political effect. Silence on this score may well suggest a belief in the impossibility of arguing for immigration on political grounds. But resignation to the idea that immigrants are political liabilities is unnecessary. In fact, it can be maintained that immigrants are good for democratic political systems; at a minimum they do not disrupt the political order, and they may serve to make it stronger. In itself this is not an argument for the elimination of all immigration controls, but if an informed immigration policy is to be established, this argument is a factor to consider.

In the final analysis, the present essay issues a call to liberalism, to the toleration of diversity essential to the democratic tradition. It is ironic that Mill, one of the greatest advocates of the principle of freedom, was a firm believer in the necessary connection between ethnic homogeneity and political stability. Mill denied the comprehensive application of the principle of freedom for reasons of political expediency; order, he thought, required cultural unity. The dilemma for democratic theory is to reconcile these two conflicting impulses: diversity of belief and behavior, on the one hand, and discouragement of cultural diversity, on the other. Normatively, an open immigration policy is appealing. It acknowledges both the freedom of movement and the freedom to live one's life without the social pressure to conform. Yet in practice the ethical case in favor of immigration has paled before the notion that immigrants upset the democratic order. On the basis of what has been argued herein, such fears are unfounded. Liberalism and political pragmatism can be squared. It is not only morally appropriate to welcome immigrants, but politically advantageous as well.

This insight is especially pertinent to the United States, where the commitment to toleration has remained less than complete. In its relationship with the foreign-born, America reveals the fundamental duality of its political character: staunchly liberal in sentiment but frequently illiberal in practice. The United States has received a greater number of immigrants than any other country in the Western Hemisphere; in that respect its promise of sanctuary has not been empty. But the virtues of the "golden door" have never been uniformly accepted. Nativism and prejudice are ignoble aspects of America's heritage. Immigrants have often been treated uncharitably, in part because of their political convictions. When agreement on the liberal political ethos is universal, liberalism itself is betrayed by an exclusivity of belief. Immigrants illustrate the paradox: solicited for their labor, offered asylum on humanitarian grounds, immigrants have also been the target of cultural and political bigotry.

With respect to immigration, the United States should affirm the more generous side of its nature. That magnanimity can bring tangible benefits is not an exceptional idea. Numerous scholars have documented immigration's contribution to America's cultural and economic vitality. What has been missing, however, is a forceful statement of immigration's political value. An initial step toward that end has now been taken. Not only have immigrants built America and defined the texture of American life, but they have also been instrumental in the preservation of the democratic order. That assertion is rarely heard, but it deserves to be heard.

Notes

1. Zig Layton-Henry, *The Politics of Race in Britain* (London: George Allen and Unwin, 1984), pp. 170–74.

2. See Carol Schmid, "Economic Necessity and Social Marginality," *Ethnic Groups*, 3, No. 4. (1981), 355–71; also Ray C. Rist, *Guestworkers in Germany: The Prospects of Pluralism* (New York: Praeger, 1978).

3. Nathan Glazer and Daniel Patrick Moynihan, *Beyond the Melting Pot: The Negroes, Puerto Ricans, Jews, Italians, and Irish of New York City,* 2nd ed. (Cambridge: M.I.T. Press, 1970); Michael Novak, *The Rise of the Unmeltable Ethnics: Politics and Culture in the Seventies* (New York: Macmillan, 1972); Andrew Greeley and William McCready, *Ethnicity in the United States: A Preliminary Reconnaissance* (New York: John Wiley and Sons, 1974).

4. See, for example, Richard D. Lamm, "English Comes First," *New York Times,* 1 July 1986, Sec. 1, p. 23, cols. 1–2.

Appendix A: Biographical Schedule

Note: All data are based on information given by the subjects themselves. Certain of the responses seem open to question, primarily those concerning years of education before coming to America.

209

BIOGRAPHICAL SCHEDULE

Respondent	Gender	Age	Last Residence in Laos	Years of Education Before Coming to U.S.	Occupation Laos	Years in U.S.	U.S. Citizen
1	M	28	Vientiane Province	6	student	4	no
2	M	39	Vientiane	12	clerical	11	yes
3	M	34	Luang Prabang	13	teacher	4	no
4	M	51	Vientiane	12	civil servant	6	no
5	M	41	Sithadone Province	12	student	21	no
6	F	48	Savannakhet	5	clerical	8	yes
7	F	48	Khammouane Province	15	teacher	6	yes
8	M	37	Vientiane	17	civil servant	10	no
9	M	28	Vientiane	13	student	3	no
10	M	35	Khammouane Province	10	tailor	6	no
11	M	31	Vientiane	14	student	5	no
12	M	36	Vientiane Province	6	Buddhist priest	5	no
13	M	54	Vientiane	13	teacher	4	no
14	F	38	Vientiane	10	nurse	10	yes
15	M	48	Sam Neua	12	civil servant	3	no
16	M	60	Champassak Province	10	policeman	6	no
17	F	20	Vientiane	7	student	5	no
18	M	41	Champassak Province	12	army nurse	2	no
19	F	28	Savannakhet	9	student	6	no
20	M	26	Vientiane	8	student	5	no
21	M	72	Savannakhet	14	judge	6	no
22	M	22	Luang Prabang	9	student	6	no
23	M	46	Vientiane	14	policeman	6	no
24	F	34	Vientiane	8	army nurse	6	no
25	F	39	Sayaboury	12	sawmill owner	6	no
26	M	37	Vientiane	12	warehouse worker	5	no
27	M	33	Vientiane	14	accountant	7	yes
28	M	56	Vientiane	7	civil servant	2	no
29	M	36	Luang Prabang	12	airplane mechanic	3	no
30	M	46	Vientiane	5	soldier	3	no

[a] Exclusive of English language and any citizenship courses.
[b] Exclusive of any public assistance.

Formal Education in U.S.[a]	Occupation U.S.	Individual Income ($)[b]	Household Income ($)[b]	Public Assistance	Number of Members in Household
some vocational	furnace operator	9-10,000	18-19,000	yes	4
university	insurance agent	30,000	30,000	no	2
none	janitor	9,000	18-19,000	no	4
some vocational	clergyman	14,000	n.a.	no	6
university	teacher	23,000	53,000	no	n.a.
none	assembly line worker	9-10,000	19-20,000	no	7
general educa. diploma (g.e.d.) (high school equiva.)	assembly line worker	10,000	30,000	no	3
some univ.	teacher	22,000	45,000	no	4
some univ.	student	—	6,000	yes	4
none	machine operator	n.a.	19-20,000	no	4
some vocational	machine operator	10,000	18,000	no	4
none	pottery maker	n.a.	15,000	no	3
none	unemployed	—	n.a.	yes	2
some univ.	nurse	15,000	30-32,000	no	4
some high school (g.e.d.)	production helper in factory	25,000	30,000	no	7
none	unemployed	—	10-11,000	yes	9
high school	student	—	n.a.	no	3
some vocational	unemployed	—	8-9,000	yes	5
none	waitress	4-5,000	20-21,000	no	3
some univ.	welder	15,000	15,000	no	4
none	retired	—	20,000	yes	6
high school, some univ.	student	—	9-10,000	yes	2
some univ.	janitor	10,000	15,000	no	5
none	unemployed	—	29,000	no	5
none	assembly line worker	9-10,000	21-22,000	no	4
some vocational	machine operator	25,000	38,000	no	4
g.e.d., some univ.	job couns.	19-20,000	19-20,000	no	1
none	unemployed	—	n.a.	yes	4
none	furniture upholsterer	12,000	19-20,000	no	5
none	unemployed	—	12,000	yes	n.a.

Appendix B:
Construction of the Research Project

The research method employed in the current study does not aspire to the quantitative sophistication necessary to place the thesis on the firmest empirical ground. Rather, the approach is consciously exploratory, appropriate given the somewhat speculative nature of the hypothesis under consideration. The intent is only to illuminate the thesis in a manner that might guide further investigations, not to provide definitive answers to causal questions. Certainly, the effect of immigrant status on political orientations is the causal relationship at the heart of the thesis. But the evidence presented here seeks only to demonstrate the plausibility of the relationship; farther than that it cannot go.

Instead of a quantitative examination of political behavior or attitudes, the present study undertakes what might be termed *qualitative social research*.[1] The particular instrument selected to explore the validity of the thesis is the "intensive interview." As John and Lyn Lofland describe it, the intensive interview is

> a guided conversation whose goal is to elicit from the interviewee rich, detailed materials that can be used in qualitative analysis. In contrast to "structured interviewing" (such as opinion polling), where the goal is to elicit choices between alternative answers to preformed questions on a topic or situation, the intensive interview seeks to *discover* the informants' *experience* of a particular topic or situation.[2]

The Lofland's use of the term *structured interviewing* is, perhaps, unfortunate, as it implies that researchers employing the intensive interview do so in an unstructured or undisciplined fashion. Yet in fact the preparation and execution of intensive interview sessions require a good deal of forethought. Care must be exercised in the selection of interviewees, question construction, administration of the interviews, and collection and analysis of the verbal testimony.

After it was determined that Laotian refugees would be the focus of investigation, the initial step in the preparation of the research project was to make contact with those individuals who would agree to be interviewed. Given limitations of time and resources, and not requiring the large sample of respondents on which quantitative studies rely, it was determined that thirty Laotians should be interviewed. It was further decided that those interviewed should have resided in the United States for at least two years, a sufficient period of time, it was thought, for immigrants to have formed more definite impressions of America and thus to give better-considered answers to interview questions.

Two intermediaries assisted the author in gaining access to the Laotian community. One of these individuals was a Laotian student attending an American university; the other, a longtime American resident of Laos. Each provided the author with invaluable introductions and served as interpreters during the interview sessions. Most of the individuals chosen for the study were first approached by these intermediaries, though on occasion the interviewees themselves furnished introductions to others. Prospective respondents were asked if they were willing to take part in a study of Laotian immigrants. They were told that they would be invited to relate their experiences in Laos and the United States and that the interview would take an hour or so of their time. They were also promised that their identities would be kept in strictest confidence. If still reluctant, they were assured they were not being tested in any manner and that the interviewer simply wished to know something of their personal histories, beliefs, and attitudes. Fearing that mention of the word *politics*—a concept suspected to be rich with pejorative connotations—would cause many refugees to refuse to be interviewed, the interviewer said little at this initial stage about the political nature of the questions to be asked. Almost all of those who were contacted agreed to be interviewed.

As the interview sample was so small, those taking part in the project cannot be said to represent the population from which they are drawn in any statistical sense. Nevertheless, care was taken to be sensitive to the diversity of the Laotian community. So, for example, while the largest number of respondents were from Vientiane City, all regions in Laos were represented. Similarly, respondents were taken from a variety of age groups, though all were at least twenty years old.

In addition, those who were interviewed shared certain demographic characteristics with Laotian populations considered in research of roughly the same period. This was especially true with respect to employment and occupational status. Among the interview sample, 23 percent of Laotians were unemployed but seeking new employment; other surveys confirm that Laotians have a higher unemployment rate than the national average, though these surveys usually cite a figure even higher than 23 percent.[3] A decline in occupational status is also apparent. Among the interview sample, 82 percent held middle- or upper-middle-class jobs in Laos, while only 35 percent of those Laotians employed in the United States could say the same.[4] Moreover, the literature on Indochinese refugees suggests, and the present study supports the finding, that the greater part of the Indochinese refugee population is involved in manufacturing; 50 percent of the current study's population were so employed.[5]

In other respects, however, the Laotians interviewed for this study were better situated than many of their compatriots. This was particularly the case with regard to household income. Only 12 percent of the twenty-five individuals for whom such data were available came from households falling below the United States government's definition of the poverty line; other investigations reveal that poverty is a concern for a much higher proportion of Indochinese refugees.[6] Relatedly, the percentage of individuals receiving government assistance was proportionately less than the number cited in other research; only 30 percent of the Lao participants in the current study received public aid (though most had done so earlier during their stay in America).[7] Educationally, too, the sample group seems advantaged. With respect to their academic background in Laos, those who were interviewed appeared atypical of their compatriots, most attesting to at least a secondary school level of instruction, and several, quite a bit more. Their education has continued in America: twenty-six of the thirty respondents had at least some formal academic training in the United States, including vocational education, study for high school general equivalency degrees, college and university experience, or enrollment in English-language courses.[8] Finally, the interview population was exceptional in that most had spent less than two years in the refugee camps in Thailand. Accordingly, on average, the refugees on whom this study is based seemed more economically secure, less apt to draw public welfare, more likely to have had at least some formal education, and less likely to have endured as long a period of uncertainty concerning resettlement as their countrymen and countrywomen.

If the current study reveals bias in the choice of respondents, therefore, it would seem to be on the side of political sophistication. the overrepresentation of the economically and educationally advantaged, as well as the disproportionate number of male respondents (twenty-three of those interviewed), suggests that result. This does not necessarily challenge the validity of the study, however. If individuals with a greater likelihood of paying attention to and participating in American politics do not do so, it is improbable that other Laotians, who have even fewer resources to expend on political activity, will be disposed to participate. Of course it might still be expected that those who were interviewed would express more enthusiasm for America than their compatriots, the consequence of the group's comparative good fortune. Nevertheless, high unemployment rates, a decline in occupational status between Laos and the United States, and general cultural insecurity seem enough to temper unqualified praise for life in America, even among these immigrants.

Although the interview sessions followed a relatively flexible format, a central guide was used to focus the discussions. Many questions were generated by adapting questionnaires used in research with similar concerns.[9] Not all questions on the guide were asked in each case, the particular direction of the interview being dictated by the sorts of responses given. But five basic areas of questioning were covered in all instances: (1) general perspectives concerning the United States; (2) attitudes toward the constituent elements of the American creed—participatory democracy, individualism, freedom, equality, capitalism; (3) specific orientations to political participation; (4) political socialization experiences; (5) basic demographic information. Within each category of inquiry several types of questions were posed; some asked respondents to evaluate certain aspects of American political practice or principles, some invited affective responses to those same practices and principles, several probed the immigrant's level of knowledge about the American political system, and still others requested simple factual data regarding political behavior.

Interviews were conducted over a period of two and one-half weeks during the summer of 1986. The great majority of the interviews were held in private homes, though a public library and a YMCA provided interview sites on two occasions. Although the author's preference would have been to conduct all interviews at a common "neutral" location, this was found to be impractical, and as the main objective in choosing an interview site was to place respondents at ease, allowing the immigrants to suggest a meeting place seemed a wise rule of thumb.

On average, each interview session lasted between one and two hours. All but five of the interviews were conducted in both Lao and English, the remainder in English alone. In most cases, at least one of two interpreters was present. Naturally, the sessions were prolonged by the necessity to translate from English to Lao and back again, yet the interview process itself rarely seemed belabored by a language barrier. Although the presence of an interpreter might be thought intimidating or intrusive, the author found little evidence of this. If the interpreters had any effect on the interview sessions at all, it was likely in the opposite direction; in several cases respondents seemed more forthcoming because they knew the interpreters quite well, a rapport transferred to the author.

The great majority of questions were open-ended, permitting follow-up inquiries and responses. Even so, all interviews followed a predetermined course. First, the interviewer made a uniform introductory statement, thanking the interviewee for agreeing to participate in the study, explaining something of the nature of the research project, and once again allaying fears about confidentiality. Next, a series of questions were asked centering on the departure from Laos—the reasons for leaving, the circumstances of departure, and conditions and time spent in the refugee camps. Subsequent categories of questioning were raised in the following order: (1) general thoughts about America, (2) the American creed, (3) participatory orientations, (4) socialization experiences, (5) demographic data.

This order of procedure was constructed around two considerations. First, questions proceeded from the nonthreatening to those of a more unsettling nature. For instance, questions concerning the departure from Laos were not very controversial and seldom met with a hesitant response. Conversely, several questions about political activities in the United States, as well as those asking for particular types of demographic data, were more delicate; their placement toward the end of the interview allowed for a certain boldness and trust to develop in the relationship between the interviewer and respondent. Second, the interview tended to move from descriptive to evaluative and affective questions, concluding with cognitive and factual inquiries. Again the desire was to put the respondents at ease. Cognitive and factual questions often appear as a test of the respondent's intellect and can thus be intimidating. The placement of such questions toward the end of the interview enabled the respondent to feel more confident before such questions were asked.

Prior to the beginning of the sessions, respondents were asked if they would grant permission for the interview to be taped. All agreed to this, having once again been assured of anonymity. Indeed, the author was somewhat surprised at the readiness with which immigrants would speak even on subjects of a controversial nature. On only one occasion did a respondent request that the tape machine be switched off, and this was for only a brief period. The author's overall impression was that respondents were very willing to discuss their political beliefs and opinions and in certain instances seemed quite pleased to be asked about such matters.

All thirty of those individuals interviewed for the study are cited in Chapter 5, some more than others. There is, perhaps, an inevitable predisposition to favor those interviewees who give more thorough and articulate responses. An effort has been made to make the responses that do appear more representative than exhaustive. In many instances, individuals make a similar point in only slightly different language; though germane, in such cases the entire quantity of testimony is not recounted. Hence, in the interest of space and narrative flow, much of the empirical support for the thesis remains out of view. As in all research of this kind, the evidence presented is the product of the investigator's discretion, disciplined by a commitment to represent faithfully his subjects' views. Only further research can determine whether the author's judgments, and the arguments that emerge from them, are correct.

Notes

1. John Lofland and Lyn H. Lofland, *Analyzing Social Settings: A Guide to Qualitative Observation and Analysis*, 2nd ed. (Belmont: Wadsworth, 1984), pp. 1–3.

2. Ibid., p. 12.

3. For example, Strand and Jones found an unemployment rate of 31.9% among the Laotians they surveyed, whereas Van Esterick cites a 1983 Office of Refugee Resettlement survey that discovered that 38% of the ethnic Lao in the sample population were unemployed. Paul Strand and Woodrow Jones, *Indochinese Refugees in America: Problems of Adaptation and Assimilation* (Durham: Duke University Press, 1985); John L. Van Esterick, "Lao," in *Refugees in the United States*, ed. David W. Haines (Westport: Greenwood Press, 1985).

4. Cf. Linda Gordon, "Southeast Asian Refugee Migration to the United States" (Paper prepared for the Conference on Asia-Pacific Immigration to the United States, September 20–25, 1984, East-West Population Institute, Honolulu, Hawaii), p. 21; Strand and Jones, *Indochina Refugees*, p. 85; and Nathan Caplan, John K. Whitmore, and Quang L. Bui, "Economic Self-Sufficiency

Among Recently Arrived Refugees from Southeast Asia," *Economic Outlook USA,* 12, No. 3 (1985), 61.

5. Cf. Gordon, "Southeast Asian Refugee," p. 21.

6. Caplan, Whitmore, and Bui, "Economic Self-Sufficiency," p. 62.

7. Ibid., p. 61.

8. The Strand and Jones study cites the following figures for Laotians: no formal education, 13.8%; less than elementary school, 38.8%; some high school, 31.3%; high school graduate, 11.9%; post–high school, 4.4%. Strand and Jones, *Indochinese Refugees,* pp. 78–79.

9. Particularly useful as sources for questions were: Gabriel Almond and Sidney Verba, *The Civic Culture* (Boston: Little, Brown, 1965); Samuel Barnes and Max Kaase, *Political Action: Mass Participation in Five Western Democracies* (Beverly Hills: Sage, 1979); Robert Bellah et al., *Habits of the Heart* (Berkeley: University of California Press, 1985); Angus Campbell, Gerald Gurin, and Warren Miller, *The Voter Decides* (Evanston: Peterson, 1954); Donald R. Matthews and James W. Prothro, *Negroes and the New Southern Politics* (New York: Harcourt, Brace, and World, 1966); Richard Solomon, *Mao's Revolution and the Chinese Political Culture* (Berkeley: University of California Press, 1971).

Bibliography

Abbot, Edith. *Historical Aspects of the Immigration Problem: Select Documents.* Chicago: University of Chicago Press, 1926.

Abramowitz, Alan I. "The United States: Political Culture Under Stress." In *The Civic Culture Revisited.* Ed. Gabriel Almond and Sidney Verba. Boston: Little, Brown, and Co., 1980, pp. 179–207.

Addams, Jane. "Why the Ward Boss Rules." *The Outlook,* 58 (1898), rpt. in *The Irish: America's Political Class.* Ed. James B. Walsh. New York: Arno Press, 1876, pp. 879–82.

Ainsa, Fernando. "Utopia, Promised Lands, Immigration and Exile." *Diogenes,* No. 119 (1982), 49–64.

Alba, Richard. *Italian-Americans: Into the Twilight of Ethnicity.* Englewood Cliffs: Prentice-Hall, 1985.

Allswang, John M. *Bosses, Machines, and Urban Voters.* Baltimore: Johns Hopkins University Press, 1986.

_____. "Immigrant Ethnicity in a Changing Politics: Chicago from Progressivism to FDR." In *Voters, Parties, and Elections.* Ed. Joel H. Sibley and Samuel T. McSeveney. Lexington: Xerox College Press, 1972, pp. 274–88.

Allum, P. A. *Italy: Republic Without Government.* New York: Norton Press, 1974.

Almond, Gabriel A., and G. Bingham Powell, eds. *Comparative Politics Today: A World View.* Boston: Little, Brown, and Co., 1980.

Almond, Gabriel A., and Sidney Verba. *The Civic Culture: Political Attitudes and Democracy in Five Nations.* Boston: Little, Brown, and Co., 1965.

Archer, Dane, and Rosemary Gartner. *Violence and Crime in Cross-National Perspective.* New Haven: Yale University Press, 1984.

Bailyn, Bernard. *The Ideological Origins of the American Revolution.* Cambridge: Harvard University Press, 1967.

Ball, Terence, and Richard Dagger. "The 'L-Word': A Short History of Liberalism." *The Political Science Teacher,* 3, No. 1 (1990), 1–6.

Banfield, Edward C., and James Q. Wilson. *City Politics.* Cambridge: Harvard University Press, 1965.

Barker, Ernest. *Reflections on Government.* Oxford: Oxford University Press, 1942.

Barnes, Samuel, and Max Kaase. *Political Action: Mass Participation in Five Western Democracies.* Beverly Hills: Sage Publications, 1979.

Barton, Josef J. *Peasants and Strangers: Italians, Rumanians, and Slovaks in an American City, 1890–1950.* Cambridge: Harvard University Press, 1975.

Beard, Charles A. *An Economic Interpretation of the Constitution of the United States.* 1913; rpt. New York: Macmillan, 1935.

Bell, Daniel. *The End of Ideology: On the Exhaustion of Political Ideas in the Fifties.* Glencoe: The Free Press, 1960.

Bell, David, and Lorne Tepperman. *The Roots of Disunity.* Toronto: McClelland and Stewart, 1979.

Bellah, Robert N., et al. *Habits of the Heart: Individualism and Commitment in American Life.* Berkeley: University of California Press, 1985.

Bennett, David H. *The Party of Fear: From Nativist Movements to the New Right in American History.* Chapel Hill: University of North Carolina Press, 1988.

Benson, Lee. *The Concept of Jacksonian Democracy: New York as a Test Case.* Princeton: Princeton University Press, 1961.

Bentley, Arthur F. *The Process of Government: A Study of Social Pressures.* 1908; rpt. Bloomington: Principia Press, 1935.

Berelson, Bernard R., Paul F. Lazarfeld, and William N. McPhee. *Voting: A Study of Opinion Formation in a Presidential Campaign.* Chicago: University of Chicago Press, 1954.

Beyer, Gunther. "The Political Refugee: Thirty-Five Years Later." *International Migration Review,* XV, Nos. 1–2 (1981), 26–34.

Birch, Anthony H. *Nationalism and National Integration.* London: Unwin Hyman, 1989.

Blau, Francine D. "Immigration and Labor Earning in Early Twentieth Century America." In *Research in Population Economics.* Ed. Julian Simon and Julie da Vanzo. Greenwich: JAI, 1979. Vol. II.

Blegen, Theodore C. *Land of Their Choice: The Immigrants Write Home.* St. Paul: University of Minnesota Press, 1955.

Bodnar, John. *Immigration and Industrialization: Ethnicity in an American Mill Town, 1870–1940.* Pittsburgh: University of Pittsburgh Press, 1977.

_____. *The Transplanted: A History of Immigrants in Urban America.* Bloomington: Indiana University Press, 1985.

Boorstin, Daniel. *The Genius of American Politics.* Chicago: University of Chicago Press, 1953.

Boswell, Thomas D., and James R. Curtis. *The Cuban-American Experience: Culture, Images and Perspectives.* Totowa: Rowman and Allanheld, 1984.

Bridges, Amy. *A City in the Republic: Antebellum New York and the Origins of Machine Politics.* Cambridge: Cambridge University Press.

Brown, Thomas, N. *Irish-American Nationalism, 1870–1890.* Westport: Greenwood Press, 1966.

Brownstone, David M., Irene M. Franck, and Douglas L. Brownstone. *Island of Hope, Island of Tears.* New York: Penguin Books, 1986.

Brubaker, Williams Rogers. "Citizenship and Naturalization: Policies and Politics." In *Immigration and the Politics of Citizenship in Europe and North America.* Ed. Williams Rogers Brubaker. Lanham: University Press of America, 1989, pp. 99–125.

Bryce, James. *The American Commonwealth.* London: Macmillan and Co., 1895. Vol II.

Cafferty, Pastora San Juan, et al. *The Dilemma of American Immigration: Beyond the Golden Door.* New Brunswick: Transaction Press, 1983.

Caplan, Nathan, John K. Whitmore, and Quang L. Bui. "Economic Self-Sufficiency Among Recently Arrived Refugees from Southeast Asia." *Economic Outlook USA,* 12, No. 3 (1985), 60–63.

Carlson, Robert A. *The Quest for Conformity: Americanization Through Education.* New York: John Wiley and Sons, 1975.

Castles, Francis G. *Political Stability.* Milton Keynes: The Open University, 1974.

_____. "Scandinavia: The Politics of Stability." In *Modern Political Systems: Europe.* Ed. Roy C. Macridis. 5th ed. Englewood Cliffs: Prentice-Hall, 1983, pp. 387–434.

Chiswick, Barry R. "The Economic Progress of Immigrants: Some Apparently Universal Patterns." In *Contemporary Economic Problems, 1979.* Ed. William Felner. Washington: American Enterprise Institute for Public Policy Research, 1979, pp. 357–99.

Cornwall, Elmer E. "Bosses, Machines and Ethnic Groups." *The Annals of the American Academy of Political and Social Science,* 353 (1964), 27–39.

Crevecouer, J. Hector St. John de. *Letters from an American Farmer.* 1782; rpt. London: John M. Dent, 1912.

Crick, Bernard. *In Defense of Politics.* 2nd ed. Harmondsworth: Pelican Books, 1964.

Critchlow, Donald T., ed. *Socialism in the Heartland: The Midwestern Experience, 1900–1925.* Notre Dame: University of Notre Dame Press, 1986.

Croly, Herbert. *The Promise of American Life.* 1909; rpt. Cambridge: The Belknap Press of Harvard University Press, 1965.

Dahl, Robert A. *Democracy and Its Critics.* New Haven: Yale University Press, 1989.

_____. *Pluralist Democracy in the United States: Conflict and Consent.* Chicago: Rand McNally, 1967.

_____. *Polyarchy: Participation and Opposition.* New Haven: Yale University Press, 1971.

_____. *Who Governs? Democracy and Power in an American City.* New Haven: Yale University Press, 1961.

Dahrendorf, Ralf. *Class and Class Conflict in Industrial Society.* Stanford: Stanford University Press, 1959.

Daniels, Roger. *Coming to America: A History of Immigration and Ethnicity in American Life.* New York: Harper Collins, 1990.

Devine, Donald J. *The Political Culture of the United States: The Influence of Member Values on Regime Maintenance.* Boston: Little, Brown, and Co., 1972.

Diggins, John Patrick. *The Lost Soul of American Politics: Virtue, Self-Interest, and the Foundations of Liberalism.* New York: Basic Books, 1984.

Dinnerstein, Leonard, Roger L. Nichols, and David M. Reimers. *Natives and Strangers: Ethnic Groups and the Building of America.* New York: Oxford University Press, 1979.

Dinnerstein, Leonard, and David M. Reimers. *Ethnic Americans: A History of Immigration and Assimilation.* New York: Harper and Row, 1975.

Domhoff, G. William. *Who Rules America Now? A View for the '80s.* Englewood Cliffs: Prentice-Hall, 1983.

Dommen, Arthur J. *Laos: Keystone of Indochina.* Boulder: Westview Press, 1985.

Dworetz, Steven M. *The Unvarnished Doctrine: Locke, Liberalism and the American Revolution.* Durham, NC: Duke University Press, 1990.

Easterlin, Richard. "Immigration: Economic and Social Characteristics." *Harvard Encyclopedia of American Ethnic Groups.* (1980).

Easton, David. *A Systems Analysis of Political Life.* New York: John Wiley and Sons, 1965.

Ebenstein, William. *Today's Isms: Communism, Fascism, Capitalism, Socialism.* 8th ed. Englewood Cliffs: Prentice-Hall, 1980.

Eckstein, Harry. *Division and Cohesion in Democracy.* Princeton: Princeton University Press, 1966.

The Economist. *World Human Rights Guide.* New York: Facts on File, 1986.

Ehrmann, Henry W. *Politics in France.* Boston: Little, Brown, and Co., 1983.

Emmons, David M. *The Butte Irish: Class and Ethnicity in an American Mining Town, 1875-1925.* Urbana: University of Illinois Press, 1989.

Enloe, Cynthia. "The Growth of the State and Ethnic Mobilization: The American Experience." *Ethnic and Racial Studies,* 4, no. 2 (1981), 123–36.

Erie, Stephen P. *Rainbow's End: Irish Immigrants and the Dilemma of Urban Machine Politics, 1840-1985.* Berkeley: University of California Press, 1988.

Erikson, Robert, Norman R. Luttberg, and Kent L. Tedin. American Public Opinion: Its Origins, Content, and Impact. New York: John Wiley and Sons, 1980.

Evans, Grant. *Lao Peasants Under Socialism.* New Haven: Yale University Press, 1990.

Fauriol, Georges. "U.S. Immigration Policy and the National Interest." *The Humanist,* 44, no. 5 (1984), 5–26.

Femia, Joseph V. "Elites, Participation, and the Democratic Creed." *Political Studies,* 27 (1979), 1–20.

Finer, S. E. "Politics of Great Britain." In *Modern Political Systems: Europe.* Ed. Roy C. Macridis. 5th ed. Englewood Cliffs: Prentice-Hall, 1983, pp. 17–82.

Foner, Eric. *Politics and Ideology in the Age of the Civil War.* New York: Oxford University Press, 1980.

Ford, Franklin L. *Political Murder: From Tyrannicide to Terrorism.* Cambridge: Harvard University Press, 1985.

Fuchs, Lawrence H. *The American Kaleidoscope: Race, Ethnicity, and the Civic Culture.* Hanover: University Press of New England, 1990.

_____. *The Political Behavior of American Jews.* Glencoe: The Free Press, 1956.

Gans, Herbert. *The Urban Villagers: Group and Class in the Life of Italian-Americans.* Glencoe: The Free Press, 1962.

Garcia, John A., and Carlos H. Arce. "Political Orientations and Behaviors of Chicanos: Trying to Make Sense Out of Attitudes and Participation." In

Latinos and the Political System. Ed. F. Chris Garcia. Notre Dame: University of Notre Dame Press, 1988, pp. 125–51.

Garis, Roy L. *Immigration Restriction.* New York: Macmillan, 1927.

Gerstle, Gary. *Working-Class Americanism: The Politics of Labor in a Textile City, 1914–1960.* Cambridge: Cambridge University Press, 1989.

Glazer, Nathan, and Daniel Patrick Moynihan. *Beyond the Melting Pot: The Negroes, Puerto Ricans, Italians, and Irish of New York City.* 2nd ed. Cambridge: M.I.T. Press, 1970.

Gleason, Philip. "American Identity and Americanization." *Harvard Encyclopedia of American Ethnic Groups.* (1980). "Americans All: World War II and the Shaping of American Identity." *The Review of Politics,* 43, no. 4 (1981), 483–518.

Golab, Caroline. *Immigrant Destinations.* Philadelphia: Temple University Press, 1977.

Goldberg, David J. *A Tale of Three Cities: Labor Organization and Protest in Paterson, Passaic, and Lawrence, 1916–1921.* New Brunswick: Rutgers University Press, 1989.

Gordon, Linda. "Southeast Asian Refugee Migration to the United States." Paper prepared for the Conference on Asia-Pacific Immigration to the United States, September 20–25, 1984, East-West Population Institute, Honolulu, Hawaii.

Gosnell, Harold F. *Getting Out the Vote: An Experiment in the Stimulation of Voting.* Chicago: University of Chicago Press, 1927.

_____. "Non-Naturalization: A Study in Political Assimilation." *American Journal of Sociology,* 33 (1928), 930–39.

Grant, Madison. *The Passing of the Great Race.* New York: Charles Scribner's Sons, 1916.

Grant, Madison, and Charles Stewart Davison. *The Founders of the Republic on Immigration, Naturalization and Aliens.* New York: Charles Scribner's Sons, 1928.

Greeley, Andrew et al. "Political Participation Among Ethnic Groups in the United States." In *Ethnicity in the United States: A Preliminary Reconnaissance.* Ed. Andrew Greely and William C. McCready. New York: John Wiley and Sons, 1974, pp. 121–55.

Griffiths, Ernest S., John Plamenatz, and J. Roland Pennock. "Cultural Prerequisites to a Successfully Functioning Democracy." *American Political Science Review,* L, No. 1 (1956), 276–94.

Gunn, Geoffrey C. *Rebellion in Laos: Peasants and Politics in a Colonial Backwater.* Boulder: Westview Press, 1990.

_____. "Theravadins and Commissars: The State and National Identity in Laos." In *Contemporary Laos: Studies in the Politics and Society of the Lao People's Republic Democratic Republic.* Ed. Martin Stuart-Fox. New York: St. Martin's Press, 1982, pp. 76–100.

Gurr, Ted Robert. "The History of Violent Crime in America: An Overview." In *Violence in America: The History of Crime.* Ed. Ted Robert Gurr. Newbury Park: Sage Publications, 1989, pp. 11–20. Vol. I.

Hagwood, John A. *The Tragedy of German-America*. London: G. P. Putnam, 1940.

Hamilton, Alexander, James Madison, and John Jay. *The Federalist.* 1778; rpt. New York: Tudor Publishing Co., 1947.

Hancock, M. D. *Sweden: The Politics of Post-Industrial Change*. Hinsdale: Dryden Press, 1975.

Handlin, Oscar. *Boston's Immigrants: A Study in Acculturation*. 2nd. ed. Cambridge: The Belknap Press of Harvard University Press, 1959.

_____. "Education and the European Immigrant, 1820–1920." *In American Education and the European Immigrant: 1840–1940.* Ed. Bernard J. Weiss. Urbana: University of Illinois Press, 1982, pp. 4–16.

_____. "The Immigrant and American Politics." In *Foreign Influences in American Life*. Ed. David F. Bowers. New York: Peter Smith, 1952.

_____. *The Uprooted*. Boston: Little, Brown, and Co. 1951.

Hansen, Marcus Lee. *The Atlantic Migration, 1607–1860.* Cambridge: Harvard University Press, 1940.

_____. *The Immigrant in American History*. 1940; rpt. New York: Harper and Row, 1964.

Hanson, Russell L. *The Democratic Imagination in America: Conversations with Our Past*. Princeton: Princeton University Press, 1985.

Hartz, Louis. *The Founding of New Societies*. New York: Harcourt, Brace, and World, 1964.

_____. *The Liberal Tradition in America: An Interpretation of American Political Thought Since the Revolution*. New York: Harcourt, Brace, and World, 1955.

Herson, Lawrence J. R., and C. Richard Hofstetter. "Tolerance, Consensus, and the Democratic Creed: A Cultural Exploration." *Journal of Politics*, 37 (1975), 1007–32.

Higham, John. *Strangers in the Land: Patterns of American Nativism, 1860–1925.* Revised ed. New York: Atheneum, 1978.

Hobsbawm, E. J. *Nations and Nationalism Since 1780: Programme, Myth, Reality*. Cambridge: Cambridge University Press, 1990.

Hofstadter, Richard. *The Age of Reform: From Bryan to F.D.R.* New York: Vintage Books, 1955.

_____. *The American Political Tradition and the Men Who Made It*. New York: Alfred A. Knopf, 1948.

_____. "The Pseudo-Conservative Revolt." In *The Radical Right: The New American Right*. Ed. Daniel Bell. Garden City: Anchor Books, 1964, pp. 76–99.

_____. *The Progressive Historians: Turner, Beard, Parrington*. New York: Alfred A. Knopf, 1968.

Holt, Michael F. *Forging a Majority: The Formation of the Republican Party in Pittsburgh, 1848–1860.* New Haven: Yale University Press, 1969.

Huntington, Samuel. *American Politics: The Promise of Disharmony*. Cambridge: Harvard University Press, 1984.

Hurwitz, Leon. "Contemporary Approaches to Political Stability." *Comparative Politics*, 5 (1973), 449–63.

Ichioka, Yuji. *The Issei: The World of the First Generation Japanese Immigrants, 1885–1924.* New York: The Free Press, 1988.

Jackman, Robert W. "Political Elites, Mass Publics, and Support for Democratic Principles." *Journal of Politics,* 34 (1972), 753–73.

Jasso, Guillermina, and Mark R. Rosenzweig. *The New Chosen People: Immigrants in the United States.* New York: Russell Sage, 1990.

Jensen, Merrill. *The Articles of Confederation: An Interpretation of the Social-Constitutional History of the American Revolution, 1774–1781.* Madison: University of Wisconsin Press, 1959.

_____. *The Making of the American Constitution.* Princeton: D. Van Nostrand, 1964.

Jones, Maldwyn A. *American Immigration.* Chicago: University of Chicago Press, 1960.

_____. *The Old World Ties of American Ethnic Groups.* London: H. K. Lewis, 1976.

Joselit, Jenna Weissman. *Our Gang: Jewish Crime and the New York Jewish Community, 1900–1940.* Bloomington: Indiana University Press, 1983.

Kaelble, Hartmut. *Social Mobility in the 19th and 20th Centuries: Europe and America in Comparative Perspective.* New York: St. Martin's Press, 1986.

Kallen, Horace M. *Cultural Pluralism and the American Idea.* Philadelphia: University of Pennsylvania Press, 1956.

Kantowicz, Edward T. *Polish-American Politics in Chicago, 1888–1940.* Chicago: University of Chicago Press, 1975.

_____. "Voting and Parties." In *The Politics of Ethnicity.* Ed. Stephan Thernstrom. Cambridge: The Belknap Press of Harvard University Press, 1982, pp. 29–68.

Karst, Kenneth L. *Belonging to America: Equal Citizenship and the Constitution.* New Haven: Yale University Press, 1989.

Katznelson, Ira. *City Trenches: Urban Politics and the Patterning of Class in the United States.* Chicago: University of Chicago Press, 1981.

Kelley, Robert. *The Cultural Pattern of American Politics: The First Century.* New York: Alfred A. Knopf, 1979.

Kessner, Thomas. *The Golden Door: Italian and Jewish Immigrant Mobility in New York City, 1880–1915.* New York: Oxford University Press, 1977.

Kessner, Thomas, and Betty Boyd Caroli. *Today's Immigrants, Their Stories: A New Look at the Newest Americans.* New York: Oxford University Press, 1981.

Ketcham, Ralph. *Individualism and Public Life: A Modern Dilemma.* Oxford: Basil Blackwell, 1987.

Kettner, James H. *The Development of American Citizenship, 1608–1870.* Chapel Hill: University of North Carolina Press, 1978.

Kim, Illsoo. *New Urban Immigrants: The Korean Community in New York.* Princeton: Princeton University Press, 1981.

Kirk, Gordon W. *The Promise of American Life: Social Mobility in a Nineteenth Century Immigrant Community, Holland, Michigan, 1874–1894.* Philadelphia: American Philosophical Society, 1978.

Kleppner, Paul. *The Cross of Culture: A Social Analysis of Midwestern Politics, 1850–1900.* New York: The Free Press, 1970.

_____. *Who Voted? The Dynamics of Electoral Turnout, 1870–1980.* New York: Praeger Publishers, 1982.

Kohn, Hans. *American Nationalism: An Interpretative Essay.* New York: Macmillan, 1957.

Kolko, Gabriel. *Main Currents in Modern American History.* New York: Harper and Row, 1986.

LaGumina, Salvatore J. *The Immigrants Speak: Italian Americans Tell Their Story.* New York: Center for Migration Studies, 1979.

Lamm, Richard D. "English Comes First." *New York Times,* 1 July 1986, Sec. 1. p. 23, cols. 1–2.

Lane, A. T. *Solidarity or Survival? American Labor and European Immigrants, 1830–1924.* Westport: Greenwood Press, 1987.

Lane, Robert E. *Political Life: Why and How People Get Involved in Politics.* New York: The Free Press, 1959.

Lane, Roger. "On the Social Meaning of Homicide Trends in America." In *Violence in America: The History of Crime.* Ed. Ted Robert Gurr. Newbury Park: Sage Publications, 1989, pp. 55–79. Vol. I.

"Laos." *The Europa Yearbook.* (1990 ed.)

"Laotians Consider Their Future." *Refugees,* No. 84 (April 1991), 28.

Laski, Harold J. *The American Democracy: A Commentary and Interpretation.* New York: Viking Press, 1948.

Layton-Henry, Zig. *The Politics of Race in Britain.* London: George Allen and Unwin, 1984.

Lee, Gary Y. "Minority Policies and the Hmong." In *Contemporary Laos: Studies in the Policies and Society of the Lao People's Democratic Republic.* Ed. Martin Stuart-Fox. New York: St. Martin's Press, 1982, pp. 197–217.

Leifer, Eric M. "Competing Models of Political Mobilization: The Role of Ethnic Ties." *American Journal of Sociology,* 87 (1981), 23–47.

Lerner, Max. *America as a Civilization: Life and Thought in the United States Today.* 2nd ed. New York: Henry Holt, 1987.

Levine, Edward M. *The Irish and Irish Politicians.* Notre Dame: University of Notre Dame Press, 1966.

Lieberson, Stanley. *A Piece of the Pie: Blacks and White Immigrants Since 1880.* Berkeley: University of California Press, 1980.

Lienesch, Michael. *New Order of the Ages: Time, the Constitution, and the Making of Modern American Political Thought.* Princeton: Princeton University Press, 1988.

Light, Ivan. "The Ethnic Vice Industry, 1880–1944." *American Sociological Review,* 42 (1977), 464–79.

Lijphart, Arend. *Democracies: Patterns of Majoritarian and Consensus Government in Twenty-One Countries.* New Haven: Yale University Press, 1984.

_____. *Democracy in Plural Societies: A Comparative Exploration.* New Haven: Yale University Press, 1977.

Lipset, Seymour Martin. *Continental Divide: The Values and Institutions of the United States and Canada.* New York: Routledge, 1990.

_____. *The First New Nation: The United States in Historical and Comparative Perspective.* New York: Basic Books, 1963.

Lipset, Seymour Martin, and Earl Raab. *The Politics of Unreason: Right-Wing Extremism in America, 1790–1970.* New York: Harper and Row, 1970.

Lipson, Leslie. *The Democratic Civilization.* New York: Oxford University Press, 1964.

Litt, Edgar. *Ethnic Politics in America.* Glenview: Scott, Foresman and Co., 1970.

Loescher, Gil, and John A. Scanlon. *Calculated Kindness: Refugees and America's Half-Open Door, 1945 to the Present.* New York: The Free Press, 1986.

Lofland, John, and Lyn H. Lofland. *Analyzing Social Settings: A Guide to Qualitative Observation and Analysis.* 2nd ed. Belmont: Wadsworth Publishing, 1984.

Lopata, Helen Z. *Polish-Americans: Status Competition in an Ethnic Community.* Englewood Cliffs: Prentice-Hall, 1976.

Lopreato, Joseph. *Italian-Americans.* New York: Random House, 1970.

Lowi, Theodore. *The End of Liberalism: Ideology, Policy, and the Crisis of Public Authority.* New York: W. W. Norton, 1969.

Luebke, Frederick C. *The Bonds of Loyalty: German-Americans and World War I.* DeKalb: Northern Illinois University Press, 1974.

_____. *Immigrants and Politics: The Germans of Nebraska, 1880–1900.* Lincoln: University of Nebraska Press, 1969.

Lyman, Stanford M. *Chinese-Americans.* New York: Random House, 1974.

Mackay, Alexander. *The Western World.* 1849; rpt. New York: Negro University Press, 1968. Vol. III.

MacPherson. C. B. *The Real World of Democracy.* Toronto: Canadian Broadcasting Company, 1965.

Martineau, Harriet. *Society in America.* Ed. Seymour Martin Lipset. Garden City: Anchor-Doubleday, 1962.

Matthews, Donald R., and James W. Prothro. *Negroes and the New Southern Politics.* New York: Harcourt, Brace, and World, 1966.

McClosky, Herbert. "Consensus and Ideology in American Politics." *American Political Science Review,* LVIII (1964), 361–82.

McClosky, Herbert, and John Zaller. *The American Ethos: Public Attitudes Toward Capitalism and Democracy.* Cambridge: Harvard University Press, 1984.

McClymer, John F. "The Americanization Movement and the Education of the Foreign-Born Adult." In *American Education and the European Immigrant: 1840–1940.* Ed. Bernard J. Weiss. Urbana: University of Illinois Press, 1982, pp. 96–116.

McDonald, Forrest. *Novus Ordum Seclorum: The Intellectual Origins of the Constitution.* Lawrence: University Press of Kansas, 1985.

Merriam, Charles E., and Harold F. Gosnell. *Non-Voting: Causes and Methods of Control.* Chicago: University of Chicago Press, 1924.

Milbrath, L. W. *Political Participation: How and Why Do People Get Involved in Politics?* Chicago: Rand McNally, 1965.

Mill, John Stuart. *Considerations on Representative Government.* 1867; rpt. London: J. M. Dent and Sons, 1972.

Miller, Kirby A. *Emigrants and Exiles: Ireland and the Irish Exodus to North America.* New York: Oxford University Press, 1985.

Miller, Mark. "Political Participation and Representation of Noncitizens." In *Immigration and the Politics of Citizenship in Europe and North America.* Ed. Williams Rogers Brubaker. Lanham: University Press of America, 1989, pp. 129–44.

Miller, Sally. "Casting a Wide Net: The Milwaukee Movement to 1920." In *Socialism in the Heartland: The Midwestern Experience, 1900–1925.* Ed. Donald T. Critchlow. Notre Dame: University of Notre Dame Press, 1986, pp. 18–41.

Miller, Warren E., and Teresa E. Levitin. *Leadership and Change: The New Politics and the American Electorate.* Cambridge: Winthrop Publishers, 1976.

Mink, Gwendolyn. *Old Labor and New Immigrants in American Political Development: Union, Party, and State, 1875–1920.* Ithaca: Cornell University Press, 1986.

Monkkonen, Eric H. "Diverging Homicide Rates: England and the United States, 1850–1875." In *Violence in America: The History of Crime.* Ed. Ted Robert Gurr. Newbury Park: Sage Publications, 1989, pp. 80–101. Vol. I.

Montero, Daniel. *Vietnamese Americans: Patterns of Resettlement and Socio-Economic Adaptation in the United States.* Boulder: Westview Press, 1979.

Montgomery, David. *The Fall of the House of Labor: The Workplace, the State, and American Labor Activism, 1865–1925.* Cambridge: Cambridge University Press, 1987.

Morawska, Ewa. *For Bread with Butter: The Life-Worlds of East Central Europeans in Johnstown, Pennsylvania, 1890–1940.* Cambridge: Cambridge University Press, 1985.

_____. "The Sociology and Historiography of Immigration." In *Immigration Reconsidered: History, Sociology, and Politics.* Ed. Virginia Yans-McLaughlin. New York: Oxford University Press, 1990, pp. 187–238.

Morris-Jones, W. H. "In Defence of Apathy: Some Doubts on the Duty to Vote." *Political Studies,* II, No. 1 (1954), 25–37.

Myrdal, Gunnar. *An American Dilemma: The Negro Problem and Modern Democracy.* New York: Harper and Brothers, 1944.

Nelli, Humbert S. *The Business of Crime: Italians and Syndicate Crime in the United States.* Chicago: University of Chicago Press, 1976.

_____. *From Immigrants to Ethnics: the Italian Americans.* Oxford: Oxford University Press, 1983.

_____. *Italians in Chicago: A Study in Ethnic Mobility.* New York: Oxford University Press, 1970.

Nguyen, Liem, T., and Alan B. Henkin, "Vietnamese Refugees in the United States: Adaptation and Transitional Status." *Journal of Ethnic Studies*, 9 (1982), 101–16.

Norton, Anne. *Alternative Americas: A Reading of Antebellum Political Culture.* Chicago: University of Chicago Press, 1986.

"No Refuge." The Economist, 21 February 1987, p. 41, cols. 2–3; p. 42, col. 1.

Novak, Michael. *The Rise of the Unmeltable Ethnics: Politics and Culture in the Seventies.* New York: Macmillan Publishing, 1972.

Olson, John Stuart. *The Ethnic Dimension in American History.* New York: St. Martin's Press, 1979. Vol. I.

Osborne, Milton. *Southeast Asia: An Introductory History.* Sydney: George Allen and Unwin, 1979.

Ostergren, Ray C. *A Community Transplanted: The Trans-Atlantic Experience of a Swedish Immigrant Settlement in the Upper Middle West, 1835–1915.* Madison: University of Wisconsin Press, 1988.

Paine, Thomas. *Common Sense and Other Political Writings.* Ed. Nelson F. Adkins. 1783; rpt. New York: The Liberal Arts Press, 1953.

Pangle, Thomas L. *The Spirit of Modern Republicanism: The Moral Vision of the American Founders and the Philosophy of Locke.* Chicago: University of Chicago Press, 1988.

Parenti, Michael J. *Democracy for the Few.* 5th ed. New York: St. Martin's Press, 1988.

____. *Ethnic and Political Attitudes: A Depth Study of Italian Americans.* New York: Arno Press, 1975.

Parrington, Vernon L. *Main Currents in American Thought: An Interpretation of American Literature from the Beginnings to 1920.* New York: Harcourt Brace, 1927.

Pennock, J. Roland. *Democratic Political Theory.* Princeton: Princeton University Press, 1979.

Perlman, Selig. *Theory of the Labor Movement.* 1928; rpt. New York: Augustus M. Kelley, 1949.

Peterson, William. "Concepts of Ethnicity." *Harvard Encyclopedia of American Ethnic Groups.* (1980 ed.)

Pickles, Dorothy. *Democracy.* New York: Basic Books, 1970.

Pocock, J.G.A. *The Machiavellian Moment: Florentine Political Thought and the Atlantic Republican Tradition.* Princeton: Princeton University Press, 1975.

Portes, Alejandro, and Rafael Mozo. "The Political Adaptation Process of Cubans and Other Ethnic Minorities: A Preliminary Analysis." In *Latinos and the Political System.* Ed. F. Chris Garcia. Notre Dame: University of Notre Dame Press, 1988, pp. 152–70.

Portes, Alejandro, and Ruben G. Rumbaut. *Immigrant America: A Portrait.* Berkeley: University of California Press, 1990.

Potter, David. *People of Plenty: Economic Abundance and the American Character.* Chicago: University of Chicago Press, 1954.

Powell, G. Bingham. "American Voter Turnout in Comparative Perspective." *American Political Science Review,* 80, no. 1 (1986), 17–43.

_____. *Contemporary Democracies: Participation, Stability, Violence.* Cambridge: Harvard University Press, 1982.

Prothro, James W., and Charles M. Grigg. "Fundamental Principles of Democracy: Bases of Agreement and Disagreement." *Journal of Politics,* 22 (1960), 276–94.

Rischin, Moses. *The Promised City, New York's Jews, 1870–1914.* Cambridge: Harvard University Press, 1962.

Rist, Ray C. *Guestworkers in Germany: The Prospects for Pluralism.* New York: Praeger Publishers, 1978.

Rogg, Eleanor M. *The Assimilation of Cuban Exiles: The Role of Community and Class.* New York: Aberdeen Press, 1974.

Rose, Richard. *Politics in England.* 3rd. ed. Boston: Little, Brown, and Co., 1980.

Rosenblum, Gerald. *Immigrant Workers: The Impact on American Labor Radicalism.* New York: Basic Books, 1973.

Rosenthal, Uriel. *Political Order.* Aalphen den Rijn: Sijthoff and Noordhoff, 1978.

Safran, William. *The French Polity.* New York: Longman Press, 1977.

Saxton, Alexander. *The Indispensable Enemy: Labor and the Anti-Chinese Movement in California.* Berkeley: University of California Press, 1971.

Schmid, Carol. "Economic Necessity and Social Marginality." *Ethnic Groups,* 3, No. 4 (1981), 351–71.

Schumpeter, Joseph. *Capitalism, Socialism, and Democracy.* 3rd. ed. New York: Harper and Row, 1950.

The Select Commission on Immigration Policy. *U.S. Immigration Policy and the National Interest.* Washington, D.C.: G.P.O., 1981.

Sesser, Stan. "Forgotten Country." *The New Yorker,* 20 August 1990, pp. 39–68.

Shafer, Byron E. "'Exceptionalism' in American Politics?" *Political Science and Politics,* 22, no. 3 (1989), 588–94.

Shannon, William V. *The American Irish.* New York: Macmillan Publishing, 1963.

Shapiro, Steven R. "Ideological Exclusion Closing the Border to Political Dissidents." *Harvard Law Review,* 100 (1987), 930–45.

Silbey, Joseph, and Samuel T. McSeveney, ed. *Voters Parties, and Elections: Quantitative Essays in the History of American Voting Behavior.* Lexington: Xerox College Press, 1972.

Skerry, Peter. "The Ambiguity of Mexican American Politics." In *Clamor at the Gates: The New American Immigration.* Ed. Nathan Glazer. San Francisco: ICS, 1985, pp. 241–56.

Smith, Allan. "National Images and National Maintenance: The Ascendancy of the Ethnic Idea in North America." *Canadian Journal of Political Science,* 14, no. 2 (1981), 227–59.

Smith, Gordon. *Democracy in Western Germany: Parties and Politics in the Federal Republic.* London: Heinemann, 1979.

Smith, James Allen. *The Spirit of American Government; A Study of the Constitution: Its Origin, Influence, and Relation to Democracy.* 1907; rpt. New York: Macmillan, 1911.

Smith, Rogers M. "The 'American Creed' and American Identity: The Limits of Liberal Citizenship in the United States." *The Western Political Quarterly,* 41 (1988), 225–52.

Solomon, Richard. *Mao's Revolution and the Chinese Political Culture.* Berkeley: University of California Press, 1971.

Sowell, Thomas. *Ethnic America: A History.* New York: Basic Books, 1981.

Steinberg, Stephen. *The Ethnic Myth: Race, Ethnicity, and Class in America.* New York: Atheneum, 1981.

Stouffer, Samuel A. *Communism, Conformity, and Civil Liberties.* Gloucester: Peter Smith, 1963.

Strand, Paul J., and Woodrow Jones, Jr. *Indochinese Refugees in America: Problems of Adaptation and Assimilation.* Durham: Duke University Press, 1985.

Stuart-Fox, Martin. *Laos: Politics, Economics, Society.* London: Frances Pinter, 1986.

Taylor, Charles Lewis, and Michael Hudson. *World Handbook of Political and Social Indicators.* New Haven: Yale University Press, 1972.

Taylor, Philip. *The Distant Magnet: European Emigration to the U.S.A.* New York: Harper and Row, 1971.

Teske, Raymond H. C., and Bardin H. Nelson. "Acculturation and Assimilation: A Clarification." *American Ethnologist,* I (1974), 351–67.

Thernstrom, Stephan. *The Other Bostonians: Poverty and Progress in the American Metropolis, 1880–1970.* Cambridge: Harvard University Press, 1973.

_____. *Poverty and Progress: Social Mobility in a Nineteenth Century City.* Cambridge: Harvard University Press, 1964.

Thistlethwaite, Frank. "Migration from Europe Overseas in the Nineteenth and Twentieth Centuries." In *Population Movements in Modern European History.* Ed. Herbert Moller. New York: Macmillan, 1964, pp. 73–92.

Thomas, William I., and Florian Znaniecki. *The Polish Peasant in Europe and America.* 1918; rpt. New York: Dover, 1958. Vol. II.

Tocqueville, Alexis de. *Democracy in America.* Trans. Henry Reeve. Revised Francis Bowen. Ed. Phillips Bradley. New York: Vintage Press, 1945.

Torres, Maria de los Angeles. "From Exiles to Minorities: The Politics of Cuban-Americans." In *Latinos and the Political System.* Ed. F. Chris Garcia. Notre Dame: University of Notre Dame Press, 1988, pp. 81–98.

Trollope, Fanny. *Domestic Manners of the Americans.* Ed. Richard Mullen. 1839; rpt. Oxford: Oxford University Press, 1984.

Truman, David B. *The Governmental Process: Political Interests and Public Opinion.* New York: Alfred A. Knopf, 1965.

Tsai, Shi-Shan Henry. *The Chinese Experience in America.* Bloomington: Indiana University Press, 1986.

Tumin, Melvin. "Some Unapplauded Consequences of Social Mobility in a Mass Society." *Social Forces,* 36 (1957), 32–37.

Ueda, Reed. "Naturalization and Citizenship." *Harvard Encyclopedia of American Ethnic Groups.* (1980).

United Nations Development Program. "The Economy of Laos: An Overview." In *Laos: Beyond the Revolution.* Eds. Joseph J. Zasloff and Leonard Unger. New York: St. Martin's Press, 1991, pp. 67–83.

United States Bureau of the Census. *Historical Statistics of the United States: Colonial Times to 1970.* Washington, D.C.: G.P.O., 1975.

United States Bureau of the Census. *Statistical Abstract of the United States: 1986.* Washington, D.C.: G.P.O., 1985.

United States Bureau of the Census. *Statistical Abstract of the United States: 1990.* Washington, D.C.: G.P.O., 1990.

United States Department of Health and Human Services. *Profiles of the Highland Lao Communities in the United States.* Washington, D.C.: G.P.O., 1988.

United States Immigration and Naturalization Service. *1989 Statistical Yearbook of the Immigration and Naturalization Service.* Washington, D.C.: G.P.O., 1990.

Van-es-Beeck, Bernard. "Refugees from Laos 1975–1979." In *Contemporary Laos: Studies in the Politics and Society of the Lao People's Democratic Republic.* Ed. Martin Stuart-Fox. New York: St. Martin's Press, 1982, pp. 324–34.

Van Esterick, John. "Lao." In *Refugees in the United States.* Ed. David W. Haines. Westport: Greenwood Press, 1985.

Vecoli, Rudolph J. "Immigration, Naturalization and the Constitution." *News for Teachers of Political Science,* No. 50 (1986), 9–14.

Verba, Sidney, and Norman Nie. *Participation in America.* New York: Harper and Row, 1972.

Weber, Max. *The Theory of Social and Economic Organization.* New York: Oxford University Press, 1947.

Whitaker, Donald P. et al. *Area Handbook for Laos.* Washington, D.C.: Foreign Area Studies of the American University, 1972.

Whitfield, Stephen J. *Voices of Jacob, Hands of Esau: Jews in American Life and Thought.* Hamden: Archon Press, 1984.

Wilentz, Sean. *Chants Democratic: New York City and the Rise of the American Working Class, 1788–1850.* New York: Oxford University Press, 1984.

Wilkinson, Rupert. *The Pursuit of American Character.* New York: Harper and Row, 1988.

Wittke, Carl. *We Who Built America: The Saga of the Immigrant.* New York: Prentice-Hall, 1940.

Wolfinger, Raymond E., and John Osgood Field. "Political Ethos and the Structure of City Government." In *Perspectives on Urban Politics.* Ed. Jay S. Goodman. Boston: Allyn and Bacon, 1970, pp. 454–95.

———. *The Politics of Progress.* Englewood Cliffs: Prentice-Hall, 1974.

———. "Why Political Machines Have Not Withered Away and Other Revisionist Thoughts." *The Journal of Politics,* 34 (1972), 364–98.

Wolfinger, Raymond E., and Steven J. Rosenstone. *Who Votes?* New Haven: Yale University Press, 1979.

Wood, Gordon S. *The Creation of the American Republic, 1776 1787.* Chapel Hill: University of North Carolina Press, 1969.

Yans-McLaughlin, Virginia, ed. *Immigration Reconsidered: History, Sociology, and Politics.* New York: Oxford University Press, 1990.

Yarnold, Barbara M. *Refugees Without Refuge: Formation and Failed Implementation of U.S. Political Asylum Policy in the 1980's.* Lanham: University Press of America, 1990.

Zasloff, Joseph J. "Political Constraints on Development in Laos." In *Laos: Beyond the Revolution.* Eds. Joseph J. Zasloff and Leonard Unger. New York: St. Martin's Press, 1991, pp. 3–40.

Zucker, Norman L., and Naomi Flink Zucker. *The Guarded Gate: The Reality of American Refugee Policy.* New York: Harcourt Brace Jovanovich, 1987.

Zunz, Oliver. *The Changing Face of Inequality: Urbanization, Industrial Development, and Immigrants in Detroit, 1880–1920.* Chicago: University of Chicago Press, 1982.

About the Book and Author

As an ethnically heterogeneous but stable democracy, the United States is a puzzle for students of politics. Typically, the literature of democratic theory regards ethnic diversity as disruptive of a democratic polity. However, the United States has so far avoided the system-threatening consequences of heterogeneity experienced by other democratic states—it appears to be distinctive in the extent of its political integration.

Politics in the Lifeboat argues that the secret to America's success lies in the immigrant origins of its population. Voluntary migration, not forcible incorporation, has been the major source of America's ethnic diversity, and this, the author maintains, has had positive political consequences. Drawing on an investigation of immigrant political values and behavior in general, and on a qualitative study of Laotian refugees in particular, he contends that, far from being disruptive, immigrants have been an essential part of the relatively stable American democratic order.

Assessing immigration's impact on the American political system from the perspective of democratic theory, *Politics in the Lifeboat* opens a new dialogue on the challenges of democratization currently facing countries all over the world.

John C. Harles is associate professor of political science at Messiah College in Grantham, Pennsylvania.

Index

237